Practical social work

Published in conjunction with
the British Association of Social Workers
Series Editor: Jo Campling

B A S W

Social work is at an important stage in its development. The profession is facing fresh challenges to work flexibly in fast-changing social and organisational environments. New requirements for training are also demanding a more critical and reflective, as well as more highly skilled, approach to practice.

The British Association of Social Workers has always been conscious of its role in setting guidelines for practice and in seeking to raise professional standards. The concept of the *Practical Social Work* series was conceived to fulfil a genuine professional need for a carefully planned, coherent series of texts that would stimulate and inform debate, thereby contributing to the development of practitioners' skills and professionalism.

Newly relaunched, the series continues to address the needs of all those who are looking to deepen and refresh their understanding and skills. It is designed for students and busy professionals alike. Each book marries practice issues and challenges with the latest theory and research in a compact and applied format. The authors represent a wide variety of experience both as educators and practitioners. Taken together, the books set a standard in their clarity, relevance and rigour.

A list of new and best-selling titles in this series follows overleaf. A comprehensive list of titles available in the series, and further details about individual books, can be found online at:
www.palgrave.com/socialworkpolicy/basw

Series Standing Order ISBN 0-333-80313-2

You can receive future titles in this series as they are published by placing a standing order. Please contact your bookseller or, in the case of difficulty, contact us at the address below with your name and address, the title of the series and the ISBN quoted above.

Customer Services Department .... Ltd, Houndmills, Basingstoke

D1093400

Practical social work series

New and best-selling titles

Robert Adams *Empowerment, Participation and Social Work* (4th edition) **new!**

Sarah Banks *Ethics and Values in Social Work* (3rd edition)

James G. Barber *Social Work with Addictions* (2nd edition)

Suzy Braye and Michael Preston-Shoot *Practising Social Work Law* (2nd edition)

Veronica Coulshed and Joan Orme *Social Work Practice* (4th edition)

Veronica Coulshed and Audrey Mullender with David N. Jones and Neil Thompson
 Management in Social Work (3rd edition)

Lena Dominelli *Anti-Racist Social Work* (3rd edition) **new!**

Celia Doyle *Working with Abused Children* (3rd edition)

Tony Jeffs and Mark Smith (editors) *Youth Work*

Joyce Lishman *Communication in Social Work*

Paula Nicolson, Rowan Bayne and Jenny Owen *Applied Psychology for Social
 Workers* (3rd edition)

Judith Phillips, Mo Ray and Mary Marshall *Social Work with Older People*
 (4th edition)

Michael Oliver and Bob Sapey *Social Work with Disabled People* (3rd edition)

Michael Preston-Shoot *Effective Groupwork*

Steven Shardlow and Mark Doel *Practice Learning and Teaching*

Neil Thompson *Anti-Discriminatory Practice* (4th edition)

Derek Tilbury *Working with Mental Illness* (2nd edition)

Alan Twelvetrees *Community Work* (4th edition) **new!**

robert adams

Empowerment, participation and social work

fourth edition

First published as *Self Help, Social Work and Empowerment* 1990
Second edition published as *Social Work and Empowerment* 1996
Third edition 2003
Fourth edition published as *Empowerment, Participation and Social Work* 2008

Published by
PALGRAVE MACMILLAN
Houndmills, Basingstoke, Hampshire RG21 6XS and
175 Fifth Avenue, New York, N.Y. 10010
Companies and representatives throughout the world

PALGRAVE MACMILLAN is the global academic imprint of the Palgrave Macmillan division of St. Martin's Press, LLC and of Palgrave Macmillan Ltd. Macmillan® is a registered trademark in the United States, United Kingdom and other countries. Palgrave is a registered trademark in the European Union and other countries.

ISBN-13: 978–0–230–01999–7
ISBN-10: 0–230–01990–4

This book is printed on paper suitable for recycling and made from fully managed and sustained forest sources. Logging, pulping and manufacturing processes are expected to conform to the environmental regulations of the country of origin.

A catalogue record for this book is available from the British Library.

A catalog record for this book 1s available from the Library of Congress.

10 9 8 7 6 5 4 3 2 1
17 16 15 14 13 12 11 10 09 08

Printed in China

To James George Adams (1908–96) and
Winifred Mary Adams (1917–79)

Contents

List of figures and tables

Figures

Tables

Introduction to the fourth edition

I am so pleased for this invitation from the publishers to create a fourth, more inclusively international edition of this book, which has benefited from major changes since it was first published in 1990 and, excitingly, still stimulates messages to me from people in different parts of the world, and is now translated into several languages, notably Japanese and Korean. The changing nature and history of the book is reflected in its changing title. In its first edition it was *Social Work, Self-help and Empowerment*, in its second and third editions *Social Work and Empowerment* and, enlarged and much rewritten, it has now become *Empowerment, Participation and Social Work*. The participants to whom this refers are the people who use services, clients or carers who should benefit from the practice of social workers. One major prediction I made in those early years has come to pass, namely the growing participation in services and growing power of these people who use services. We cannot speak complacently about their empowerment, because in some areas the rhetoric still exceeds the reality and much remains to be achieved, but at least debates about how to achieve it are taking place in the centre ground now, rather than on the margins of practice.

The book grew partly from personal experiences of the need for self-help to contribute to the care of my own relatives and partly from my efforts to support the self-help initiatives of Mind, as the then chairperson of Mind's advisory committee in Yorkshire and Humberside. To that chance initiation into the politics of empowerment in mental health, I owe a debt to Norman Jepson and the late John Crowley. My involvement in Mind Your Self in Leeds and collaboration with Gael Lindenfield, who founded it, led to several books and other publications. The book also began partly with the awareness that despite the growing numbers of handbooks on self-help, there was a need for an accessible yet critical text, which would provide a framework for the development of more effective relationships between professionals and self-helpers.

Several years later, during study leave, I started to write on the basis of a series of visits to a wide variety of self-help groups and organizations throughout the UK. I should like to record my appreciation of the many people I spoke to about the subject matter of this book during the process. The list is too long to mention everyone, but thanks are due to Helen Allison, Mike Archer, Don Barton, the late David Brandon, Francis Conway, Gilly Craddock, Dave Crenson, Parul Desai, Nick Ellerby, John Errington, Alec Gosling, John Harman, Gerry Lynch, Peter McGavin, Sam McTaggart, Jim Pearson, Tom Rhodenberg, Alan Robinson, Gill Thorpe, Bob Welburn and Tom Woolley. For the ideas about how to tackle oppression, I am indebted to Julia Phillipson, whose publication (1992) contributes much to the latter part of Chapter 4. For the ideas about community profiling, thanks are due to Mark Baldwin who has rekindled my reading in this area. My thinking about participation and empowerment has benefited from many carers and people who use services with whom I have talked during this period, meetings and discussions with representatives of service user and carer organizations as well as with my academic colleagues Wade Tovey and Pat Watson. I am also particularly grateful to Dorothy Whitaker and Terence O'Sullivan for their comments on earlier drafts of the first edition, Paddy Hall for his ideas on community education and Dr Raymond Jack and Jane Thompson for reading and commenting on drafts of the second edition. Jo Campling, who I collaborated with on the first edition of this book many years ago, and Catherine Gray at Palgrave Macmillan have been as encouraging as ever. It is with great sadness that I record the death of Jo in the summer of 2006, predating the publishing of this fourth edition. For more than 20 years I benefited from her friendship and support. I also owe an enormous debt to members of my family. Notwithstanding all these acknowledgements, it goes without saying that, while much of the content of the book reflects the various contributions of those mentioned, among many others, all the opinions expressed in it, and any errors, are entirely my own.

ROBERT ADAMS

Glossary

Glossary terms are highlighted in **bold** in the text.

Capacity building: ways of improving the abilities, skills and related resources of individuals, groups, organizations and communities, to enable people to take part to meet their own needs and those of other people

Carer: person who gives care informally and unpaid, usually as partner, other household members, friend and neighbour

Citizen engagement: that early stage in the process of involvement where citizens and officials are in regular or continuous interaction that the citizens regard as significant

Citizenship: the status of citizens, with its related rights, privileges, powers, duties and responsibilities of social, political and community involvement and participation

Collaboration: people working together and sharing power and decision-making

Community capacity building: the means by which communities build on their existing knowledge, skills and expertise and develop so as to meet the needs and priorities perceived as necessary by community members

Community profile: an assessment of need that is mapped with the participation of local people, at the level of the community in which they live

Community work: working with people in communities on goals they define to enable them to achieve them

Consultation: seeking people's views as one source of influencing decisions, policy and practice

Deconstruction: digging away at discourses about a concept so as to probe beyond the dominant or widespread ideas contributing to them, to find out what lies behind or beyond them

Discourse: a system of beliefs and practices sustained by being passed on between individuals, groups and organizations in society and helping to construct the social arrangements that people regard as reality

Empowerment: the capacity of individuals, groups and/or communities to take control of their circumstances, exercise power and achieve their own goals, and the process by which, individually and collectively, they are able to help themselves and others to maximize the quality of their lives

Empowerment in practice: the continuous interaction between critical reflection and empowering practice, that is, the continuous in and out cycle of reflecting-acting-evaluating and the interplay between thinking and doing

Exclusion: the lack of participation in, and segregation from, the mainstream of social and economic life of individuals, groups and communities

Governance: how policy is sustained in practice

Infrastructure: the systems, procedures and processes for supporting staff in their work

Involvement: the entire continuum of taking part, from one-off consultation through equal partnership to taking control

Learning organization: an organization geared to rapid changes in working practices that enable it to tackle many issues and problems

Mutual help: means by which individuals, groups or organizations come together and share an experience or problem, with a view to individual and mutual benefit

Participation: forms of involvement where people play a more active part, have greater choice, exercise more power and contribute significantly to decision-making and management

Participatory culture: one where participation is central and fundamental to the functioning of the organization

Qualitative methodology: the collection and analysis of non-quantitative data, using non-traditional research methods, which may be based on assumptions from the critical social sciences that the researcher can become a research instrument through subjective involvement in the research process

Reflexivity: using the impact of a situation or experience on oneself to help understanding and feed into future activity

Reticulists: people who are committed to achieving change through their skills in crossing organizational and professional boundaries, strengthening existing networks and forming new networks involving individuals and groups

Self-empowerment: people taking power over their own lives

Self-help: the means by which people help themselves

Service user: person who is eligible to receive social care and social work services either from professionals or through direct payments, which enable her or him to buy these services

Stakeholder: person with an interest in, or power to influence, a policy, project, organization, service or activity

part **I**

Theories, models and methods for empowering practice

1 | Understanding empowerment

I attended a meeting of women in a deprived urban area, running their own project to cater for their under-five children. At the meeting, several women voiced their frustration that experience in the project did not provide them with an empowering ladder to qualify themselves as play workers alongside the women project workers. A local professional declared his view that experiencing the process of working in an empowering way could be as valid for them as achieving an empowering outcome. He said it was probably sufficient for them to feel better, rather than to achieve material advancement to a professional role. The responses of the women after he had left the meeting left no doubt that this professional had fallen into the trap of treating empowerment as though it can be put into a compartment so that one aspect does not affect any others. This started me thinking about empowerment as a contested concept. It reminds me of two crucial realities:

- the meaning of empowerment can be taken from the people by the professionals who are meant to be working with them in an empowering way, and returned to them in a diluted way, so that they actually feel disempowered
- a book about the development of empowerment and participation in practice must be holistic and cover all dimensions, from personal, interpersonal, group, through to organizational, community and political aspects. To attempt to work at one level and separate it from others is to risk tokenism at best and, at worst, failure.

Introduction

This book sets out to provide social workers with a framework for purposeful, self-critical, empowering practice, based on a combination of critical understanding, knowledge and skills in an appropriate context of values. This chapter explores the meanings of the term 'empowerment', examining its relationship with similar concepts such as self-help, participation and user-led activities.

Empowerment is a multifaceted idea, meaning different things to different people. It has academic, rhetorical and radical associations. It is used academically to theorize about people's relationship with power and powerlessness in society (Humphries, 1996; Rees, 1991). It may be used rhetorically, to make a case for people to achieve power and assert it. To some people, empowerment has become a synonym for all that is dangerous and radical, carrying the threat of the growing nuisance value of carers and service users as they assert power in conferences, meetings and working groups, not endearing it to managers in agencies.

None of these ideas is dominant and, as a result, no final, so-called 'authoritative' definition of empowerment is possible. Empowerment does not correspond with a single, existing social work method, although it can be shown to have links with all of them. It does not derive exclusively from individually based, person-centred or problem-focused, social or environmental approaches to social work, although examples can be found in all of these. People who use services can argue that the authority for the definition of empowerment should not rest in books written by academics or practitioners. They may argue that the concept of empowerment should be constantly redefined and reconstructed not just by professionals but also through the actions and words of people who are experts by virtue of their experience, particularly vulnerable and excluded people, who want greater control over the services they receive. The authenticity of empowerment should derive from being rooted in the circumstances of those who use services, not those who commission, manage and deliver them, or those who research, write and teach about them. The following example shows how patronizing and disempowering professional practice can be.

practice study

Kiri is 61 and experiencing the early stages of presenile dementia. This morning was one of her off days and she felt confused, too rushed to speak up for herself and angry and fed up afterwards. When her sister, who visits her at home daily to do the housekeeping, met the social worker at home, they talked through the initial stages of the assessment process as though she wasn't there. Because Kiri has started to forget to put food in the fridge overnight, her sister wants to arrange for Kiri to move into a residential home. Today, it was just before the social worker left that she turned to Kiri and said, 'Don't worry love, we'll make sure you're not a risk. Then I'll give you the chance to state your views.'

commentary

Four important points about empowerment emerge from this example. First, empowerment is a means to the end of improving the quality of Kiri's social care, not an end in itself, one more item to be ticked on the checklist of things the worker has done. Second, there is a risk that empowerment will be tacked onto bad practice in a tokenistic way rather than making a difference to practice as a whole.

Third, although empowerment is vital to successful social work, its position is uncertain, or problematic. At its strongest, it is a challenging concept, pointing to the imperative for those who have least and are treated most unjustly in society to take power and rise up against that injustice, against the people and the structures that oppress them. At its weakest, it may be diluted or taken over altogether by professionals and others in powerful positions, so that it fits neatly and benignly into professional frameworks and does not change the way people receiving services are controlled, managed, assessed and treated.

Fourth, empowerment is also a paradoxical aspect of practice. In order for a practitioner to empower somebody, they need to act, even if this action is facilitation rather than intervention (Burke and Dalrymple, 2002). Parsloe (1996, xxi) acknowledges that:

> empowerment cannot always be the primary goal of social work action. Sometimes children, old people, sick people and those who are mentally disabled actually need protection. The social worker will try to act in ways which provide the necessary protection and empower the individuals, or, in the case of a young child, the parents, to have as much control of their own lives as possible. But the first imperative may be to minimise risk.

But how does the practitioner manage the tension between minimizing risk and empowering the person? Risk management may disempower, depending on whether it is planned and carried out on behalf of, or with, the service user. Or, a person may wish to assert the right to continue to live in a situation of greater risk, so as to retain greater independence and enjoy a better quality of life in other respects.

Before discussing practice any further, let us clarify what empowerment means.

Growing significance of empowerment in social work

Before 1990, 'empowerment' hardly received a mention in standard British social work texts (see, for example, Coulshed, 1991), but since the 1990s, it has achieved prominence. A spate of publications indicates the willingness of researchers, policy-makers and practitioners to apply the notion of empowerment to different aspects of the human services (see, for example, Adams, 1991, 1994, 1996, 1997, 1998a, 1998b; Braye and Preston-Shoot, 1995; Charlton, 2000; Clarke and Stewart, 1992; Green, 1991; Gutierrez et al., 2003; Holdsworth, 1991; Jack, 1995; Kemshall and Littlechild, 2000; Parsloe, 1996; Perkins and Zimmerman, 1995; Ramcharan et al., 1997; Shera and Wells, 1999; Shor, 1992; Simon, 1994; Sleeter, 1991; Stewart, 1994; Thompson and Thompson, 2004; Wolfendale, 1992). The term 'emancipation' is sometimes used to refer to empowerment and may be linked with feminism (as in Dominelli, 1997, p. 47). Emancipation is associated in Britain with the women's movement for political equality through the right to vote. In social work, emancipation means liberating a person from oppression or from undesired physical, legal, moral or spiritual restraints and obligations.

Ironically and paradoxically, this very attractiveness of empowerment to people who use services and practitioners makes it even more likely to be professionalized, and, from the viewpoint of service users, diluted, distorted and exploited as a topic by researchers or students, or colonized by one interest group, such as community care managers or practitioners. It is inherently contradictory to refer to empowering people through social work carried out by social workers employed by state agencies working in bureaucratic organizations, the balance of whose practice derives from legislation rather than from principles laid down by a professional body, let alone from the experiences of people who use services.

Empowerment and self-help: radical or reactionary?

It was the late 1980s before empowerment came of age in the UK (Adams, 1990, p. 2), at which time it was quite slow to develop. Even in the mid-1990s, it had yet to achieve maturity, either as a critically understood concept, or as reflective practice (Baistow, 1994). Empowerment in the UK social work literature has eight main roots:

1. Social activism was imported from the black civil rights movement and public protest in the US in the 1960s. The leading exponent at the time was Barbara Solomon, whose book about black

empowerment and social work was first published in 1976. Solomon's writing (1976, 1986) fuelled movements for advocacy and empowerment in the US in the 1980s (Payne, 1997, p. 267).

2. Ideas about the engagement of individuals in informal education, neighbourhood action and democracy in management were influenced by the US social worker and writer Mary Parker Follett (1868–1933), who was 'rediscovered' as an inspirational figure in adult education, management development and the study of power in organizations.

3. The term 'empowerment' was beginning to be used, linked with children's and parents' rights, by some international childcare charities in the late 1980s and, in the direct experience of the author, some of the associated ideas and practices found their way into the UK offices of, for example, Save the Children.

4. Equally important, in the UK, the concept of empowerment has drawn on ideas and practices not derived from the US. It has inherited the traditions of self-help and mutual aid (Burns et al., 2004, pp. 6–11), reflected in the setting up of many friendly societies, or mutual societies (taking a small subscription from people and paying them money in times of hardship) from the eighteenth century onwards, kept alive in credit unions. Credit unions (acting as banks for poorer people) began in Germany in the mid-1850s, soon spread to Britain, moved in 1900 to Canada and within a decade to the US. Some still flourish today as financial cooperatives owned and controlled by their members (www.abcul.org). Empowerment has benefited from the growing faith in self-help for self-made success in business, charity policy and social work support for poor people, from the mid-nineteenth century, exemplified in the writing of the Yorkshire entrepreneur Samuel Smiles (1875, 1890). Smiles (1890), writing in mid-Victorian England, saw self-help as an expression of individualism, since it denotes activities whereby individuals and small groups deal with their problems. The role of professionals is largely limited to exhorting people to take responsibility for solving their own problems, with a little material and spiritual support for those whose efforts prove they deserve it. These ideas have never been the monopoly of Western countries. Kropotkin (1842–1921), a leading theorist of the anarchist movement who was imprisoned in Russia and France before living and writing in Bromley, England for 30 years, saw the collective benefits of self-help, the goal being a nationally healthy community, aiming to fulfil the individual and provide insurance against people's loss of

control over their own lives by improving their participation in the local community (Kropotkin, 1902). In addition, he felt that self-help should set out to improve the self-awareness of individuals. In one sense, self-help has always been popular. As Tax (1976, p. 448) has pointed out, self-help and mutual aid are probably as old as the history of people living in communities. Yet in Britain, they are viewed by some people as a by-product of Thatcherism, or as an import from the self-help boom in the US, which has gathered pace over the past 50 years. While self-help groups may be seen simply as a perpetuation of long-established or even prehistoric forms of mutual aid, it is perhaps more accurate to regard them as midway between such traditional 'folk' activities and fully professional services (Killilea, 1976, p. 47).

5. In Britain, various traditions of radical and socialist political and social protest since the 1960s, feeding the growth of political pressure groups and community and social action, were enriched greatly by feminist theory and practice. From the 1990s, large-scale protests using networks through mobile phones and the internet, particularly against schemes to develop new trunk roads in countryside of outstanding beauty or special scientific interest, and groups such as Reclaim the Streets, have demonstrated that people can exercise power collectively to influence policies.

6. Specifically therapeutic movements for empowerment have arisen in Britain, driven by British psychiatrists such as R.D. Laing and Cooper with whom the term 'anti-psychiatry' was associated. These have drawn on a range of ideas from Buddhism to feminism, giving additional impetus to a range of groups, such as women's therapy groups, which give power to the patient or client.

7. People caring for a partner or relative, unpaid and not in a professional capacity, have formed groups and organizations to voice their concerns collectively.

8. People who receive a range of health and welfare services have become increasingly organized and vociferous, on behalf of the 'service user' or 'consumer' perspective. Disabled people, older people and survivors of psychiatric services are prominent in this sector, which grew alongside movements for consumer protection, founded in the US by Garland Dempsey of the Consumer Education and Protective Association in Philadelphia in 1966, and, using new information and communication technologies, diversifying throughout the world in such groups as the Consumers Association of Penang and the Third World Network (Hilton, 2003; Hilton et al., 2006).

To summarize, contemporary forms of empowerment in many parts of the developed and developing world have fed off anti-sexist, anti-racist, anti-disablist and rights-based, critical, anti-oppressive movements, whereas its historical roots lie partly in traditions of mid-Victorian self-help, which tend to reflect the dominant values of Western countries such as the US.

From the late 1970s, in the US and the UK, self-help has figured prominently as a respectable contributor to the economy, based on the free enterprise economic theories of Milton Friedman and espoused by Republicans in the US and the Thatcherite Conservative government in Britain (1979–97). At the same time, the mutual aid aspects of the concept of self-help retained some currency with socialists and democrats.

Nature of self-help

Self-help may be defined as a means by which people help themselves. Self-help may thus be viewed as one form of empowerment. At the same time, it illustrates a particular strain of anti-intellectualism, which in Britain is exemplified in a mixture of utilitarian philosophy and preference for amateurism and charitable giving over professionalism embedded in theory and the social sciences, which besets present-day social work education, training and practice. In so far as self-help is heir to a well-entrenched tradition of amateurism and voluntary effort, links can be made with the British context of mid-Victorian philanthropy in which self-help was first associated, through the Charity Organisation Society. Self-help attracts criticism because, in Britain at least, for 150 years or more it has often reflected the values of middle-class society. In the late nineteenth century, Smiles put forward an essentially bourgeois view. From his respectable middle-class position, Smiles (1875, p. 361) preached that 'poverty often purifies, and braces a man's morals'. The harmful vice of charity was expressed in mere giving, which contrasted with the more considered charity of useful philanthropy (Smiles, 1875, p. 324). Hard work provided the preferred route to overcoming poverty, through self-denial, thrift, individual self-improvement and self-denying economy:

> The spirit of self-help is the root of all genuine growth in the individual; and, exhibited in the lives of many, it constitutes the true source of national vigour and strength. (Smiles, 1890, p. 1)

The positive aspect of these ideas is that self-help still has a place in the tradition of philanthropy and voluntary action in Britain and that the movement did not die with the end of the nineteenth century. The negative feature is the persistent tendency of individualism, which proposes self-help and private provision, for example in health and community care, as a substitute for statutory services rather than as complementary with, or supplementary to, them.

In healthcare and social work, several social and economic factors may have been associated with the growth and spread of self-help:

1. the impulse towards decarceration (moving people out of residential institutions to be supported, hopefully, in the community) in mental health
2. growing disillusionment with and questioning of conventional medical and clinical practice
3. increased prominence of alternative and complementary health
4. heightened awareness of some service users beyond their situation as stigmatized 'clients'
5. greater tendency for the power and decisions of professionals in health and social services to be viewed more critically
6. motivation of some practitioners towards harnessing networks of users of health and social services in helping activities of many kinds in the community.

Self-help and voluntary action

In the past half-century, in Britain at least, self-help has gained from the increased strength of the voluntary movement. But it should be noted that although self-help often involves voluntary activity, it is not synonymous with the voluntary sector. Conversely, the enthusiasm for the welfare state after the 1940s did not see the demise of voluntary activity and self-help. In fact, the 1950s witnessed the growth of many self-help and pressure groups. A significant report on the roles of volunteers at the end of the 1960s (Aves, 1969) strengthened the base of the voluntary sector, which still provides the support and encouragement for many self-help initiatives. Although voluntarism was gaining in strength from the 1960s, it was a further decade before the Wolfenden Report (1978) set the tone for the renewed emphasis specifically on self-help that has gathered momentum in Britain since then. Wolfenden emphasized the significance of the voluntary sector in developing partnerships between individuals, informal networks of support, voluntary bodies and the statutory agencies.

We can see how empowerment rooted in self-help had become associated with political conservatism, whereas since the late 1980s, the more democratic, equality-based and left-wing elements of empowerment have benefited from movements of liberation, rights and social activism, strengthened by anti-racism, feminism and critiques of inequalities and oppressions arising from differences in social class, age, disability, sexuality, religion and others. Both advocacy and empowerment are linked with movements for users' rights and user participation (Brandon and Brandon, 1988, 2001), although they should not necessarily be regarded as the exclusive bridge between providers and users of services (the User-Centred Services Group, 1993). The notion of partnership between users and workers may actually confuse the role of advocate and undermine or even contradict empowerment.

Empowerment through self-help has found its way into health services largely dominated by the medical model and the earliest examples of health service-based empowerment tend to be found mainly in the women's health movement and progressive psychiatry.

There is another dimension to empowerment in health, which involves challenging the medical model. In psychiatry, we need to go back several decades to radical psychiatry, as formulated at the Berkeley Radical Psychiatry Centre, for a more dramatically empowering approach, emphasizing people taking action to free themselves rather than relying on therapists and social workers to rescue them. The awareness that people's problems are political leads to the teaching of political values as part of problem-solving and as a way out of oppression. Claude Steiner (1975, pp. 80–105) asserts that rescue does not empower but perpetuates oppression. It colludes with people's sense of powerlessness. This example is adapted from his writing and the work of Hogie Wyckoff to whom he refers.

---

example

Empowering practice – liberation rather than rescue
The client (victim) insists to the social worker that being the subject of parental (abuser) abuse over many years makes it impossible to form constructive let alone long-term relationships with any other adult and that this can never be resolved since both parents died without all this being taken up with them. At first, the social worker is inclined to listen, console the victim, prolong mourning and self-pity and collude with the claim that nothing

can change (acting as rescuer). Subsequently, the social worker decides to work cooperatively with the 'victim', towards self-liberation. Figure 1.1 shows how necessary it is for the social worker to enable the person to engage in self-empowerment rather than succumb to the temptation to rescue the person through some form of help.

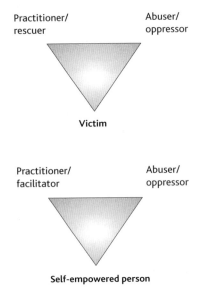

Practitioner/
rescuer

Abuser/
oppressor

Victim

Practitioner/
facilitator

Abuser/
oppressor

Self-empowered person

Figure 1.1 How rescue oppresses

Empowering elements of self-help

We have seen that self-help and empowering groups and organizations adopt and reflect a wide range of perspectives from reactionary to radical. According to Gartner and Riessman (1977, pp. 13–14), the philosophy of self-help is 'much more activist, consumer centred, informal, open and inexpensive'. It emphasizes non-professional themes: 'the concrete, the subjective, the experiential and the intuitive – in contrast to the professional emphasis on distance, perspective, reflection, systematic knowledge and understanding' (Table 1.1).

Table 1.1 Self-help and professionally led practice

Characteristic	Self-help	Professional practice
Relations between practitioner and 'client'	Democratic	Significant social distance
Degree of formality in practitioner–'client' relations	Informal	Formal
Focus of activity	Consumer/user centred	Agency and service centred
Style of communication between practitioner and client	Open	Reserved
Knowledge base	Everyday support, lay knowledge and skills	Professional knowledge, taking a perspective
Application	Intuitive	Systematic application and reflection
Level of resourcing	Inexpensive	Full cost of staff and services

The following elements of self-help all contribute to empowerment:

● advocacy and self-advocacy
● self-management
● anti-bureaucracy
● cooperation
● common experiences.

These are discussed below.

Advocacy and self-advocacy

Advocacy by professionals has its origins in the legal advocacy that solicitors and barristers provide for their clients (Payne, 1997, p. 267), while what Brandon (1995, p. 1) calls 'amateur advocacy' by any citizen can be traced back to the origins of Christianity. Advocacy is the activity of negotiating or representing on behalf of a person. Brandon defines it in relation to disability as:

> a person(s), either an individual or group with disabilities or their representative, pressing their case with influential others, about situations which either affect them directly or, and more usually, trying to prevent proposed changes which will leave them worse off. (Brandon, 1995, p. 1)

Advocacy can take a number of differing forms, such as self- or group advocacy, and can be considered as a further form of empowerment. Beresford and Croft (1993, p. 85) describe it as a process by which 'people are given a say that they have previously been denied and can turn paper entitlements into real rights'. Brandon (1995, p. 1) distinguishes three kinds of advocacy: self-advocacy by the person affected; paid or professional advocacy such as by a lawyer, accountant or trade union official; and unpaid or amateur advocacy. Payne (1991, p. 225) distinguishes case advocacy, by which the worker seeks to enhance people's access to services, from cause advocacy, which seeks to promote social change for social groups from which these people come. Rees (1991, p. 146) distinguishes advocacy relating to an individual's interests from that affecting many individuals, for example pursuing a common cause.

All aspects of advocacy and self-advocacy are potentially empowering. The roots of self-advocacy are generally regarded as stemming from advocacy in the area of learning disability (Lawson, 1991, p. 70). Self-advocacy is the process of the person representing herself or himself. Collective self-advocacy, which we discuss further in Chapter 4, involves self-help activity by groups of people on their own behalf. Thus, self-help, self-advocacy and empowerment are all linked. The self-advocate is the person who inverts the traditional view that professionals provide services for clients. The self-advocate is the client turned practitioner, the self-made advocate. Self-advocacy not only empowers the client but bypasses the professional. It demonstrates that while the client may need help, this can be obtained without dependence on a practitioner. Self-advocacy also obviates the need for a middleman, negotiator or facilitator. Self-advocacy asserts the rights of the person. In social work, the most dramatic achievements of self-advocacy are where clients have been marginalized or discriminated against, as in the cases of disabled people, older people or people with mental illnesses, and have managed to assert themselves and achieve changes in their circumstances.

Self-management

Self-management involves both an attachment to the desirability of individuals and small groups of people, face to face or through networks and email or postal contacts that can be managed from home, and the belief in problem management. In most self-help groups and organizations, there is an assumption that participants have the potential to manage their own self-help, whether through individual self-management, group leadership or other means.

Anti-bureaucracy

Self-help groups and organizations often assert the need to develop ways of organizing themselves that are different from many of the organizations with which they have come into contact as clients. This frequently involves an emphasis on avoiding hierarchical and bureaucratic patterns of organization.

Cooperation

The emphasis on mutual help or joint care (Wilson, 1988), which distinguishes much self-help activity from selfish individualism, is often expressed in a belief in democracy, equality of status and power within groups and organizations, shared leadership and cooperation in decision-making. Some self-help initiatives have much in common with cooperatives. **Mutual help** (or mutual aid) is the means by which individuals, groups or organizations come together and share an experience or problem, with a view to individual and mutual benefit.

Common experiences

Quite often a requirement of participants is a willingness to start from the common base of experience defined by the group or organization. This can involve members of a group necessarily sharing issues or problems. It also implies a resistance to internal divisions in groups between expert and lay members, therapists and clients. Although some self-help actually espouses anti-professionalism, this is not always the case. What is more often held to is the principle that the self-help process should not simply be the property of professionals but should be able to be initiated and engaged in by any of the participants. On the whole, research suggests that self-help groups tend to accept rather than reject relationships with professionals (Lieberman and Borman, 1976), while self-help may involve a profound critique of professional activities (Gartner and Riessman, 1977, p. 12).

Empowerment in social work: a changing discourse

Empowerment as a discourse in social work has changed since the late 1980s. A **discourse** is a system of beliefs and practices sustained by being passed on between individuals, groups and organizations in society and helping to construct the social arrangements that people regard as reality. In the 1980s in Britain, social work lost ground against Thatcherite individualism and experienced assaults on its credibility through various scandals and inquiries. In the 1990s, consumerism came to dominate the newly created, managed, quasi-markets for the delivery of health and social care services. In the twenty-first century, empowerment may be regarded as a means of transcending these social, political and policy limitations and liberating both workers and service users. But it could also be regarded as a rhetorical gesture, a device of government to keep the consumers of welfare in their places in the queues for dole, social security, private health and welfare, and national lottery prizes. According to Mullender and Ward (1991, p. 1), empowerment is a term 'used to justify propositions which, at root, represent varying ideological and political positions', and which 'lacks specificity and glosses over significant differences'. It 'acts as a "social aerosol", covering up the disturbing smell of conflict and conceptual division'.

An empowering practice needs to be purposeful and critical. In developing this, the first task is to clarify the concept of empowerment and relate it to other allied concepts, before examining aspects in more detail in subsequent chapters.

Working definitions of empowerment

The inherently problematic nature of empowerment is part of a wider pattern of insecurity and instability in social work, highlighted by Schön (1991, p. 23). Social work does not possess a well-researched, agreed evidence base for practice: a knowledge base that is systematically developed, scientifically proven and part of a public and professional consensus about the values, techniques and skills to be adopted by qualified and practising social workers.

The uncertainties extend to what we call the person receiving social services. Do we use the term 'consumer', 'client' or 'user'? These words conjure up different images. 'Consumer' reminds us of being a customer and purchasing goods or services. 'Client' is usually reserved for the recipient of professional services. 'User' may be applied to the person with a drug or alcohol problem as well as to the person receiving social services.

Empowerment means different things to different people, but we need a working definition to get us started. The *Dictionary of Social Work* links empowerment with self-help:

> Empowerment can refer to user participation in services and to the self-help movement generally, in which groups take action on their own behalf, either in cooperation with, or independently of, the statutory services. (Thomas and Pierson, 1995, pp. 134–5)

Empowerment literally means 'becoming powerful', but in social work it has come to mean much more than that. It embraces both theory and method. According to the *Dictionary of Social Work*, empowerment is:

> theory concerned with how people may gain collective control over their lives, so as to achieve their interests as a group, and a method by which social workers seek to enhance the power of people who lack it. (Thomas and Pierson, 1995, p. 134)

Bringing these statements together, **empowerment** may be defined as: the capacity of individuals, groups and/or communities to take control of their circumstances, exercise power and achieve their own goals, and the process by which, individually and collectively, they are able to help themselves and others to maximize the quality of their lives.

It is important to recognize that our definition includes the three elements of people's capacity, the process by which they exercise power and their achievement, not just individually but also mutually through empowering experience with others. Self-empowerment is not just individually based and self-directed, but involves mutual support to empower other people. In order to be empowered, people need the power to change key aspects of their environment and an understanding of themselves as well as the motivation to work individually and collectively towards change (Lord and Hutchison, 1993, p. 3).

Empowerment is a political concept, although the extent to which this is apparent to those involved depends on their approach and the circumstances in which the empowering work takes place. The political dimension of the concept of empowerment is not party political because its activist tone transcends party politics; it is not a legal term (such as intermediate care, community care and so on) derived from the law; it is a concept that is rapidly being colonized by professionals, which carries the risk, of course, of marginalizing and perpetuating the exclusion of service users; it is a generic concept, which can be attached to any aspect of social work, in areas such as disability, mental health and anti-racist and anti-sexist practice. According to Mullender and Ward (1991, p. 6):

Empowering practice, like the demands of the user movements it serves, seeks change not only through *winning power* – bringing to those who have been oppressed the exercise of control over what happens to them – but through transforming it.

There is a tension between the view that it is sufficient to *feel* empowered and the view that the outcomes of empowerment are important. A useful paper by Ruth Alsop and Nina Heinsohn (2005, p. 4) provides criteria by which empowerment can be measured. They argue that empowerment is 'a person's capacity to make effective choices [and] ... the capacity to transform choices into desired actions and outcomes'. They suggest that this individual empowerment is affected by two factors: personal agency and opportunity. Personal agency is composed of the following assets: psychological, informational, organizational, material, social, financial and human, and the opportunities a person has are affected by legislation, various regulatory frameworks and rules and the social norms governing behaviour in society; in other words, 'degrees of empowerment are measured by the existence of choice, the use of choice and the achievement of choice' (Alsop and Heinsohn, 2005, p. 4).

Related concepts

The multifaceted nature of the concept of empowerment makes it necessary for us to try to deconstruct it. **Deconstruction** means digging away at discourses about a concept so as to probe beyond the dominant or widespread ideas contributing to them, to find out what lies behind or beyond them. Empowerment is holistic and non-hierarchical. Empowerment is about taking control, achieving self-direction, seeking inclusiveness rooted in connectedness with the experiences of other people. It concerns individual achievement and social action. One aspect feeds another. Before exploring this, let us excavate some of the main themes in empowerment writing and practice.

Democratization

In an important way, empowerment concerns participation. Beresford and Croft are among the best-known exponents in Britain of service user participation and this tends to be linked with the process of empowerment. Their two early projects, which contributed greatly to this area, are the study of a patch-based approach to delivering welfare services (Beresford and Croft, 1986) and the research into citizen involvement funded by the Joseph Rowntree Foundation (Beresford and Croft, 1993). The latter research illustrates the barriers to participation, progress towards which is an uphill struggle that is still ongoing. On a related tack, Sainsbury (1989, pp. 105–6) has written of the need not to create a false dichotomy between the roles of social work in furthering participation by people and those of protection of people, both of which are necessary in social work. He cautions against unrealistically anticipating that social work will be able to fight effectively against the tendency of society to promote differences between people in terms of income and power. He notes that this may be unattainable at present, since it is only possible to pursue social justice through achieving equality if citizens' social rights are equated with systems for allocating resources based on principles of social justice.

Normalization/social role valorization

Normalization and social role valorization refer to processes by which disabled people and people with mental health problems have engaged in movements towards maintaining and promoting their own independence and managing their own lives (Sinclair, 1988, quoted in Payne, 1991, p. 226; Towell, 1988; Wolfensberger, 1972, 1982).

Reflexivity and criticality

By its nature, empowerment is a critical activity. Self-empowerment and self-advocacy necessitate reflexivity by the individual. **Reflexivity** involves using the impact of a situation or experience on oneself to help understanding and feed into future activity.

Consciousness-raising

Although empowerment does not always figure explicitly in the literature concerning consciousness-raising, it is implicit in the process. One illustration of this is the women's therapy group movement, involving individuals benefiting therapeutically but also gaining awareness of the social context of their problems and developing ways of addressing these. Another example is community work, which, despite its difficult history in local authority-funded practice since the mid-1970s (Jacobs and Popple, 1994), is a presence in the 2000s.

Carer and service user-led practice

A range of approaches, both traditional and new, conservative and radical, come under this heading. From the 1970s, there has been a trend towards people in receipt of welfare benefits and health and personal social services demanding more control over the services provided for them. As Craig notes, this is located in the wider context of community action by poorer people (Craig, 1989), and the gap between the encouragement by government of participation by service users on the one hand and the lack of resources to underpin such participation on the other (Craig, 1992). Undoubtedly, taking the initiative by engaging in user-led activities is one route to self-empowerment and the empowerment of others. But it is necessary to distinguish the objective judgement that one person may make about another person necessarily being empowered, because of involvement in a user group, and the subjective experience of that person. For example, participation by a family carer in a partnership board (which brings professionals, people with learning disabilities and their carers together to discuss and improve their services) or an adult carer in a carers' self-help group may initially reinforce the experience of being excluded, isolated and powerless before the person moves on to acting positively to tackle these problems.

Radical social work

We need to beware of calling empowerment radical. It is difficult to establish the relationship between empowerment and other concepts, such as those rooted in a range of radical ideas. 'Radicalism' is a generic term for a wide range of standpoints, which space only allows a brief mention of here. The word 'radical' comes from the Latin meaning 'a root', so radicals are concerned to dig up existing arrangements by their roots. However, radical in one context is not radical in another. In a conservative setting, socialism is radical and vice versa. In a traditional setting, change is radical, and yet traditionalists – such as the American Homer Lane (1875–1925), who, in 1913 in Dorset, England, founded the pioneer Little Commonwealth childcare community for 'problem' children from the towns – are radical to the extent that they seek to replace present-day arrangements (in his time, these were the workhouses, reformatories and orphanages for children in need) with a utopian vision of self-governing communities as they imagined them to be before the industrial society brought about the social problems of urban society.

Marxist socialist perspectives can be viewed as radical and generally seek empowerment as a means of promoting contradictions in society, with a view to eventually achieving change (Payne, 1991, p. 225). In this connection, Rojek (1986) argues that advocacy and empowerment have their origins in fundamentally different objectives from the Marxist and radical perspectives to which they are closely related. Adherents to radical social work have propounded empowerment. One version of collective action in practice is linked with a more explicitly socialist agenda, such as the Marxist view expounded by Walker and Beaumont (1981, pp. 174–95). This radical critique of probation work, which relies heavily on social and environmental explanations of people's problems, is an alternative to those that are individually based (Walker and Beaumont, 1981, pp. 89–93). Thompson (1993, p. 32) links empowerment with radical social work, describing it as:

> an approach to social work which seeks to locate the problems experienced by clients in the wider social context of structured inequalities, poverty, inadequate amenities, discrimination and oppression. It sees social work as primarily a political venture, a struggle to humanise, as far as possible, the oppressive circumstances to which clients are subject. It is premised on the key notion of empowerment, the process of giving greater power to clients in whatever ways possible – resources, education, political and self-awareness and so on.

This extract glosses over the inherent paradox of professional involvement in empowerment, which revolves round the desirability of professionals giving power to other people. It would be unfortunate if powerful people were able to dismiss advocacy and empowerment as radical, and therefore marginal, ideas. We need to incorporate them into the mainstream of practice.

Anti-oppressive practice

Critiques of oppression from black, feminist, anti-ageist and disability perspectives have all converged on the concept of, and need for, empowerment. Empowerment may be used as the defining feature of work with particular groups, such as gay and lesbian people (Tully, 2000) and has contributed to the growing body of literature on anti-oppressive practice in social work. Empowerment is anti-oppressive, as Ward and Mullender (1991) rightly observe, although we should exercise caution about claiming that user-directed groups, no matter how empowered, will change the structural features of the world in which their members live (Page, 1992).

Postmodernism and empowerment

Leonard (1997) has linked the continuing importance of empowerment and emancipation with the direction of social work in the postmodern era. The fragmentation of service provision through the multiplication of service providers in the public, private and independent sectors is one feature of postmodern welfare. In the early twenty-first century, for example, the gradual spread of direct payments to people in the UK, enabling them to buy their own care services, by employing carers or 'personal assistants', is both empowering and a fragmentation of the labour market. It creates a growing number (more than 50,000 in 2007) of small employers of between one and six personal assistants and it distances the state from direct service provision.

The wider changes that have produced the fragmentation of socialist movements, one manifestation being the changing political complexion of European countries since the disappearance of the Iron Curtain, can be linked with the dissolution in many countries during the latter part of the twentieth century of the dichotomy between the single political options of Left and Right. The postmodern era, some commentators claim, provides opportunities for a politics that transcends the grand theories, such as those of Marx, and gives space to a multiplicity of diverse voices. The fragmentation of the personal social services into many small providers could be seen as one manifestation of the breaking up of the large, all-providing local authority providers.

The term 'anti-oppressive work' has provided a language for the paradigm of empowerment, which transcends the policies and politics of the many different groups and interests involved in social work. In the postmodern era, empowerment has the potential to become either a unifying or a divisive theme of social work, in the sense that not all managers of children's and adult social services will embrace the empowerment of service users with enthusiasm.

International developments

Some of the literature on participation and empowerment reflects Western democratic values rather than the richness of global diversity. Payne (1991, p. 227) makes the point that empowerment is rationalistic, that is, it has links with humanist and existential theory and practice, in that it emphasizes self-knowledge and self-control, accepting that people can control their own lives by rational, cognitive means and assuming that the environment can be changed directly, in favour of the service user. One immediate consequence of the rationalistic basis for empowerment approaches is that failure to achieve immediate major changes in the conditions of their lives is likely to make people feel disappointed and therefore disillusioned with empowerment. Parsloe (1996, xvii) reminds us that 'empowerment in social work is a western concept', which means that it is rooted in Western notions of individualism and self-advancement. It is part of Western culture to associate empowerment with democracy and the paramount importance of individual choice and freedom. If we accept that these ideas are relative to particular cultures and not absolute, we may conclude that empowerment is rationalistic only if you start from the individual's thoughts and plans, rather than from traditional values based on the paramount importance of the continuance of the state, the community and the family. Seeking power is just as likely to be values based, reflected in principles believed in by people, rather than an outcome of rational debate and thought. In Eastern societies such as Japan, self-help is likely to conflict with the lack of democratic pluralism and the importance of hierarchies in administering organizations (Oka, 1994).

Empowerment in China, Hong Kong and other Chinese communities outside China has advanced in theoretical debates (Yip, 2004) and in specific areas of practice such as empowerment groups for divorced women (Chan et al., 2002), but there is a relative lack of research literature (Mok et al., 2006), some difficulty in reaching consensus over general social work concepts (Hutchings and Taylor, 2007) and a need for development with appropriate cultural sensitivity in order to avoid different types of false empowerment (Yip, 2004). In part, this reflects cultural and political diversity and in part religious and philosophical differences between East and West (Ng and Chan, 2005).

While empowerment is associated in the West with individualism and the rights of the individual, in many developing societies mutual help and traditions of family life and community are as important. However, there is no clear-cut division between different beliefs and geographical locations. Emancipatory ideas are not bound by geographical boundaries and the growing social and financial freedom of people to travel, plus the spread of the internet, has accelerated existing trends towards their global accessibility.

Empowerment is associated with the struggles of people against divisions and inequalities. Disabled people, people who are mentally ill, people who are older and people in particular ethnic groups all have formed groups and organizations to promote their causes. Women have challenged the oppressiveness of patriarchal laws, policies and societies. The history of empowerment in many developed and developing countries coincides with movements to emancipate women and through them many other parts of the community.

There is a continuum between the 'softer' end of patient and public involvement in healthcare and patient empowerment. The authorities may introduce a little consultation – the focus group or citizens' jury, with members chosen randomly or by government; the representative of clients or their carers invited to join a working party or steering group as the token consumer. Patients, and to a lesser extent the public, have been encouraged towards greater participation in health in many Western countries, including Germany, Denmark, Norway (Heikkilä and Julkunen, 2003), France, the UK, Australia, Canada and the US (Simces, 2003). Of course, patient involvement in their own healthcare is very different from public involvement in taking strategic decisions about policy and organization of health services (Florin and Dixon, 2004). The latter is relatively uncommon.

There are continuities between empowerment and participatory initiatives in many parts of the world (Steeves and Melkote, 2001). Mohan and Stokke (2000) argue that Western countries have tended to focus on work in developing countries which concentrates more on local participatory development and empowerment projects. The dangers of focusing too narrowly on partnership with, and listening to, the voices of those receiving services, as Stewart (2003) argues, include losing sight of factors such as how to structurally improve the circumstances of the most excluded and poor people and how to combat deep-rooted inequality, the unequal exercise of power, and national and transnational economic and social influences. Empowerment should, and sometimes does, increasingly engage with global challenges, notably in work with poor, hungry, oppressed and sick people in the developing nations, such as some African countries (Botchway, 2001). This is compatible with the portrayal of empowerment by Lee (2001, p. 401) as a universal rather than as an ethnocentric or Eurocentric concept. Empowerment concepts and practices are not the invention solely of the developed world. They cross regional and national boundaries and provide strategies to tackle problems posed by global inequalities. Responses to these inequalities need to engage not only with individuals but with groups, organizations, laws and policies. Empowering people implies tackling individual problems and structural – including sociopolitical and economic – divisions and inequalities. The World Bank, with the US its majority stakeholder among 184 countries, funds more than 1,800 projects, its partners being governments and other public bodies and private commercial organizations. The critical question, however, has been posed starkly by Waring (2004, p. 5), who wonders whether there has been any 'genuine grassroots participation' in 'the identification of the goals and the objectives, the parameters of the project, or the outcomes desired of the project by those directly impacted', despite the World Bank's consultation with more than 60,000 poor men and women in more than 50 countries to inform its strategy.

The influence of the US on Western Europe is no more significant than what has been learned from the developing countries. The mushrooming literature in the US and UK on empowerment and participation of adults, children and young people in the health and social care field indicates a high level of interest in both these countries. The problems of Western industrial societies tend to arise from overproduction and overconsumption, whereas in developing countries, the reverse is true. Here, self-help and mutual aid commonly make up not just the core of health and social services but also of the economic and social fabric itself. This applies from agriculture to education, from housing to the supply of energy. In most areas, the majority of the people since time immemorial have had to provide their own tools, buildings, skills and other resources, or run the risk of deprivation or death.

In the developing countries, empowerment by poor people is as much a political issue as anywhere else. For instance, the shift to community-based, local, non-professionally led campaigns or programmes to change lifestyles, reduce environmental hazards or deal effectively with personal health and social problems may involve confronting the exploitive power in societies either apathetic or actively hostile towards any activity implying changes in their policies or practices (Afshar, 1998). In many countries, self-help and self-care are much more of a substitute for non-existent health and social services rather than complementary to existing provision.

Oka (1994) shows how, in Japan, political obstacles such as lack of pluralism and centralization of administrative power combine with cultural factors to discourage individualistic self-help. On the other hand, in other countries, self-help essentially operates as an alternative to, or a substitute for, social work. Much self-help activity, especially in groups, is referred to as user led. User-led groups may be supportive of, indifferent towards or critical of social work. In the latter case, whether the user group is fairly long-lived or has a limited life, it tends to function as a critical presence in the field of helping services. That is, its presence generally implies criticism of existing services. This critical presence may be with regard to the practice of the individual social worker, the agency, the entire service, or indeed several services.

In the developing countries, participatory research (see Chapter 9) and social development (see Chapter 8) go hand in hand. Here, participatory approaches to development operate in many forms. One of the best known is PRA (participatory rural appraisal/participatory relaxed appraisal/participatory reflection and action) (Holland and Blackburn, 1998), which is promoted and published by Intermediate Technology Publications (103–5 Southampton Row, London WC1B 4HH, England).

Mohan and Stokke (2000) refer to a tendency towards more localized approaches to participation and empowerment. They highlight the danger that focusing on local conditions and initiatives may divert attention from inequalities and structural power relations, locally and more widely. Despite this warning about the fragmentation illustrated by the diversity of local practice in different countries and regions, there is a sense in which empowerment initiatives include some that are engaging with some major barriers to people being free from famine and poverty, overcoming inequality and attaining personal and social freedom.

Conclusion

This brief review shows that the complex field of empowerment in social work relates to many diverse, and to some extent problematic, concepts and areas of practice. Not least, there is a divergence between contemporary anti-oppressive and equality-driven influences on empowerment and the traditions of self-help and mutual aid. Additionally, a critical understanding of empowerment needs to take account of the wider international context of the developing countries, as well as developments in Western Europe and the US.

putting it into practice

Activity 1

Identify and explain each of the main elements of empowerment.

Activity 2

Write your own definition of empowerment.

Activity 3

List what you regard as the main themes of empowering practice in social work.

Further reading

Gutierrez, L. and Lewis, E.A. (1999) *Empowering Women of Color*, New York, Columbia University Press.

Gutierrez, L., Parsons, R. and Cox, E. (eds) (2003) *Empowerment in Social Work Practice: A Sourcebook*, Belmont, CA, Wadsworth. These two books by Gutierrez and colleagues contain useful general analysis about discrimination, oppression and empowerment and specific guidance on practice development.

Humphries, B. (ed.) (1996) *Critical Perspectives on Empowerment*, Birmingham, Venture. A stimulating series of essays in contemporary contextual and theoretical aspects of empowerment.

Parsloe, P. (ed.) (1996) *Pathways to Empowerment*, Birmingham, Venture. A useful collection of studies of empowerment approaches and practice.

Rees, S. (1991) *Achieving Power: Practice and Policy in Social Welfare*, London, Allen & Unwin. A detailed exposition of a framework for conceptualizing and practising empowerment.

Shera, W. and Wells, L.M. (eds) (1999) *Empowerment Practice in Social Work*, Toronto, Canadian Scholars Press. An edited collection of conference papers examining theories, applications, critical issues and future directions for empowerment.

2 | Understanding participation by people who use services and by carers

In my current work with colleagues in the university and with groups of carers and people who use services, I have been consultant to a social care organization implementing a strategy for enabling carers and people who use services to take an active part in the work. Some staff in the organization have concerns that this participation by people may get out of control, in the sense of costing too much and giving people too much power to dictate policy and practice in inappropriate areas. In contrast, a commonly expressed view by carers and service users is that, provided their out-of-pocket expenses are met, they are less concerned about payment of fees than about having their views heard. Many regard empowerment as feeling valued and having their views recognized and acknowledged as making a significant contribution. Many of them do not seek participation to the point of taking control of any aspect of running the organization. In this chapter, by the way, I sometimes use the term 'service users' to include carers and people who use services.

Introduction

As we noted in Chapter 1, people were engaged in self-help and mutual help before the nineteenth century. User involvement and participation was a logical development from these trends and, from the 1960s, was heightened in the US, the UK and other Western European countries by several factors linked with the growing tendency of members of the public to question the expertise and power of practitioners:

- heightened voice of the consumer
- emergence of pressure groups
- development of individual and group self-advocacy
- spread of neighbourhood campaigns and protests and community action.

Participation by people in policy and service development and delivery is becoming the accepted orthodoxy, not just in social work but across the health and welfare services, in the US, Canada, Australia and many Western European countries. Even where many people distance themselves from formal participation in politics, informally and at the interpersonal level, research in the UK, for example, indicates that there is a great deal of participation going on (Pattie et al., 2004). There is similarity between the growing strength of participation in policy and practice and the move towards participatory research methods (Cornwall and Jewkes, 1995). In the twenty-first century, health and welfare policy in the UK has advocated increasing the participation in providing organizations by carers and people who use services, as part of the government's agenda for modernizing health and social services. In England, the Commission for Patient and Public Involvement in Health (CPPIH), an independent, non-departmental public body, was established in 2003 and led to over 400 Patient and Public Involvement (PPI) forums being set up, one for each NHS Trust, with the aim of improving people's say in local health services. In 2007, this system was replaced by Local Involvement Networks (LINks), which extended to social care, under the Local Government and Public Involvement in Health Act 2007. All 30 member countries of the Organisation for Economic Co-operation and Development (OECD), which includes many European countries and also South Korea, Mexico, Japan, Iceland, New Zealand, Turkey and the US, are committed to increasing the representation and participation of citizens, and evaluations of public participation in different OECD countries have produced lessons for practice (OECD, 2005). While participation is not synonymous with empowerment, the two concepts overlap significantly. More often than not, a service user or carer needs to be empowered in order to participate, or at least is likely to become empowered through participating.

The key question is what the evidence tells us about the most and least effective ways of enabling carers and people who use services to participate. This chapter draws on the evidence first to examine some of the barriers and second to discuss some pointers towards empowering people by enhancing their participation in social work and social care.

We should be in no doubt, however, that the task of improving participation by patients, clients, people using services and carers is not straightforward, for two reasons:

1. There is no consensus that it is always a good thing. For example, Salmon and Hall (2004) conclude from a critical analysis of patient participation in treatment decisions (or, in rare cases, patient-controlled treatment) in the UK that it does not fit the prevailing medical ideology that 'doctor knows best', it may not be what patients want and may confuse rather than clarify what patients need.

2. Participation cannot be presented as a series of simple tasks to be carried out as a taken-for-granted part of the responsibilities of practitioners. There is a lack of consensus among managers, professionals and people receiving services about what participation means. There is no readily available strategy for achieving participation in the great number and variety of health and social services organizations and there are no generally agreed milestones for implementing such a strategy.

Having said this, both outside and inside health and welfare providing agencies there is a huge and dynamic wealth of activity and energy created and sustained by people who use services and carers themselves. Change is happening and much of it is significant. Our task in this chapter is to provide a basis for understanding what is going on.

Participation and involvement: contested concepts

Participatory approaches undoubtedly can challenge traditional and even oppressive power structures in families, groups, organizations and society and provide excluded and seldom heard people with access to power. On the other hand, participation can also be used to serve a wide range of political and social interests, which can be implemented by those in power as an instrument of reinforcing oppressive and exclusive practices (Kesoy, 2005). Less obvious, but no less insidious, in respect of participation initiatives involving black and minority ethnic service users, is the tendency, pointed out by Begum (2006, p. vii), for policy-makers and practitioners often to seek the participation of professionals and leaders among black and minority ethnic communities rather than engaging service users directly.

What do we mean by participation and involvement?

The word 'participation' means different things to different people. Similarly, the words 'participation' and 'involvement' often are used as though they are interchangeable. At best, this misses an opportunity, while at worst it creates confusion. To avoid confusion in this book, we use these words in the following ways:

- **Involvement** refers to the entire continuum of taking part, from one-off consultation through equal partnership to taking control.
- **Participation** refers to that part of the continuum of involvement where people play a more active part, have greater choice, exercise more power and contribute significantly to decision-making and management.

This means that while participation probably is empowering, some less intensive forms of involvement, such as one-off, occasional consultation, may be tokenistic and disempowering. By **consultation** we mean seeking people's views as one source of influencing decisions, policy and practice.

The term 'citizen engagement' is sometimes used. Phillips and Orsini (2002) regard this as a form of involvement in which citizens, politicians and professionals constantly interact and discuss together. The key element to engagement, however, is that the citizens feel their interaction with officials is meaningful. **Citizen engagement** can be defined, therefore, as that early stage in the process of involvement where citizens and officials are in regular or continuous interaction that the citizens regard as significant.

Models of participation

We can view participation from different viewpoints, according to whether we are policy-makers, managers, professionals, people on the receiving end of services or people who are excluded altogether. We can also view participation in terms of its overall purpose. The goal of the authorities may be (Jackson, 2004, p. 4) to enable people to participate *politically*, by influencing political decision-making, or to enable them to participate *socially*, by engaging in everyday policy and practice. Thus, the purpose of participation may be to educate people, enable them to adjust, empower them to take decisions, manage resources and influence policy, or ensure they conform (Jackson, 2004, p. 4).

Why participation?

Participation in policy and practice can be justified because:

- people have a right to participate

- people will gain from participating
- services will improve in quality
- services will become more inclusive
- people's interpersonal and social skills will improve
- people will learn more democratic ways of working
- wider participation will be encouraged.

Article 26 of the European Union (EU) *Charter of Fundamental Rights* asserts the right of people with disabilities to participate in the life of the community (European Parliament, 2000). Children and young people have rights under the UN *Convention on the Rights of the Child* (United Nations, 1989), wherein Article 12 states that it is the duty of governments and professionals to consult young people in the planning and delivery of services.

Cohen and Emanuel (2000, p. 5) point out that the following other rights of children and young people under this UN Convention also involve participation. They include a longer list such as non-discrimination (Article 2), which does not explicitly involve participation. The following are items that more obviously include participation:

- the freedom to associate with other people (Article 15)
- the right of access to appropriate information (Article 17)
- the right to periodic review of treatment (Article 25).

Differences between the structure and functioning of health services in different countries, as well as historical and cultural variations, make for a wide variety of emphases. In the UK, since the early 1990s, there is a tendency towards patient participation being more institutionalized, driven by policy and legislation and by pressure from patients and members of the public. In countries such as Germany, there is a tendency towards patient and public involvement through self-help. In a publication by the Social Care Institute for Excellence (SCIE) on participation by black and minority ethnic service users, Begum (2006, p. 5) observes that participation by service users across the board in England is now positioned 'at the heart of social care policy and practice'. However, this publication highlights the difficulty of establishing the precise status of participation in practice. What is this positioning? Does it mean the aim of participation is accepted? Participation in what? Is it, as in the health area in the US and the UK, patient involvement in one's own treatment, or is it public participation in policy, management and planning? And to what extent is this participation actually achieved?

We must distinguish between public involvement in healthcare, which concerns the participation of members of the public in influencing local, regional or national policy and management decisions, and patient involvement, which concerns individual patients becoming involved with professionals who treat them, so as to affect decisions about their own healthcare (Florin and Dixon, 2004, p. 159). Despite the widespread acceptance in policy and practice in the UK of the desirability of carers and people who use services participating fully in service provision and delivery, there is limited evidence of this being adopted wholeheartedly in health and social care services in the public, private and voluntary sectors. Why is this the case? We can make five general points:

1. Not everybody is interested in being empowered. Among individuals, groups and organizations described as service users, a number are involuntary or unwilling users of services. People should be free to choose for themselves what they do or do not engage in.

2. It is hard to achieve representation across the wide variety of service user and carers. Some categories of service use are more prominent than others and some service users, notably people who are disabled, occupy the foreground of debates, while others are in the background or, as we say, are 'seldom heard'. So any involvement of carers and service users is more likely than not to include disabled people, since they seem to have made particular progress towards having their voices heard. Yet even in this sector, in a major study of participation by disabled people, Barnes and Mercer (2006, p. 72) note:

> The historical denial of any significant participation of disabled people in running voluntary organisations, as well as statutory services, has been sustained despite claims of a shift towards more user involvement by the mainstream sectors during the 1990s.

3. The widespread use of plans and strategies for increasing the participation of service users and carers in the work of health, education and social services agencies is positive, in that it raises the agency and practitioner profile of empowerment. At the same time, paradoxically, it makes more obvious the power differential between practitioners and people using services and creates enormous complications, for example in debates about how to reward those on benefits. Ironically (see below), a person on benefits cannot receive more than a few pounds a week as payment for taking part, without losing entitlement to benefits.

4. There is no consensus among managers, practitioners and people we work with about how we should refer to them. Should we say they are users, service users, consumers, customers, service advisers, experts through experience, or people who use services? We have a tendency, in the common phrase 'service users and carers', to refer first to the service user and mention the carer as an afterthought.

5. Service users and carers do not change at one stroke from a state of disempowerment to being fully empowered. The reality is that our identities are not constructed from single experiences. We may feel empowered in one situation and continue to feel disempowered in another. We may shift along the continuum between empowerment and disempowerment. Quite often, carers and people who use services may be able to participate, using their identities as carers and service users. Without these labels, they may be excluded from participation. It would be preferable, perhaps, if people were able to continue to participate, while their identities as carers or service users could change.

The lack of universally agreed terms for people who receive welfare services is not a coincidence, but is a sign of the problematic status of the client in the health and social services and the somewhat controversial nature of their claimed right to participate in the shaping and delivery of the services they receive. While we can find reasonably straightforward, simple definitions for social work service users and carers, a term to describe them does not exist, in the UK at any rate. **Service users**, or people who use services, are people who are eligible to receive social care and social work services either from professionals or through direct payments, which enable them to buy these services. **Carers** are people who give care informally and unpaid, usually as partners, other household members, friends and neighbours.

Different kinds of participation

Participation takes place in two main territories:

1. *Service providing organizations:* People who receive services and carers may aspire to controlling services; health service managers may view it as patients taking a fuller, that is, more knowledgeable and informed, part in their treatment; social work and social care providers may see it as seeking the views of consumers before professionals make the decisions.

2. *Self-help, user-led and carer-led organizations:* Alongside health and welfare organizations, there are a growing number of groups and organizations led by service users, whose members aim to support each other. In 2005, for example, Colin Barnes (2005, p. 1) stated that there were 85 such organizations in Britain controlled and run by disabled people.

Participation activities cover a wide span:

- One-off consultation
- Ongoing consultation
- Working with decision-making groups
- Working individually and in groups with professionals, for example in case reviews, where an individual's services are planned, delivered and reviewed
- Contributing to quality assurance, for example taking part in inspections
- Acting as contributor to service provision, that is, as co-provider to other people
- Acting as educator of other people
- Acting as mentor to other people
- Leading an activity
- Managing a group of people in an activity.

Perspectives on involvement and participation

Beresford and Croft (1993) put forward two main models of involvement and participation:

1. *The consumerist model:* This regards the individual service user as no more than a consumer, who is able to make choices in the marketplace of available goods and services that influence what is made available, but, as a net consumer of services, is segregated from the general public who are able to be net creators of the wealth of society.
2. *The democratic model:* This regards the individual service user as an equal citizen with other members of the general public, who, through greater participation, is able to gain power and more control over his or her life and contribute to the development of better services.

These two models have been referred to in the literature on citizen involvement in welfare since the mid-1990s in the UK. We can summarize the two models in Table 2.1.

Table 2.1 Consumerist and democratic models of participation

Aspect of empowerment	Nature of model	
	Consumerist	Democratic
Identity of person using services	Consumer	Active citizen
Role	Exercising choice	Empowered contributor
Net gain or loss to GDP or society	Consuming services	Creating capital and revenue

Notes:

1 GDP is the gross domestic product or total amount of wealth, totalling goods and services, produced in society over a given period.

2 The idea of net consumers and wealth creators is drawn from Beresford 2001 p. 502, who argues that New Right arguments since the 1990s have been used to justify the consumerist model as the underpinning for the contract-based system of commissioning and delivering social care services increasingly through the independent, that is private and voluntary, sectors.

Johnson (2006) proposes four orientations to participation by people in shaping policy: scientific, managerial, market and social justice as shown in Table 2.2.

Table 2.2 Four orientations towards participation

Model	Characteristics
Scientific	Improving outcomes of services
	Ensuring effectiveness of services
Managerial	Improving cost-effectiveness
	Increasing efficiency
	Improving safety and quality
Market	Increasing share of the market
	Providing services that meet customers' needs
Social justice	Promoting human and democratic rights
	Achieving power shifts/empowerment
	Achieving equity
	Enhancing citizenship
	Maintaining public accountability

We can add to the richness of understanding about participation by exploring the ideas of Mary Parker Follett (1918, 1924), who developed a theory of participatory democracy (Table 2.3), focusing on the neighbourhood as the main setting for institutionalizing participation. She described the 'circular response' of continual interaction between the individual and the environment.

Table 2.3 Components of participatory democracy

Component	Characteristic
Authentic participation	**Authentic participation is the process of building a sense of community**
Circular experience	Continual interaction between individual and environment
Building public	Building up the public through a process of engaging people cumulatively over a period of time
Integration	Different interests may oppose, leading to domination, compromise or, preferably, integration of different views
Process	Integration, like democracy, is a group process
Creative democracy	Everyone participates and is empowered through self-government

Follett argued that democracy is built by the cumulative process of increasing people's participation, through building up the general public before institutions are developed. She proposed authentic participation as the main vehicle of democracy, in which each person took part in self-government. It was authentic in the sense that it was seen as

- more than just a technical task
- not merely a means by which both professionals and public tried to achieve what they wanted
- not just a way in which staff manoeuvred the public to gain consent to their wishes (Morse, 2007, pp. 2–6).

Process of participation

There is a good deal of movement of ideas between the literature on empowerment in developed and developing countries. A report appraising the attempts between 2001 and 2004 by the United Nations Development Programme (UNDP) to encourage the empowerment of people living with HIV/AIDS in the Asia Pacific region identifies three stages in the move from more modest involvement to empowerment: first-, second- and third-generation responses (Table 2.4), associated with receiving help, a policy commitment to involvement and the implementation of involvement respectively (Kumar, 2004, p. 18). This is a useful clarification of the assumptions embedded in practice, which emphasizes that the fullest implementation of a policy of participation is linked with acknowledging that people have the right to empowerment.

Table 2.4 Charting the process: from low level involvement to empowerment

Stage	Process	What is involved
First-generation response	Experience translated into principles	Early victims of HIV/AIDS receive help from people
Second-generation response	Principles translated into policy	At an AIDS summit in Paris in 1994, the principle of greater involvement of people living with HIV was adopted
Third-generation response	Policy translated into rights	Bankok Declaration on HIV/AIDS in Asia Pacific region 2004, that people who live with HIV should have the right to full empowerment along with other vulnerable people, such as sex workers, trafficked women, migrant workers and drug users

The practice of participation is socially constructed from a complex mix of carer and service user-led initiatives and statements of policies and principles by government and service providers.

Principles of participation by service users and carers

In England, the General Social Care Council (GSCC), the Commission for Social Care Inspection (CSCI), Skills for Care (SfC) and the Social Care Institute for Excellence (SCIE) signed up in 2005 to a joint statement of eight principles concerning what any carer or service user should expect when working with them:

1. We will be clear about the purpose of involving service users or carers in aspects of our work.
2. We will work with people who use social care and health services to agree the way they are involved.
3. We will let service users and carers choose the way they become involved.
4. We will exchange feedback about the outcome of service users' and carers' involvement in appropriate ways.
5. We will try to recognise and overcome barriers to involvement.

6. We will make every effort to include the widest possible range of people in our work.
7. We will value the contribution, expertise and time of service users and carers.
8. We will use what we have learned from working with service users and carers to influence changes in our ways of working, to achieve better outcomes.

The seventh principle in this list was linked with various initiatives aiming to achieve a commonly agreed policy for paying people fees and expenses for their involvement and trying to negotiate with the Department of Work and Pensions to ensure that people paid for this involvement did not have their benefits cut as a consequence of immediately being regarded as fit to work.

The four stages of participatory work with people described by Wilcox (1994) are initiation, preparation, implementation and continuation. However, many factors can interrupt or prevent progress through these stages. Let us examine these.

Factors inhibiting and encouraging empowerment through participation

Greater involvement of carers and service users does not automatically empower them. On the positive side, they gain from being in attendance where some decisions are made. However, on the negative side, they could feel even more disempowered by this and, consequently, this could make the relationship between social workers and service users even more problematic. This is largely due to tensions between the relatively powerful practitioner and the relatively powerless service user, in the context of strongly employer-led service provision, in effect, backing off the goal of developing practice that empowers carers and service users. It is vital that strategies for greater participation by people are accompanied by capacity building, in order to enable those who have been excluded to be included and in order that their views are heard, are influential and the results are fed back to them. This capacity building should aim to ensure that participation avoids being tokenistic, impoverished and ineffective. The goal of capacity building is to enrich the range of people contributing to decisions, enhance their power and widen the scope of their roles. According to Lee (2001, pp. 62–3):

> the roles of a *partner*, *collaborator*, *co-teacher*, *co-investigator*, *dialogist*, *critical question poser*, *bridge builder*, *guide*, *ally* and

power equalizer, *co-builder*, *co-activist* and *co-worker* are needed by both practitioners and clients in empowering practice ... [in addition to] those of *mediator*, *advocate*, *resource broker*, *clinician*, *mobilizer*, *organizer*, *innovator*, *coach*, *facilitator* and *enabler* that are used in direct social work practice ... we are partners against oppression, but in this dance leading and following may be fluid and interchangeable. The concept of co-teaching implies that clients and workers teach each other what they know about the presenting problem and about the oppression(s) faced.

practice study

A group of young carers who cared for their parents decided to write to the local director of adult services asking for a meeting with the staff responsible for adult care, to discuss ways of improving their situation. After declaring her amazement, the director did not know how to respond, apart from handing the letter to the manager of adult services in the carers' locality and asking him to deal with it diplomatically, bearing in mind that local councillors would not be pleased if they saw signs that young people were taking over and running adult services.

commentary

It would have been preferable if the director signalled directly to the young carers and staff in the organization that a positive response was necessary, participation by young carers was desirable, but that the precise level of participation would need to be worked out. The director met with the young people and staff to discuss this agenda. A list of barriers to and opportunities for participation was made by the young carers and by staff. The director considered that the subject of participation was sufficiently important to the entire organization to warrant her participation. She prepared a briefing paper in language accessible to the young people, setting out the goals of a participation strategy as a means to empower children and young people.

Factors inhibiting empowerment of carers and people who use services

One ironic result, perhaps, of the speedy moves of some agencies, organizations, professions and individuals in the UK towards embracing participation and empowerment as goals for staff, service users and carers is that little attention has been paid to evaluating the effect this may have on the quality of social care and social work services. Carr (2004a, p. vi) observes that:

> there is some knowledge about participation techniques but little or no examination of the relationship between the process and the achievement of tangible user-led change. This is not to say that certain participation initiatives are not contributing to the improvement of services for the people who use them, but that those changes are not being monitored and evaluated.

What does evidence from research tell us works best, in attempts to engage service users in more meaningful participation? Carr's (2004a) review of relevant research rests on six literature reviews of participation in the major service areas (Barnes et al., 2003; Crawford et al., 2003; Danso et al., 2003; Janzon and Law, 2003; Rose et al., 2003; Williams, 2003). The conclusions of these are summarized in Table 2.5.

Table 2.5 What works in participation by service users

Aspects	Findings (summarized from Carr, 2004a)
Means not ends	Participation should be introduced as a means to the end of empowering people, rather than as a goal in its own right (p. 9)
Improving services	What people desire from participating is being able to bring about improvements in their own service provision (p. 9)
Feedback	People want and need feedback on how their participation is affecting services. The absence of feedback can have a disempowering effect (p. 9)
Agency culture change	Organizational and agency cultures and professional practices need to change in major ways so as to enable changes and improvements in services to take place as a consequence of participation by people (pp. 14–17)
Diversity	Particular attention should be paid to engaging with the diversity of service users and carers (p. 14–17)
People who are seldom heard	The engagement should be sought especially of people perceived as 'hard to reach' or 'seldom heard', in participation initiatives (pp. 18–22)

The evaluation of service user participation usually focuses on gathering their perceptions of the process of participation rather than on whether their participation has made a difference (Carr, 2004b, p. 24). A parallel study of carer participation (Roulstone et al., 2006) identifies a range of indicators as to what does and does not work well, summarized in Table 2.6.

Table 2.6 What works in participation by carers

Aspects	Findings (summarized from Roulstone et al., 2006)
Lack of conceptual clarity	The lack of definition of what constitutes good practice or carer participation
Consultation not participation	There is a tendency to consult carers rather than empower them to participate
Lack of support services	Resources such as respite care to enable carers to participate tend to fall short of carers' expectations
Seldom heard carers excluded	Carers who are 'hidden' or marginalized tend not to be identified and enabled to participate
Organizational cultures	Carers are not perceived as 'core business' by organizations; organizational cultures and funding tend to block working in partnership with them
Limited budgets	Carers and professionals complain of lack of resources as inhibiting participation

We summarize now the most important barriers to greater participation and empowerment of service users and carers.

Structural imbalance of power

Despite the growing trend towards participation by service users and carers in health and social services in the UK, some practitioners are unwilling to take initiatives that may lead to them losing power to their service users, as demonstrated by research into users' perceptions of mental health services (Rogers et al., 1993). The authors conclude that 'the greatest limitation of legal regulation is its inability to break the structural power imbalance which exists between professionals and patients' (Rogers et al., 1993, p. 172). Whereas professionals are a concentrated interest, with continuity built into their relatively powerful position, in contrast, most service users are in a dispersed situation. That is, they have relatively slight chances of meeting to develop a common approach to negotiating with practitioners. How often do groups of people meet to compare notes on their visits to the same outpatient clinic, general practitioner surgery or social services office? Each service user and carer tends to function in isolation from others, unless a member of a group, organization or network. People are often fragmented by divergences of local beliefs and practice, competitiveness and petty squabbles (Robinson and Henry, 1977, p. 130).

Discrimination against carers and people who use services

Carr's comprehensive critical review of research into participation in all major areas of health and social care concludes that 'exercise of choice as an individual "welfare consumer" remains restricted, particularly if you are from a black or minority ethnic group or are lesbian or gay' (Carr, 2004a, p. 10). The main barriers to empowering people through enhanced participation continue to be 'power differentials and dynamics between service users and professionals' (Carr, 2004a, p. 14). Specifically, 'exclusionary structures, institutional practices and attitudes can still affect the extent to which services users can influence change. It appears that power sharing can be difficult within established mainstream structures, formal consultation mechanisms and traditional ideologies' (Carr, 2004a, p. 14).

Defensiveness by professionals and organizations

Three forms of defensiveness by practitioners are likely (Table 2.7): a person-centred focus may be reinforced; practitioners as service providers may opt out; or self-help or user-led activities may retreat into alternativism. We discuss these now.

Table 2.7 Three forms of defensiveness towards empowerment

Nature of defence	Characteristic
Person-centred focus	Individualization Neglecting context
Opting out	Cutting costs Erosion of services
Alternativism	Retreating Flight

Reinforcing the person-centred focus

The threat to the quality of helping services and activities, as has been noted in the health field, is that most self-help or user-led groups hold the same view of health and illness as do more conventional helpers (Robinson and Henry, 1977, p. 126). In the activities they studied, Robinson and Henry found that the focus is upon helping individual people with problems rather than upon the broader structural features of the situation in which they live, such as the problems of homelessness, overcrowding, loneliness, stress and so on. In such circumstances, self-help or user-led activities actually may make more pronounced the very health problems they seek to alleviate (Robinson and Henry, 1977, p. 126), by meeting immediate needs, deluding people into thinking that local action will solve their problems, diverting people from seeking their proper share of potential services and giving officials and agencies an excuse to neglect the provision that is due to people.

Practitioners may opt out

Cooperation in the form of working partnerships between paid social workers and carers, for example in the interweaving of statutory and voluntary services, may be welcomed in principle. But care needs to be taken that the participation of users is not seen as a way of cutting costs by the erosion of statutory services (Darvill and Munday, 1984, p. 5). The paid worker and the service user and carer both have distinctive contributions to make to services and each may enrich what the other provides.

Alternativism

The rationale for self-help or user-led activity seems to imply that it flourishes when disenchantment with existing services and associated supporting organizations and networks is running high. But more than that, self-help or user-led activity may be infused with the distinct but often connected strains of alternativism or even anti-professionalism. This is not to deny that many prac-titioners themselves may allow, facilitate, encourage, participate in or even stimulate user-led activities. But sometimes action by service users – as in the campaigns of the 1990s in the UK to establish legislation promoting disabled people's rights – goes hand in hand with antagonism towards an individualistic, priva-tized, competitive social environment, which disempowers people rather than giving them power to allocate adequate resources to the services they choose and need. In general, the more rooted in genuine empowerment the activity, the more tenuous and poten-tially conflict-ridden its links with professional workers are likely to be.

Corruption by professionals and organizations

The relationship between social workers and service users and carers is vulnerable to corruption from three directions: exploitation of service users; professionalization of service users; or imperialism by professionals, which involves practitioners taking over the territory of service users (Table 2.8). We now discuss these in turn.

Table 2.8 Three forms of corruption of empowerment

Nature of corruption	Characteristic
Exploitation	Picking off people 'Using' representatives Tokenistic consultation
Professionalization	Cooption Recruitment of service users and carers
Imperialism	Extending the organization Taking over arguments of service users and carers

Exploitation of non-practitioners

There is a risk that service users and carers may be seen just as another kind of volunteer, propping up inadequately resourced services such as community care, for example through informal caring for relatives at home. In short, they may be treated as additional volunteers. On the whole, in the UK, the main role of volunteers working with social workers has been in befriending and practical services, while in the probation service they have been involved in befriending and counselling (Holme and Maizels, 1978, p. 88). Experience in New York of using indigenous non-practitioners as aides in mental health has served the function of providing psychological first aid and acting as a means of intervention in community health issues. Aides may thus improve service delivery and help to increase the understanding of mental health problems held by more traditional staff. In addition to providing direct services, community action and community education, it is suggested that aides may also take on the role of social planners (Hallowitz and Riessman, 1967).

The use of non-practitioners should not be undertaken lightly. In the New York example noted above, some aides feared exploitation and felt relatively ignorant of basic skills such as routine recording. These aides remain inescapably subservient, secondary in importance to, and dependent on, professionals. Knight and Hayes advocate the use of non-practitioners or indigenous workers in the light of limited but encouraging research, indicating that:

> non-professional or indigenous workers have a number of advantages over professionals. Living in the same neighbourhood, they do not commute, and have a knowledge of their locality that can only come from living there. They are of the same social class as those they are trying to help, do not have narrowly defined professional roles, and can offer friendship rather than just a service, they are less threatening to local people because they do not have elements of control or

power, or the association with the state, that workers in official social work agencies have. (Knight and Hayes, 1981, p. 96)

They admit that indigenous workers do tend to take on too much work and risk burning out, but that proper professional support can alleviate this.

Professionalization of service users

Self-help or user-led activities may be prone to the insidious process of professionalizing the participants. At the point where members achieve control over their own problems, they are in a position to manage aspects of their own lives independently from the practice of practitioners. But it has been observed that many healthcare groups fail to capitalize on this opportunity. They do not work out the implications of the power they possess. The consequence is that group members give themselves help that does not differ significantly from that offered to them by practitioners. The only difference is that they are administering it themselves (Robinson and Henry, 1977, p. 129).

Imperialism by practitioners

The biggest threat to self-help or user-led activities is of a takeover by professional practice. Takeovers may occur in any setting where the power of one group over a market is affected by the existence of successful competitors. The more effective self-help or user-led activities become, the more they are at risk of cooption by practitioners. Self-appointed experts, media personalities, researchers, writers and practitioners in many fields appear from time to time, riding on the backs of service users. Practitioners can make only a limited contribution to self-help or user-led endeavours before they begin to take over and reduce other people's belief in their ability to break out of constraints and empower themselves.

But in spite of these risks, there is room for optimism, especially in the case of the more resilient self-help or user-led activity. Marieskind's (1984, pp. 31–2) observation on women's groups probably has wider relevance:

> Despite the vulnerability to co-option, the self-help group is an invaluable concept. It is not just a personal solution for individual women's needs – although that alone is a valid reason for its existence. The self-help group is a tool for inducing collective thought and action, and radical social change.

The gains from collaboration between practitioners and service users may be counterbalanced by the potential dangers. We use the term **collaboration** to refer to situations where people are working together and sharing power and decision-making. Through this process, service users may gain credibility, support and resources from professional help, but may sacrifice independence. Kleiman et al. (1976) record some of the hazards of partnerships between users and practitioners. In the American Cancer Society project examined by Kleiman et al., professionals tended to criticize helpers for their lack of counselling skills and volunteers did not have the motivation and assertiveness to take charge of the running of the project themselves.

Conclusion

This chapter has introduced the notion of participation. We have uncovered enough to be aware that there is a lot of rhetoric about encouraging greater participation by people who use services and carers. However, research demonstrates that participation will not happen in isolation from a considered approach to empowering people, which is broadly based in their circumstances and experiences. It is not adequate to set up mechanisms whereby people can participate, in isolation from a broader based commitment in agencies and organizations, linked with a well-considered participation strategy.

We devote Chapter 3 to surveying different perspectives on empowerment and participation, explore the ways these different ideas are linked and generate a framework which identifies different domains for practice. In Chapters 4 to 8, we go through the domains, examining their connections with social work practice.

putting it into practice

Activity 1
Define what you mean by 'participation' in social work.

Activity 2
List as many activities as you can think of which are participatory in practice.

Activity 3
List the factors you regard as the main barriers to implementing participation in social work.

Further reading

Barnes, M. and Warren, L. (eds) (1999) *Paths to Empowerment*, Bristol, Policy Press. A useful discussion of aspects of empowerment.

Beresford, P. and Croft, S. (2001) 'Service Users' Knowledges and the Social Construction of Social Work', *Journal of Social Work*, **1**(3): 295–316. A relevant examination of theoretical aspects of service user participation.

Burke, B. and Dalrymple, J. (2002) 'Intervention and Empowerment', in R. Adams, L. Dominelli and M. Payne (eds) *Critical Practice in Social Work*, Basingstoke, Palgrave Macmillan, pp. 55–62. Covers aspects of empowerment in social work.

Burns, D., Williams, C.C. and Windebank, J. (2004) *Community Self-help*, Basingstoke, Palgrave Macmillan. A study of the practice of community self-help containing three useful chapters (1, 2 and 3) discussing the relationship between self-help, mutual aid and empowerment.

Carr, S. (2004a) *Has Service User Participation Made a Difference to Social Care Services?*, position paper 3, London SCIE. A critical review of the literature on participation by service users.

Haslar, F. (2003) *Users at the Heart: User Participation in the Governance and Operations of Social Care Regulatory Bodies*, report No. 5, London, SCIE. A useful study of user participation in social care.

Kemshall, H. and Littlechild, R. (eds) (2000) *User Involvement and Participation in Social Care: Research Informing Practice*, London, Jessica Kingsley. A relevant collection of chapters on aspects of participation by people who use services.

Slocum, R., Wichhart, L., Rocheleau, D. and Thomas-Slayter, B. (eds) (1995) *Power, Process and Participation: Tools for Change*, London, Intermediate Technology Publications. A practical book on participation in diverse settings, with Chapters 1, 2 and 3 examining aspects of participation, empowerment and development.

Thomas, N. (2000) *Children, Family and the State: Decision-making and Child Participation*, Bristol, Policy Press. A thought-provoking study of theories and practice of children's involvement, or not, in decision-making.

3 | Frameworks for empowerment

After several months of university-based involvement in some consultancy with a group of carers and people using services, we seemed to be engaging in the work as an increasingly close-knit team. Then we encountered difficulties within our group. There were some tense meetings and written messages between us. The upshot was a particularly painful period of self-examination. It emerged that we had to accept the reality that we were not a homogeneous team who fundamentally shared our perspective on the health and social services but occasionally differed. On the contrary, despite our shared goals, we were fundamentally two groups, separated by the difference of structural power between the university employees and the carers/service users, who most of the time managed to patch over this division and work together. Outwardly, there may be nothing different about our behaviour to distinguish between these two perspectives. I am simply arguing that from my 'conflict' perspective, our underlying interests were in conflict, rather than being in consensus. This crucial distinction contributes to the theoretical perspective on empowering social work developed in the second part of this chapter.

Introduction

We saw in Chapter 1 that the concept of empowerment is rooted in a mixture of traditions of mutual aid and self-help as well as more recent liberation, rights and social activist movements and offers social work the richness of these ingredients. Alternatively, of course, it risks offering all things to all people and in the event satisfying nobody. Empowerment concepts, approaches and practices since the 1960s have tended to cross national boundaries. The process of sharing ideas has accelerated since the mid-1990s, with the spread of the internet. This chapter briefly surveys different theo-

ries and approaches and sets out a framework for empowering practice. This provides a structure for discussing the diversity of levels
and settings (I call them domains in this chapter to avoid ranking one
above another) where empowerment can be applied. We begin,
though, by surveying briefly the main currents of theorizing about
empowerment in social work.

Theories and models

The practice of empowerment in the UK has been strongly influenced by theories and approaches in different continents, notably
North and South America (Table 3.1), and these are now discussed.

Table 3.1 Contributors to empowerment and participation theories
and practice

Participatory democracy	Follett, 1918, 1924
Black empowerment: USA	Solomon, 1976, 1986
Consciousness-raising: South America	Freire, 1972, 1973, 1990; Illich, 1975
Disabled people movements	Morris, 1993, 1997
Consumer rights	Dempsey Garland, founder of US version of Consumers Association in 1966; Hilton, 2003; Hilton et al., 2006
Women's self-help	Marieskind, 1984
Advocacy	Brandon 1988; Brandon and Brandon, 2001
Pupil participation and protests	Adams, 1991
User participation	Beresford and Croft, 1993
Prisoners' rights	Scraton et al., 1991; Adams, 1992
Feminist women's therapy	Krzowski and Land, 1988
Women's mental health	Nairne and Smith, 1984; Women in MIND, 1986
Anti-psychiatry	Sedgwick, 1982
Radical therapy	Agel, 1971; Steiner, 1974
Survivors' movements	Survivors Speak Out, 1988
New paradign research	Reason, 1994; Reason and Rowan, 1981
Participatory research	Marsden and Oakley, 1990
Participatory rural appraisal	Chambers, 1997
Integrative	Mullender and Ward, 1991; Lee, 2001; Rees, 1991; Labonte, 1993; Rissel, 1994; Cutler, 2002; Tibbitts, 2002; Saleeby, 2005

Black empowerment: originating in the US

The most influential early developments in social work empowerment have come from the US through writing and practice, exemplified in the writing of Barbara Solomon (1976, 1986) in the area of black empowerment and the movement for civil rights in the US. The late 1960s saw the civil rights movement and campaigns for black power in the US, student protests against the Vietnam War and more widespread protests that also spread through several parts of Western Europe, notably Britain, France and Germany. It is difficult to improve on the vigour and clarity of Solomon's conceptualization of how empowerment works. She defines empowerment as activities aiming to reduce the powerlessness created by being a member of a stigmatized group. Empowerment aims to achieve this by identifying direct and indirect power blocks contributing to the problem. Whereas individuals need to obtain and use resources to achieve personal goals, groups and communities need to achieve collective goals. Direct blocks include things such as a lack of funds and political sanctions. Indirect blocks include the underdeveloped personal resources and interpersonal skills of group members. They also include factors such as power blockages because of stigmatization from wider society, preventing the local community developing strong resources such as schools, community associations, parks and civic societies (Solomon, 1976, pp. 20–1). Solomon identifies some individuals and groups as having been exposed to negative valuations so intensely that they accept them as correct or inevitable and do not make the effort to exert any power. Their powerlessness is 'power lack' rather than 'power failure' (Solomon, 1976, p. 21). Some people have such strong family or group relationships that they are cushioned from negative valuations and still achieve goals by using a variety of personal, interpersonal and technical resources. Solomon states that this concept of empowerment is 'culture-specific', in that it assumes the subjects have 'the experience of belonging to a socially stigmatized category' (Solomon, 1976, p. 22). She concludes that empowerment is an appropriate concept for social intervention with any individual, group or community where there is a 'present and pervasive condition of systematic, institutionalized discrimination' (Solomon, 1976, p. 21).

The strength of Solomon's work lies in two aspects: the application of theory to practice and the transforming of individual negative experiences of being subjected to stigmatization or institutional discrimination into positive social action to take power.

Consciousness-raising and empowerment: South America

Paulo Freire's work (1972, 1973, 1990) is the starting point for many liberationist and participatory approaches to empowerment, especially in the areas of community work (Chapter 8) and collaborative research (Chapter 9). It is remarkable that Freire's methodology, developed from his close proximity to poverty in his home country of Brazil at the time of the Great Depression of the 1930s, crossed disciplinary and conceptual boundaries with such ease, an achievement partly due to his ability to synthesize contributions from theorists such as Sartre, Fromm, Althusser, Marx and Mao Zedong and social and political activists such as Che Guevara and Martin Luther King. Freire's significance in the area of empowerment lies in three areas:

1. He advocated democracy as a method of educating people rather than simply as an ingredient in education.
2. He advocated reciprocity in the relationship between the teacher and the student, in the idea of the teacher as learner and the learner as teacher. Policy and practice in social care and social work in Western countries has not tackled this in relation to blurring boundaries between practitioners, carers and people who use services.
3. His best-known concept, 'conscientization', has been widely quoted and adopted in many fields. His notion of conscientization (*conscientizacao* in Portuguese, meaning the growth of critical consciousness, or consciousness-raising) strengthens the theoretical underpinning of the empowerment process and provides a bridge between individual and collective empowerment.

Ivan Illich (1926–2002), who left Vienna and Rome to settle first in Puerto Rico and then in South America, proposes consumer advocacy and people organizing for a healthier way of life as a countermeasure to deficiencies he identifies in health services (1975, pp. 166–7). The free school initiatives arising from the work of progressive and radical educationalists were given a boost by Freire and Illich, but ultimately were retrograde because they enabled important ideas to be marginalized as 'alternatives' rather than mainstream.

Radical therapy

Some important critiques of traditional therapies and medically dominated psychiatry were linked with radical movements to empower patients (Sedgwick, 1982). In the early 1970s, the Radical

Therapy Collective, which grew from radical psychiatry, was described by Claude Steiner (1974) as setting out to challenge psychiatry as it was predominantly practised. The main target was the authority of the psychiatrist as a powerful professional, but a broad-based movement in mental health to empower patients did not make significant inroads for another 15 years.

Marxist critiques

From the 1970s, social theorists took on board theories rooted in critiques of the status quo in society, influenced by Marxism. Student protests, anti-poverty demonstrations, civil rights movements and black power direct action overlapped into activism by people on the receiving end of services. For example, the prisoners' rights movements, and associated prison riots, spread through the USA, the UK, Scandinavia and other countries from the early 1970s (Adams, 1994). Power may be expressed invisibly through the culture and institutions of society. Marxist theory as developed by Antonio Gramsci discusses hegemony, which includes a range of more and less subtle ways in which the ruling class in society dominates. Gramsci (1971) describes how hegemony is ensured by the domination of more powerful people, which is established and maintained with such subtlety and persuasiveness that people do not question its legitimacy and the basis for its authority. Further, the people subjugated and oppressed by it actually seem to accept the fact that they are subordinated and dominated. In order to understand how people are subjugated in this way, Marx uses the concept of 'ideology'. Ideology, which means the set of ideas and beliefs on which the system is based, ensures that people who are older, disabled, vulnerable or mentally ill accept a view of their world that is not borne out by their experience, is not in their interests and which they may even believe is misplaced.

Feminist theories

Feminists have made important contributions to challenging the male dominance and gender imbalances of sociological theories, not least Marxism (Rowbotham et al., 1980), and mainstreaming theories and practices of protest and empowerment. In England, the anti-nuclear protest at Greenham Common came to symbolize women's activism and enabled many people to learn from women's experiences in networking and non-macho styles of resistance (see, for instance, Lowry, 1983). The Women's Therapy Centre used workshops and self-help groups as a way of enabling women to tackle depression, agoraphobia and problems in relationships (Krzowski and Land, 1988). Women in mental distress formed Women in MIND, which included groups such as the Women Prisoners Resource Centre, Leeds Women's Counselling and Therapy Service, Peckham Women's Group and Glasgow Women's Network and Support Project. These enabled them to share common experiences and begin to take control of their own health (Women in MIND, 1986). These initiatives by women, linked with other feminist critiques of aspects fundamental to social work, such as ethics and values (Wise, 1995), community care (Orme, 2001), anti-racist and anti-sexist practice (Dominelli, 2002) and education and training (Phillipson, 1992), demonstrate among other things how the empowering potential of ideas cannot be segregated from the mainstream of theorizing and practice. Carr (2003) shows the contribution of feminist perspectives to putting empowerment in a social, historical and political context, when theorizing and carrying out research.

Development studies

Many initiatives and projects empowering poor people and excluded groups, including women in countries where they are oppressed, have led to publications in the field of development studies. Chambers (1997) and colleagues such as Blackburn and Holland (Blackburn and Holland, 1998; Holland and Blackburn, 1998) have been responsible for institutionalizing participatory approaches to social development and evaluation in the many developing countries, through the Intermediate Technology Centre.

Perspectives based on the voice of the service user, the excluded and the stigmatized

Since the 1960s, theoretical perspectives on empowerment have been linked consistently with advocacy as a means of empowering people (Leadbetter, 2002). The late David Brandon (1995), not a theorist but a pragmatic activist in mental health partly as a conseq-uence of his own experiences of mental health problems, distin-guished three main forms: advocacy, self-advocacy and citizen advocacy. Self-advocacy received a boost from increasingly popular movements gathering experiences of people on the receiving end of social services (Mayer and Timms, 1970; Page and Clark, 1977). They contributed to a rich tradition of oppressed people, notably

prisoners, writing in US and European literature, from the imprisonment of Socrates to Thomas More, Cervantes, Donne, Bunyan,
Defoe, Voltaire, Oscar Wilde, Jack London, Bertrand Russell,
Solzhenitsyn, Brendan Behan and, in a leading contribution to black
power movements in the US, Malcolm X (Franklin, 1978, p. 233).
The popularity of seeking the voice of the service user, the excluded,
or what Goffman (1963) calls 'the expelled', has its roots in
phenomenology (the philosophical view that reality is defined by the
meanings a person attributes to what he or she experiences) and
existentialism (the philosophical view that a person's experience is
the authentic basis for reality rather than externally based, objective
scientific descriptions and tests), and was reflected in the interac-
tionist sociological theories that underlay Goffman's (1963) study of
residential – 'total', as he called the more closed ones – institutions.

Empowerment theory and practice benefited from the increasing
strength of justice and rights-based approaches, rooted in the experience of the individual on the receiving end of services. Consumer
protection movements have been active in the public, health and
human services since the early 1970s. Related concerns arise over
unequal, discriminatory or oppressive treatment of some people and
are often associated with empowerment. However, it is important to
base the eradication of discrimination and oppression on more than
liberal principles and to seek what Owusu-Bempah (2001, p. 48)
calls 'genuine empowerment'. He is referring to the need to base fair
and non-discriminatory services on principles of challenging and
overcoming structural barriers in society preventing people
achieving their potential.

The contribution of Peter Beresford and Suzy Croft in the UK
over the past 20 years has been to push consistently for the viewpoint
and presence of service users to be taken seriously in any consider-
ation of the delivery of personal social services. Beresford, a long-
term mental health service user and professor of social policy and
director of the Centre for Citizen Participation, Brunel University, has
campaigned to achieve significant citizen participation in social care
and social work services. With Croft, he explores self-help, libera-
tional, professional, managerialist and market models of empowerment, emphasizing their regulatory and liberatory potential (Croft
and Beresford, 2000, p. 117). According to this view, empowerment
is an inherently political idea in which issues of power, the ownership
of power, inequalities of power and the acquisition and redistribution
of power are central (Croft and Beresford, 2000, p. 117). Being
concerned with a shift of power and an emphasis on meeting the

needs and rights of people who are often marginalized or oppressed, the term 'empowerment' is often used to cover a whole range of activities from consulting with service users to involvement in service planning. Beresford and Croft recognize the inherent differences between practitioner and service user discourses. They are optimistic, however, that the increasing involvement of service users in social work education, research, theory-building and practice is likely to offer a means of developing more inclusive practice and restoring social work to its core values (Beresford and Croft, 2001, pp. 295–316). While Beresford and Croft have concentrated on adult participation, from the late 1960s, the rights of young people (Franklin, 1986, 2001), including young carers (Dearden and Becker, 2004), have received increasing attention, in Western countries in particular. Cutler (2002) envisages an integrated model such as the Seattle Youth Involvement Networks as producing synergies from the interaction between different projects and initiatives. Specifically, this means transferring knowledge about how to develop leadership skills, improve academic performance, develop groupwork, raise self-esteem and find ways of serving the local community.

Integrative approaches to empowerment

A number of authors have developed approaches integrating theories from different traditions. Gutierrez et al. (2003) illustrate the diversity of perspectives on empowerment at the macro-, mezzo- and micro- (societal, local and interpersonal) levels, examining practice, research, evaluation, policy and administrative aspects. The second edition (2001) of Lee's encyclopedic work, her US-based empowerment approach to social work, is a reminder of the huge literature in Canada and the US in this field. She states that empowerment is 'the keystone of social work'. It has three interlocking dimensions: developing a 'more positive and potent sense of self'; constructing knowledge and the 'capacity for a more critical comprehension of the web of social and political realities of one's environment'; and cultivating 'resources and strategies, or more functional competence, for attainment of personal and collective goals' (Lee, 2001, p. 34). Mullender and Ward (1991) have written about how user-led groupwork brings together themes of anti-oppressiveness and non-discriminatory practice with the traditions of self-help and group therapy; Stevenson (1996, pp. 81–91) has examined empowering work with older people; Boushel and Farmer (1996, pp. 93–107) have explored empowering work with children and families; and

Burke and Cigno (2000, pp. 110–21) have given detailed attention to empowering work with children with learning disabilities.

Rees sets out to provide an integrated approach to empowerment that engages with the personal as well as the political aspects. This is not novel. Rappaport (1984) proposed empowerment at the personal, group and community levels (Lord and Hutchison, 1993, p. 4). Rees (1991, p. 10) has theorized an approach to empowerment, regarding empowerment as a political activity composed of five essential concepts: using people's biographies; developing the use of power; developing political understanding; deploying skills in evaluation, administration, negotiation and advocacy; and recognizing the interdependence of policy and practice. Labonte (1993) envisages five equally important, partly overlapping spheres of empowerment activity, possibly involving several practitioners: personal care; small group work; community organization; building coalitions; and advocacy and political action. Rissel (1994) attempts a similar task, but indicates that the sense of community sphere lies within the sphere of psychological empowerment, which lies within the larger sphere of community empowerment. Thus, psychological empowerment at the individual level takes over from the development of a sense of community through working in groups and finally is incorporated into community empowerment and collective action. Rissel envisages a progression from an empowerment 'deficit' to health, by moving through personal development, mutual support groups, identifying issues, participating in organizations and collective political and social action, leading to gaining control over resources.

Cutler (2002, p. 57) distinguishes between the youth development model of empowerment prevalent in the US and the rights-based model more common in the UK. The youth development model sets out to empower young people to make their contribution to adult-run organizations by equipping them with knowledge and skills. The rights model, widespread in Scandinavia, focuses on changing organizations so that they listen to the contribution of young people. Tibbitts (2002) discusses three different models of human rights education, which vary according to the target group: the values and awareness model, which targets public awareness; the accountability model, which targets the awareness of professionals of their responsibilities; and the transformational model, which aims to empower the individual by raising awareness of abuses of human rights and working to eliminate them. Many of these initiatives relate to a strengths-based perspective (Saleeby, 2005), which depends on the people involved developing knowledge, resources and skills through what is called 'capacity building' of oneself (Chapter 4) and community capacity building (Chapter 8).

Although they are not explicitly theoretical statements, some of the prescriptive packages advocating the development of participatory practices make reference to empowering aspects that presume a theoretical base. For example, Kirby et al. (2003a) carried out research, involving case studies of a broad sample of organizations, to analyse how children and young people have been involved in decision-making. The report concludes that positive lessons can be drawn from the experiences of developing a range of participation initiatives. The same authors (Kirby et al., 2003b) have developed a practical handbook from the research, summarizing the lessons for practice. Pasteur (2001) writes about social development in developing countries, but much of the advice about changing the culture of organizations to enhance participation applies in developed countries.

We can draw four conclusions from this brief survey of empowerment theories and approaches to practice:

1. There is no general consensus about the appropriate concepts and models of empowerment and approaches to it in particular settings. The continued growth in diversity of theories and models of empowerment reflects the lack of a single definition of the concept and a consensual, unified approach to practice.
2. There is little coherent mapping of diverse empowerment theories and practices across the human services, particularly health and social care.
3. There is a general assumption in the literature that empowerment is a 'good', that people benefit from as much of it as possible and that, by implication, we do not need to ask the question 'Empowerment, for what?' However, significant groups of people, including employers in health and social care, show no enthusiasm for giving up their power wholesale to carers and service users.
4. At a modest level of participation and empowerment in individual and group-based social work, there is much enthusiasm for methods, checklists, procedures and sequences, which, it is hoped, if followed will lead automatically to greater empowerment and/or participation by those currently excluded, by carers or people who use services.

Before moving forward, we need to refer to one more problematic aspect and that is the concept of power, which lies at the heart of empowerment.

Problems of power and empowerment

The failure of many so-called empowerment initiatives has been noted and also the lack of attention in the literature to the nature of power itself (Hardy and Leiba-O'Sullivan, 1998). As a starting point for disempowered people, powerlessness is in the foreground and social workers need a framework to enable them to understand issues of power and powerlessness in their work with people (Tew, 2006).

The concept of power is 'masculine'

We can make the following points about the way power is conceptualized:

1. Writers on power in the social sciences have developed different theoretical perspectives on power.
2. They tend to share the assumption that power is unequally shared in different parts of society and in an ideal world would be shared more equally.
3. The exercise of power is described and analysed at length, but not alternative ways in which people may gain satisfaction in their lives and work.

Advocates of empowering oppressed people include Marxist theorists and practitioners, who regard the struggle between the social classes and the overthrow of oppressive capitalists as historically inevitable. The macho nature of these ideas, emphasizing physical conflict, is apparent. If empowerment was only about seizing power in this way, this book would be lacking in the breadth and depth brought about by considering a whole variety of empowering strategies and tactics. So we need to beware of a narrow concept of empowerment that reinforces the centrality of power embedded in masculine-dominated knowledges of sociology in general and, for example, Marxist theory in particular (Adams, 1991, 1992, 1994, pp. 235–6). In research into protests by school pupils, I discovered a whole range of ways in which children and young people protested, outside the narrow confines of physically challenging the authority of the staff in the school (Adams, 1991, pp. 177–8). Again, in analysing the history of protests by prisoners, I looked beyond the period when the activists were organizing large-scale campaigns involving simultaneously orchestrated riots in different prisons. I found other ways, many non-violent, in which prisoners engaged in collective protests. We can use these analyses to 'deconstruct' (take apart) the general assumptions of Marxist analysis and go beyond it. One outcome of this deconstruction may be what Rutherford (1990) calls a 'cultural politics of difference'. This puts the diversity of prisoners and the issues of imprisonment onto the agenda of a discourse about penalties. They offer the opportunity of responding to riots in ways that transcend and transform the dominant values of hierarchy, militarism, machismo, oppression and violence in the prison systems of Britain and the US. This suggests ways of criticizing and challenging dominant views not just through displays of strength, but, as Rutherford puts it, through recognizing the otherness of ourselves, in transforming relations of subordination and discrimination (Rutherford, 1990, p. 26). This suggests that empowerment can take place in many ways that lie beyond confrontations between powerless people and those who hold power. Rutherford's ideas imply a need to hesitantly view totalizing frameworks for the concept of empowerment and any attempt to construct a global framework for the application of empowerment to practice. Further, they lay a basis for the critique of dominant knowledges of professional practice, embodied in the more tentative and anti-oppressive framework for empowerment in practice, developed below. It is about what Follett called exercising power with other people rather than power over them (Morse, 2007).

Perspectives on power: creating problems for empowerment

The nature of power is multifaceted. The word 'power' denotes a strength or force and can refer to both positive and negative aspects, as the following list shows:

● Power may be experienced within a person as a capacity or a motivating factor. This includes the ways we use our qualities and skills, which represent a sort of personal stock or capital of resources.
● Power may be exercised by one person over another, positively in terms of support or protection, or negatively in terms of coercion or abuse. This may be physical, emotional or psychological.
● Power may be distributed between different people differentially, so that one person or group possesses more than another. Thus, within a group, several people may accumulate and demonstrate collective power by acting together.
● Power may take the form of a preventive, inhibiting something from happening.

There are three main reasons why the concept of power at the heart of empowerment does not immediately suggest to practitioners how they may empower people:

1. There is no single view among theorists of what power is. Power is a problematic concept at the heart of empowerment and can be conceptualized in different ways, which affect how the exercise of power appears. In one of the shortest (49 pages of actual text) and most brilliant books in the social sciences, Lukes (1974) sets out three views of power: a one-dimensional view that focuses on behaviour and ignores how decisions and non-decisions are made and avoided, neglecting the biases and manipulations in the polit-ical context; a two-dimensional view that takes into account these biases and attempts at control; a three-dimensional view that brings a sociological perspective to the analysis of the complex, subtle and often structural ways in which some people remain powerless despite apparent attempts to encourage them to exer-cise power. Hugman (1991, p. 35) proposes an alternative view, derived from Habermas (1977), based on power being exercised through the structuring of social relationships according to the social framework in which ideas, interests and issues are constructed and perceived.

2. Social workers are not in a position simply to give people power, because social workers themselves exercise powers, duties and responsibilities that do not originate in them but in the laws and organizations which are the basis for their practice (Harris, 2002).

3. The conceptualizing of power too often focuses on its social, structural and organizational aspects and fails to connect this with an analysis of how the individual is disempowered or empowered (Servian, 1996). The previous two points could lead the practi-tioner to feel powerless to act. The constructionist perspective on empowering social work we develop below enables the practi-tioner to retain optimism about being able to change the ways structural features of a person's situation are constructed.

This richness of theorists and activists in the contemporary field of empowerment is partly responsible for the lack of synthesis in the concept and its applications to practice. There is also a tension between theorization, which is relatively impoverished, and practice, which is dominated by the related but distinct campaigns of activists to enhance the rights of service users and carers and increase their participation in health and social care services. At the heart of the lack of clarity and consensus in theorization about empowerment are two key problems: the first arising from the diversity of perspectives on power and the second arising from the concept of empowerment of people who, characteristically in the social services, are experiencing problems and weaknesses that they perceive as inherent in their circumstances.

Concept of empowerment: contradictions in practice

We may refer to the concept of empowerment in three main ways:

1. It describes an absolute, that is, involving a person or group gaining power.
2. It refers to a process that presupposes two conditions, one of relative disempowerment before and one of relative empowerment afterwards. In this situation, empowerment is not an absolute concept but relative.
3. Empowerment refers to the transfer of a capacity to exercise power, from one person or group to another.

The idea of empowerment is inherently contradictory, when set against the realities of people's lives as they encounter illness, disability, ageing, problems of poverty, unemployment and discrimination. How can the concept of empowerment overcome the central paradox that it needs to celebrate not just strength and wholeness but weakness and fragmentation?

practice study

Janet Price, writing about her experience of having to leave full-time employment through disability, expresses her doubts about whether the concept of empowerment could apply to her, since:

> my experience of my body over the last six years, during which I have been living with illness and have experienced disability, had somehow disqualified me. My 'broken body' appeared to exclude me from the realm of power, both materially – I have had to stop work and with this both my income and my status have fallen – and theoretically. I felt there was no longer any point in my aspiring to join those who had become 'empowered', for implicit within the idea of empowerment is a sense that power is something that can be gained and held, and it is only those with bodies that are potentially whole, stable and strong who can aspire to such power. (Price, 1996, p. 35)

commentary

In part, empowerment is inescapably heir to a masculine, sociological heritage, a descendant of Marx's macho predictions about how the male-dominated, working-class movements would eventually triumph over their oppressive capitalist masters. Price notes how Foucault also uses the male body as the standard, 'conflating ... humanity with maleness' (Price, 1996, p. 44). In contrast, Price candidly admits that her sense of her subjectivity is fragile, provisional and unstable. The grounds for her identity become diverse because they do not relate to a fixed unifying factor and the boundaries between factors differ:

> The meaning I give to being a disabled woman and a lesbian varies: on the club scene, access problems exclude me from many venues and, even if I do get in, the cult of the body beautiful marks me as not a 'real' lesbian; using a wheelchair to shop around town, my sexuality is denied and my lover is seen as my 'carer'; on Pride, my sexuality and disability seem to have lined up together – until I am confronted by a flight of steps at the station blocking my way to the party in the park. (Price, 1996, p. 44)

Developing a framework for empowering social work

We seek a framework that takes account of the diversity of social work perspectives, but does not complacently accept the fact that inherent in diversity in many different societies are inequalities that leave some people struggling, poor, vulnerable and excluded. A structural approach to social work does this. There is not space to consider this at length, but here is a summary of this approach. The history of survivors' groups in mental health, activist movements of disabled people, and service user groups and carers' organizations provides evidence of fundamental conflicts of viewpoint between those delivering and those receiving services. Beresford and Croft (2001) have underlined the reality that professionals and people who use services have fundamentally different perceptions and experiences, contributing both to divergent discourses of the user and the practitioner and to the nature of the construction of social work.

Contribution of a structural social work approach to empowerment

Carr's (2004) authoritative review of the research literature concludes that structural barriers exclude people from significant levels of participation and empowerment in the organizations delivering social care and social work services. Any strategy to make inroads into this situation will need to take account of these structural barriers.

Let us return to the start of this chapter, where I discussed my personal experience of working in a two-year project as a consultant in a team comprising university staff, carers and service users. I observed that employer-led organizations and service user-led groups and organizations have fundamentally different interests. From a functionalist perspective, there is a fundamental consensus of interests between practitioners and service users, interrupted by superficial differences. From a conflict perspective, there is a fundamental conflict of interests between staff and service users, with occasional, temporary truces between them, as agreements are made to work together (Figure 3.1). We need, therefore, to adopt an approach to empowerment in social work that takes account of the structural factors that reflect the fundamental conflicts of interest between people and can perpetuate barriers to full empowerment and participation.

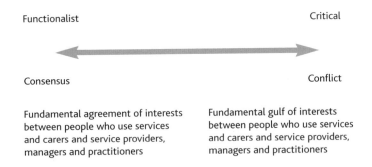

Figure 3.1 Perspectives on empowerment

The work of Gale Wood and Carol Tully, developed since the 1970s (Wood and Tully, 2006), does this by adopting a structural approach. Their approach is rooted in a social constructionist perspective. Three particular features of this contribute to empowerment:

1. It adopts a conflict-based view of society, which assumes that society is riven not just by diversity and difference but by divis-

ions based on inequalities of power, wealth, opportunity and achievement. There are areas where these divisions and inequalities are patched over, but, on the whole, most social processes are driven more by competition and conflict between people than consensus and agreement. If you have not studied sociology, we need to digress briefly. Theories about how society works fall into two camps: systems or functionalist perspectives, which assume a fundamental consensus between different people. This does not mean people do not differ widely, but the assumption is that these differences are less important than the areas of agreement. Conflict perspectives, on the other hand, assume that there are areas of agreement but, on the whole, the conflicts are more important.

2. It is strengths based, which means it endeavours to build the capacity of people to take power.

3. It is rooted in a social constructionist social work practice theory. This assumes that realities, what goes on around us including social structures, are socially constructed. This makes social constructionism a fundamentally optimistic perspective because the surrounding world is not assumed to be determined by factors beyond people's ability to challenge. Because social structures are embedded, that is, well established over years, and mutually supporting and supported by other structures does not mean they are immovable. They are socially constructed so they can change. Wood and Tully regard social constructionism as consistent with postmodernism. They emphasize the critical character of postmodernism, which encourages deconstruction of taken-for-granted ideas, beliefs and social constructions:

> A social worker cannot completely step outside of her beliefs and vested interests, and therefore the social worker's position is always somewhat compromised. Nothing can be taken to be politically neutral or theoretically innocent. (Wood and Tully, 2006, p. 17)

Understanding the social constructionist perspective

The notion of social construction became widely known in the social sciences from the mid-1960s from the writing of Berger and Luckman (1966). According to a social constructionist perspective, social concepts and social constructs – such as social work organizations, residential establishments through to ways of managing and delivering services and different social work approaches and methods – are all real to us because of how we construct, that is, construe and interpret, them between us. This sounds difficult to grasp, but an example may help. I met my school friends two years ago, whom I had not seen for several decades. We talked about our small home town, exchanging affectionate anecdotes until one of us, now living in a well-to-do city, said his memories were all totally negative and he had spent his childhood desperate to get away from that dump of a town. Our constructions and his of the same town were totally at variance. Our realities were in conflict. It was probably not the case that one of us was right and the others were wrong, or vice versa. They were simply different constructed realities in collision. That is where power and social divisions and inequalities come in. It is also why we recognize the reality of conflicts between people's viewpoints. Hence, we use a conflict and a social constructionist perspective together.

Social constructions operate in social contexts where some constructs are dominant. In a private residential establishment, for example, disempowered older people may fail to assert their construct of the establishment as a home and the unsympathetic manager may impose his view that the establishment exists as a placement for cases referred by his business colleagues. Both groups occupy the same space but their constructions are fundamentally in conflict with each other. Consequently, theories of empowerment need to be reflexive, that is, responsive to the actual practice – the ways in which practice is constructed.

Treatment and empowerment paradigms in social work

We noted in Chapter 1 that the roots of empowerment lie partly in traditions of self-help and mutual aid and partly in the unprecedented consciousness-raising and protest culture of the 1960s. But the character of empowerment in social work represents a paradigmatic change – revolution – rather than a gradual shift – evolution. This is justified by the inextricable embedding of the empowerment paradigm in anti-oppressive discourse. It makes necessary the reinterpretation of the entire social work literature through the concept of empowerment. Empowerment offers a new approach or paradigm, rather than a modification of an existing one. It involves what Kuhn (1970) terms a 'paradigm shift'. What do we mean by a paradigm shift? Kuhn uses the term 'paradigm' to describe innovations that 'define the legitimate problems and methods of a research field for succeeding generations of practitioners'. They achieve this because they have two essential features. The innovation is:

> sufficiently unprecedented to attract an enduring group of adherents away from competing modes of … activity [and] sufficiently open-ended to leave all sorts of problems for the redefined group of practitioners to resolve. (Kuhn, 1970, p. 10)

From the point of view of this book, it is a strength, although some critics in the natural sciences would say a weakness, in Kuhn's theory of how change occurs in a particular field, that a paradigm shift need not be based on a particular new piece of empirical research evidence coming to light.

The development of the paradigm of empowerment and the working out of its application to the many different areas of social work are processes that are occurring simultaneously. They have coincided with the growing importance in the UK of increasing involvement and participation of patients, carers and service users in the health and social services, due to their adoption by the Labour government since 1997 as part of the agenda of modernizing social services.

During the 1960s and 70s, the treatment paradigm dominated social work. The word 'treatment' sometimes, but not invariably, meant the application of medical terminology of diagnosis and prescription. Even apart from this particular version of the treatment paradigm, the assumption was widespread that professionals knew best what would benefit people. It is difficult to be precise, because, as we saw in Chapter 1, the notion of self-help is inherently contradictory, but during the 1970s and 80s, self-help and user-led initiatives gained ground. By the mid-1990s, the empowerment paradigm was gaining ground. This involved the equation that effective social work was the product of work with, rather than on, people.

Although it involves a somewhat artificial simplification not reflected in the complex picture of practice, we can say that social work from the 1960s onwards was concerned more with the treatment of 'clients', while from the late 1980s onwards, it was concerned more with the empowerment of service users. Space precludes an in-depth exploration of the implications of this shift. Theories and practices rooted in feminism, black liberation, social action, community work and radical politics – concerning empowerment of individuals, groups, organizations and communities – gained ground during the 1970s and 80s and had come of age by the early 1990s. The fact that commentators may disagree about the mapping of these shifts, and all the detail involved, should not obscure the fundamental gulf between the client treatment paradigm and the service user empowerment paradigm.

Different ways of linking empowerment with practice development

Empowerment may be linked in different ways with practice development. None of these are mutually exclusive, but each has distinctive features: on a continuum of partnership (O'Sullivan, 1994); as a process of reflective practice (after Schön, 1991); as a ladder or linked activities (after Arnstein, 1969; Hart, 1992; Rocha, 1997; Wilcox, 1994); as a process taking place in a number of dimensions, levels and settings (Rajani, 2001); as processes involving a number of pathways to participation (Shier, 2001); as a process of engagement in politics and policy (Connor, 1988; Dorcey and British Columbia Round Table on the Environment and the Economy, 1994; Wiedemann and Femers, 1993); as a dialogic process of consciousness-raising (after Freire, 1972); or as a generic means of anti-oppressive practice (after Phillipson, 1992). We indicate the main features of these below.

Partnership: a concept with many varieties

The notion of partnership overlaps that of empowerment. There are many forms of partnership, largely depending on how power is distributed between the partners. O'Sullivan (1994) provides a typology of possibilities on a horizontal axis: proposing that a continuum exists between total domination by the worker at one extreme and total control by the service user at the other. In between are various combinations, at a midpoint involving partnership between equal parties. To the extent that empowered people act autonomously while partners share power, entering into a partnership may actually be experienced as disempowering by some people. The question arises as to whether there are points on the continuum where a conceptual break or qualitative gulf occurs between two positions. O'Sullivan argues that such a gulf exists between partnership, which may actually be disempowering for one of the partners, who may otherwise have been autonomous and empowered, and empowerment.

In one sense, to pontificate on an 'essentially correct' view is to replicate the oppressiveness against which empowering practice often struggles. A great variety of human experiences may be viewed as empowering. The liberated consciousness of Bonhoeffer (1966), writing in a condemned cell, speaks to a view of mentally or spiritually based rather than materially based empowerment; the writing of Marx emphasizes changed material conditions as a precursor for empowerment; a more inclusive framework may involve either or both of these. It is eclectic, in that it is not bound by one theoretical perspective or approach.

Empowerment: as reflective practice

This draws on the work of Donald Schön (1991) and involves a rigorous approach to reflecting on practice, and reformulating goals and methods of working, as the action proceeds. Social work, among other human services professions, is viewed as requiring an approach to practice based on reflection-in-action, rather than the technical/ rational approach typical of those professions, such as engineering and the law, where the knowledge base is more certain and the technologies for carrying out the work are more established and clear-cut.

Empowerment: as a ladder

Arnstein (1969) distinguishes different relationships between workers and community members by reference to a hierarchical image: a ladder, with the most controlling or manipulative at the lowest rungs, moving up to the fully participative at the top rungs (Table 3.2). If the concept of empowerment were to be transposed back to the late 1960s, then it is likely that Arnstein would have conceived this typology of citizen participation in terms of the degree of empowerment or disempowerment embodied in each position. Implicitly, the image of the ladder conveys a value judgement about higher positions being preferable.

Hart (1992) relates Arnstein's image of the ladder to children's participation. He envisages eight rungs, the highest offering the greatest participation and the lowest three being non-participative (Table 3.2):

- Rung 8: shared decision-making between young people and adults
- Rung 7: action initiated and led by young people
- Rung 6: action initiated by adults and decisions shared with young people
- Rung 5: adults consulting and informing young people
- Rung 4: adults allocating young people to a particular role and informing them about how they are involved
- Rung 3: 'tokenism' – young people apparently having a say but in reality having little power over how they participate
- Rung 2: 'decoration' – young people being used indirectly to boost a project or campaign
- Rung 1: 'manipulation' – adults pretending in order to use young people to boost a cause.

It is questionable whether these divisions are as conceptually pure and distinct as they seem. For example, Hart dismisses rung 3 as non-participative, but in fact his description admits that token participation, by definition, contains an element of participation. Also, rung 1 is not so much the dishonest use of young people as manoeuvring them without their consent.

Table 3.2 Participation and empowerment: ladders, models and stances (part 1)

Arnstein (1969) Ladder of participation	Hart (1992) Ladder of participation	Rocha (1997) Model of empowerment	Wilcox (1994) Five stances (non-hierarchical)
		Community involvement	
Rung 8: citizen control	Rung 8: shared decision-making between young people and adults	Rung 5: political empowerment	Supporting independent community interests
Rung 7: delegated power	Rung 7: action initiated and led by young people		
Rung 6: partnership	Rung 6: action initiated by adults working with young people	Rung 4: socio-political empowerment	Acting together
Degrees of tokenism			
Rung 5: placation	Rung 5: adults consulting and informing young people	Rung 3: mediated empowerment	Deciding together
Rung 4: consultation	Rung 4: adults allocating young people to a particular role and informing	Rung 2: embedded individual empowerment	Consulting
Rung 3: informing	them about how they are involved		
Non-participation	**Non-participative**		
	Rung 3: 'tokenism' – young people apparently having a say but in reality having little power over how they participate		Giving information
Rung 2: therapy	Rung 2: 'decoration' – young people being used indirectly to boost a project or campaign	Rung 1: atomistic individual empowerment	
Rung 1: manipulation	Rung 1: 'manipulation' – adults pretending in order to use young people to boost a cause	**Individual involvement**	

Rocha (1997) reduces the number of rungs in the ladder to five and conceives them on a continuum between community involvement and individual involvement. At the community involvement level, the person is playing a political role, whereas at the individual level, the person is empowered without reference to the circumstances of others. Wilcox (1994, p. 4) adopts Arnstein's ladder but reduces the number of rungs to what he calls five 'stances': giving information; consulting; deciding together; acting together; and supporting independent community interests (Table 3.2). His argument is that they are not arranged in a hierarchy of preferences, but each is appropriate in different situations.

Table 3.3 Participation and empowerment: ladders, models and stances (part 2)

	Connor (1988)	Wiedemann and Femers (1993)	Dorcey and British Columbia Round Table on the Environment and the Economy (1994)
Increased	**Civic leaders** Resolution/ prevention	Public participation in final decisions	Ongoing involvement
participation	Litigation Mediation	Public participation in assessing risks and recommending	Seeking consensus
and	Joint planning	Public participation in defining interests and setting the agenda	Seeking advice
increased	**General public** Consultation	Public has the right to object	Consulting on responses
control	Feeding back information	Public is kept informed	Gathering information
by citizens	Education	Public has right to know	Educating people

Source: adapted from Schlossberg and Shuford, 2005, p. 17

Connor revises the ladder of citizen participation (Table 3.3), focusing on how civic leaders could resolve disputes, ranging from educating people to preventing conflict arising in the first place. Connor also specifies a number of methods involving different forms of participation – such as consultation and mediation – by members of the public. Wiedemann and Femers (1993) focus on the different levels of public participation in waste management decision-making, ranging from informing with little participation to a great degree of participation in the final decision-making. Dorcey and the British

Columbia Round Table on the Environment and the Economy (1994) focus on the planning process and propose a flexible hierarchy of participation, recognizing that in some cases there is a lot of public participation at the start, while in others the reverse is the case. This is helpful in reminding us that different forms of participation may be appropriate in different circumstances, according to the task and setting.

Rajani (2001) presents a model of child participation (Figure 3.2), which suggests that four linked but separate components contribute to empowerment through participation:

1. geographical setting
2. organizational structure (Rajani calls this the institutional setting)
3. role performed by the person
4. level of participation.

This enables us to clarify circumstances where the structure might be participative, but the individual might play a passive, non-empowered role while others do the participating.

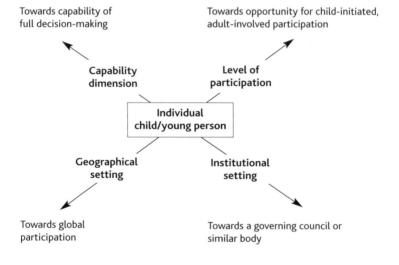

Figure 3.2 Participation and empowerment: ladders, models and stances (part 3)

Source: simplified representation of diagram in Jackson, 2004, p. 8

Shier (2001) sets out a model that links five levels of participation by children and young people (Table 3.4), focusing typically on the school setting:

1. children are listened to
2. children are supported
3. children's views are taken into account
4. children are involved in decision-making
5. children share power and make decisions.

Shier provides a pathway of questions for those involved in the process to respond to, which link the five levels (Table 3.4).

Table 3.4 Participation and empowerment: ladders, models and stances (part 4)

Level of participation	Questions on pathway from level 1 to level 5
5. Take power and responsibility for making decisions	Are adults ready to share power with children and young people?
4. Be involved in processes of making decisions	Are adults ready to allow children and young people to take part in decision-making?
3. Have views taken into account	Are adults ready to take views of children and young people into account?
2. Receive support in expressing views	Are adults ready to support children and young people in expressing their views?
1. Be listened to	Are adults ready to listen to children?

Source: simplified representation of diagram by Shier, 2001, in Jackson, 2004, p. 9

Some commentators have particular perspectives on dimensions and processes of participation and empowerment. Wilcox (1994, p. 8) offers a particularly useful and simply presented view. He suggests that participation is a unifying idea with three dimensions (Figure 3.3): the level and stance of participants, or purpose; the phase reached, or process; and who are the stakeholders, or people participating. According to Wilcox (1994, p. 16), the empowering process of participation involves initiation, preparation, particip-ation and continuation (Table 3.5).

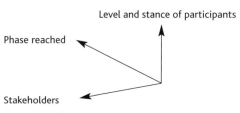

Figure 3.3 Three dimensions of participation

Table 3.5 Stages of participation

Stages	What each stage entails
Initiation	Establishing the basis for participation, agreeing about values and principles
Preparation	Setting out a strategy and planning what is to be done
Implementation	Doing the work
Continuation	Reviewing the work and ensuring it is sustained

Empowerment: consciousness-raising through a dialogic process

Freire's contribution referred to above lies in providing a model whereby the consciousness-raising process can link the circumstances of the individual with those of the social context, thereby providing a route to empowerment in the different domains, focused on the individual in society.

Empowerment: as a generic means of anti-oppressive practice

Among feminist theorists and social work practitioners, Phillipson (1992) portrays a hierarchy of anti-oppressive practice from specialist feminist practice, through the specific area of anti-sexist practice to the universal level of anti-oppressive practice. She locates empowerment at the top of this hierarchy, linking with Thompson's (1998) argument that the promotion of equality contributes to anti-discrimination and implying that it is the universal means to achieve liberation.

Framework for empowerment in practice

In order for empowerment to be more than mere tokenism, it needs to take account of two dimensions:

1. The domain of empowerment: it should be holistic and take on activity in several domains.
2. The extent to which practice is critically reflective: it should be more than a technical activity and involve the practitioner as a whole person, acting reflectively and critically (Schön, 1991).

Without this critical approach to practice, the contextual constraints referred to earlier in this chapter are likely to make empowerment a rhetorical term, without substance in practice. In this book, the term **empowerment in practice** refers to the continuous interaction between critical reflection and empowering practice, that is, the continuous in and out cycle of reflecting-acting-evaluating and the interplay between thinking and doing. It is critical and self-critical (Payne et al., 2002).

The framework takes account of Janet Price's insights, noted earlier in this chapter, about the need to theorize empowerment practice so as to encompass the diversity of views and experiences that contribute to our lives and through which we construct our worlds. If nothing else, our framework for empowerment should avoid presenting the concept as a one-dimensional technique, a simple skill or 'trick of the trade'. In contrast, it should celebrate Price's inability to reconcile the differences between the different themes of sexuality, disability and so on in her life. It should thereby encourage people to resist and subvert attempts to label them, put them down, marginalize them or dismiss them as disruptive.

Domains of empowerment

In Figure 3.4, we see the relationship between the domains of empowerment, which are covered in the next five chapters of this book: self-empowerment, empowering individuals, groups, organizations, communities and political systems. The use of the term 'domain' provides a way out of the perpetuation of the hierarchical language of levels and emphasizes the freedom to move from one domain to another or to occupy more than one simultaneously. It illustrates how the domains of empowering practice exemplify four aspects:

1. *Connectedness* (they are all linked and they all interact)
2. *Holism* (between them, they cover the full range of practice and engage the whole person)
3. *Equality* (one is not located above any other in any sort of hierarchy)
4. *Authenticity* (participation and empowerment are not merely technical procedures, but authentic explorations in democracy).

Theories supporting this view of the linked and non-hierarchical domains are being developed in the field of sustainable development. The two words that represent them are 'domains' and 'holarchy'. Figures 3.4 and 3.5 help to illustrate their meanings. We use the word domains because it is a non-hierarchical word meaning territories of ideas – theories – and practice. Figure 3.4 represents the domains as a series of broadening territories, each of which includes those inside it. Figure 3.5 shows how together they are linked non-hierarchically, each with all of the others. The word holarchy means each domain is a whole in itself, but together the different domains form a larger whole.

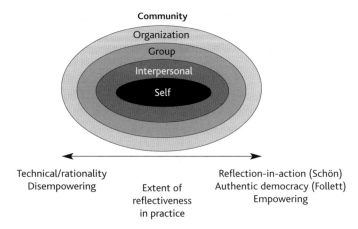

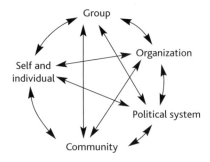

Technical/rationality
Disempowering

Extent of
reflectiveness
in practice

Reflection-in-action (Schön)
Authentic democracy (Follett)
Empowering

Figure 3.4 Domains of empowerment

Figure 3.5 Links between domains of empowerment

In Table 3.6, some of the major aspects of the divergence between technical/rationality and authentic participation and empowerment are indicated, drawing largely on insights gained through the work of Schön (see Chapter 9) and Follett. The use of the domains of the framework as the structure for the next five chapters should not be taken as implying a simple mechanistic application of the sequence from self-empowerment through to community empowerment. The adoption of a critically reflective empowering practice requires a long-term commitment by practitioners and will be a continuing struggle for the people with whom they work rather than offering a short-cut solution.

Using the framework entails assuming that all empowerment

initiatives will touch the different domains. Some will begin with self-empowerment and will progress to other domains. Others will begin with a policy decision and implementation will follow in the personal and organizational domains.

Table 3.6 Dimensions of authentic participation and empowerment

Disempowering	Empowering through participation
Personal/professional	
Fragmented	Holistic
Segregated	Integrated
Trained	Lifelong learner
Acquiescent/oppressed	Assertive/empowered
Work	
Technical/ruled by procedures	Reflective/creative, critical practice
Approaches	
Convergent	Divergent
Simplifying	Problematic focused
Checklist based	Managing complexity
Perspective	
Positivist	Postmodern
Evaluation	
Experimental (hypothesis-testing) method	Experiment-in-practice
Observer/technician	Experient/co-producer

Conclusion

This chapter demonstrates the variety of frameworks for empowerment and shows how ideas about participation contribute to the richness of practice. We acknowledge the reality that practitioners continue to hold the power and much talk about empowering practice is aspirational and rhetorical rather than achieved in practice. It is unsurprising, therefore, that many people who use services and carers experience a gulf between their experience and perceptions and the viewpoint of practitioners. Acknowledgement of this reality leads us to develop a conflict-based perspective on empowerment and participation, which gives us the realistic prospect of examining how to bridge the gulf between practitioners and people who use services and carers by developing an empowering practice. In the chapters that follow, we shall explore ideas and practice in each of the different domains we have identified here.

putting it into practice

Activity 1

Jot down the main features of empowerment practice as set out by Solomon and Freire.

Activity 2

Summarize why you think the concept of power might make the concept of empowerment more problematic.

Activity 3

Identify an example to illustrate each of the eight rungs of Hart's ladder of participation.

Further reading

Follett, M.P. (1918) *The New State: Group Organization the Solution of Popular Government*, Pennsylvania State University. This book can be ordered in a 1998 reprint using Print on Demand and contains three essays by Barber, B.R., Mansbridge, J. and Matson K. discussing the importance of Follett's writing.

Ginwright, S., Noguera, P. and Cammarota, J. (eds) (2006) *Beyond Resistance! Youth Activism and Community Change*, New York, Routledge. An edited collection, providing a rich array of contemporary examples of empowerment and protest involving young people in the US.

Humphries, B. (ed.) (1996) *Critical Perspectives on Empowerment*, Birmingham, Venture. A thought-provoking series of essays, which touch on different theoretical ingredients of the various frameworks for empowerment. Chapter 1 on contradictory aspects is particularly relevant.

Lee, J.A.B. (2001) *The Empowerment Approach to Social Work Practice: Building the Beloved Community* (2nd edn) New York, Columbia University Press. Extensively illustrated and lengthy discussion of many different aspects of empowerment theories and practice.

Rees, S. (1991) *Achieving Power: Practice and Policy in Social Welfare*, London, Allen & Unwin. A thoughtful and detailed theoretical examination of different perspectives on empowerment, accompanied by a careful explanation for, and justification of, the writer's own approach.

Skelcher, C.K. (1993) 'Involvement and Empowerment in Local Public Services', *Public Money and Management*, **13**(1): 13–20. This contains a useful analysis of a continuum of citizen involvement, from being controlled through bureaucratic paternalism, through being informed, being consulted, joint decision-making and devolved decision-making.

part **II** | **Practising empowerment**

4 | Self-empowerment

In work with groups of carers and people who use services, I have encountered several people who have experienced multiple bereavements. This has caused me to revisit my experiences of bereavements in my own family. One of the tensions which I have re-examined is between the negative and positive aspects of caring for an older relative who is dying. This applies before, during and after the death. One particular aspect is the extent to which this may be either disempowering or empowering. I tried to apply the concept of reflexivity to my reflections on my own circumstances and my understanding of what other people were going through, with some limited success, in view of the fact that my bereavement was recent and my feelings still were raw. I learnt much, especially that the process of applying learning from experience to one's knowledge and skills is not straightforward. I confirmed from experience what I had read – that self-empowerment is a complex activity, with disempowering and empowering aspects, which cannot be reduced to a series of steps or techniques.

Introduction

Everything people achieve in terms of gaining control and achieving change follows not only from outward behaviour but also from how empowered people feel. There are two quite distinct roots that feed self-empowerment in theory and practice:

- the ideas about self-help that we refer to in Chapter 1
- notions of how people's previous biographies – experiences, knowledge, skills, feelings and perceptions – shape their current and future lives.

A fully effective approach to empowering people through participation cannot begin to function until they experience empowerment.

Rees (1991, p. 10) makes the important point that people's biographies and experiences are a foundation of empowerment. People do not become empowered merely by being invited to participate. They must feel empowered. A holistic approach to empowerment requires that a person's inner experiences – feelings and thoughts – are in harmony with what they do. Self-empowerment is the central domain of empowerment and is the area where we begin to work on ourselves and take control of our lives.

Ideas of self-help and self-change often permeate traditional texts on social work and various therapies, although there may be no explicit reference to self-advocacy or self-empowerment. Neither concept is indexed, for example, in the book on brief counselling by Dryden and Feltham (1992, pp. 161–3), although they do discuss the vital role of promoting self-change in the concluding stages of counselling a person. In the classic statement of social work values and principles, Biestek (1961) includes client self-determination, which means that people receiving services have the freedom to choose how they act and make decisions for themselves. This overlaps with the notion of advocacy, which involves enabling the people receiving services to state their wants and needs and ensuring that any decisions and actions taken respect their rights. Self-determination also implies that the person, at least to some extent, is empowered. Some self-empowering organizations, such as Hemlock in the USA, which enables people with terminal illnesses to take their own lives, exist in the face of moral controversy and legal barriers (Humphry, 1996).

We are not only referring to clients, patients, service users and carers. Empowering other people is demanding work for professionals. Before empowering other people, practitioners need to become empowered themselves. Whether or not empowerment in practice begins with the self, there is certainly a place for considering one's own thoughts, feelings and situation in any work with other people. Importantly though, this does not imply a psychologized, rather than a social, vision of empowerment in practice. Adequately theorized, empowerment in practice must be realized in all domains – self, individual, group, organization and community. Also, self-empowerment, and hence this chapter, applies equally to social workers and service users. So, the purpose of this chapter is not to suggest that self-empowerment is the key to all other aspects, but to argue that the person who feels and is empowered is more likely to have the motivation and capacity to empower other people and to be empowered by them. Also, it is important to emphasize that a vision of empowerment is required, which recognizes its impact on the self, before engaging with service users and other people's movement towards their own self-realization. This chapter considers how to achieve this goal.

Concept of self-empowerment

Self-empowerment means people taking power over their own lives. Croft and Beresford (2000, p. 116) assert that 'for service users, empowerment means challenging their disempowerment, having more control over their lives, being able to influence others and bring about change'. Thus, although self-empowerment begins with the self, it cannot be considered in isolation from politics and power. Empowerment – meaning enabling people to feel better – is no substitute for liberating them from oppression.

In view of the centrality of empowering the self to the concept of empowerment, it is surprising that self-empowerment is one of the most neglected aspects of empowerment theory and practice. In one sense, this is not surprising, since in the social work literature, one of the most marginalized aspects is probably the personal and professional development of the social worker. In another sense, it demonstrates a failure to take on board the implications of the paradigm of empowerment. Yet almost every approach to self-help, self-instruction, self-development and self-education has an empowering dimension. This chapter will not attempt to survey such a vast field; instead, the focus will be upon some illustrations that have particular relevance to social work and empowerment in practice.

Activating self-empowerment

Using self-empowerment as the basis for challenging oppression

Stanton (1990, p. 122) notes that the empowerment of workers is a prerequisite, before they go on to empower other people. His argument is justified by his research into social services agencies, such as law and advice centres and Women's Aid refuges, which are attempting to manage themselves. Stanton's analysis emphasizes the need for the self-empowerment of workers to challenge a deferential and oppressive agency culture and develop a democratic way of working towards the goal of self-empowerment and the empowerment of service users. Empowerment could be used as a starting point for developing anti-oppressive practice. Stanton's analysis

(1990, pp. 124–9) can be widened to include those factors that need to be considered by practitioners, service users and carers seeking to empower themselves (Table 4.1).

Table 4.1 Factors to be considered by practitioners, service users and carers seeking self-empowerment

Factor	Description
Values	A commonly agreed value base
Analysis	An analysis of unequal or oppressive features of the situation of individuals
Strategies	Clear strategies for addressing areas of inequality and oppression
Skills	A repertoire of relevant areas of expertise to be drawn on
Learning environment	Access to learning resources and support to enable other essential expertise to be developed
Work style	An open, creative, risk-friendly style of working together
User–provider relations	A close fit between the empowerment of workers as service providers and the empowerment of people using services

Reflective practice

At the heart of empowerment in practice are two sets of ideas referred to in Chapter 3: the process of conscientization set out by Freire (1986) and the activities associated with reflection-in-practice, described by Schön (1991). Self-empowerment involves one aspect of reflective practice. In some senses, the process of experiment in practice, as described by Schön, and the investigation and critical reflection, proposed by Freire, are both attempts to capture in words what adult educators in general, and social work educators in particular, have been grappling with for years: how to facilitate learning in an empowering way. The focus on self-empowerment in this chapter means that these ideas concentrate on oneself.

The scope of self-empowerment is much broader than just social work. Health and social services apart, contemporary self-empowerment includes such aspects as agricultural self-sufficiency, alternative communities and communes and worker participation in industry (Stokes, 1981, pp. 18–19). The process of self-empowerment consists of what is often called 'capacity building'.

Capacity building

Capacity building is a much-used term in this field, which makes it more difficult to arrive at a precise, agreed definition. Capacity building can take place at the level of the individual, or at organizational or community level (see Chapter 8 for community capacity building). There are as many different types of capacity that could be built as there are perceptions of the needs and ways of meeting them. Capacity refers to the material and human resources (knowledge, skills and experience expressed in practical expertise) available for doing a task and the ways they are used in practice. We can define **capacity building** in general terms as ways of improving the abilities, skills and related resources of individuals, groups, organizations and communities, to enable people to take part to meet their own needs and those of other people. There is truth in the observation that this resembles the definition of empowerment. Capacity building can involve people gaining new skills or becoming more aware of and using new skills, promoting other people's self-confidence and ability to take responsibility and enabling them to participate more fully in the community and in wider society. Often, capacity building is linked with empowering people to tackle poverty, oppression, discrimination and exclusion. The following checklist (Table 4.2) should help us build our own capacity, before we go on to build the capacity of other people. An example from Sudan follows.

Table 4.2 Checklist for building our own capacities

Goals	Trigger questions to enable movement towards goal
Specify capacities	What kinds of capacities do I need to build in myself?
Identify appropriateness	How can I ensure that capacity building is appropriate?
Ensure accessibility	How can I make the capacity building accessible?
Establish priorities	What knowledge and skills do I need?
Set up monitoring	How do I follow them up and check what I have gained?
Provide support	What support do I need, without becoming dependent?
Evaluate outcomes	How can I check whether the capacity building has been empowering?

example

The organization South Sudan Women Concern works to enable women to empower themselves by building their capacity through education. The aim is to support their aspirations by enabling them to gain expertise in developing their knowledge and skills in practical aspects such as intermediate technology, agricultural skills, literacy skills, health promotion skills, advocacy, lobbying, negotiating, management skills, entrepreneurial skills and taking collective action (Kiden, 2004).

Process of self-empowerment

We consider now the main stages of self-empowerment, which are shown in Table 4.3.

Table 4.3 Main stages of self-empowerment

Assessment and planning

Finding a starting point

Focusing on areas for self-development

Identifying relevant skills

Clarifying learning styles and profiles

Formulating a self-empowerment plan

Action

Carrying out the self-empowerment plan

Tackling the barriers to self-empowerment

Tackling aspects of inequality

Using assertiveness, self-actualization and personal growth

Reflection

Using reflection and reflexivity

Using perspective transformation

Assessment and planning

Finding a starting point for self-empowerment

It is worth attempting to frame the situation from which our self-empowerment starts as though it was like many other learning situations. This should generate a number of key questions, which may help to clarify the potential strengths and weaknesses of the situation. Our personal profile should include details of the situation in which learning takes place. What barriers exist? What learning opportunities are there? What supports exist for the learning process? What level of resources – access to libraries, learning opportunities and other learners and colleagues – is there? How relevant are the resources of time to learn and somewhere to learn at this stage in the process? What sorts of skills, previous learning and experience can be brought to bear on the current situation?

Focusing on areas for self-development

One way forward with the planning is to continue with the educational model and develop a strategy based on the notion of adult learning. This may involve nothing more than sorting out a list of areas relevant to self-development. At the other extreme, it may lead to registering on a formal programme dealing with an aspect of personal and/or professional development, or it may involve informal, independent study on a relevant topic. The advantages of this clarification exercise, though, are in terms of the development of knowledge about our preferred personal learning style and learning needs, as well as in the possible increase in self-confidence that may result.

Identifying relevant skills

It is likely that we will be aware of unevenness and gaps in skills related to being empowered. Often, a lack of particular practical expertise prevents people from pushing themselves forward and becoming involved. These may arise from a lack of self-esteem and confidence as much as actual deficits in skills. Common areas noted include taking part in, and organizing, meetings, chairing and taking the minutes for meetings, facilitating and leading groups, speaking in public, assertiveness, negotiating and report writing.

Clarifying learning styles and profiles

People learn in different ways. Some adult learning programmes include materials enabling people to find out more about their preferred learning styles and develop learning profiles, charting particular areas of personal preference and interest. Some profiles include self-assessment schedules, to enable inventories of personal skills to be developed. One such programme for managers in health and social care, the Health and Social Services Management Programme, is published by the Open University and includes a workbook, *Learning to Learn*, in its first module 'Personal and team effectiveness' (Salaman et al., 1994). This material is designed for flexible use by an individual, who may use it for college, work or home-based study.

Formulating a self-empowerment plan

The next stage is to prepare a plan. The plan should include reference to our goals, the methods of attaining them, the areas of existing expertise on which the individual will draw, the new areas of expertise that will be needed, when and how these will be gained, what resources – including time, money and people – may be drawn on, and over what time period our plan will be carried out.

Action

Action involves doing and, at least in theory, is incompatible with reflection. But as Schön (1991, p. 275) admits, practitioners often think about what they are doing while they are doing it. The important thing is not to take this doing for granted, but to consider carefully how to make the best use of it, with the aim of self-empowerment. The following are some pointers to action.

Carrying out the self-empowerment plan

Implementing the plan typically will involve a good deal of effort, spent on aspects such as negotiating space to do the work and organizing time to complete various tasks. Access to resources, including learning materials where appropriate, will need to be found. There will be a need to manage time and effort carefully, so as not to lose these scarce resources. One's commitment to the task is vulnerable and should be nurtured in a self-interested way.

Tackling barriers to self-empowerment

Not only the practice but also the conceptual basis – the language and grammar – of self-empowerment are currently in the process of development, implying that measures for self-empowerment by individuals will involve a struggle. Sometimes the struggle will be for resources, at other times it will be against one's own attitudes or the barriers may exist at the level of the attitudes of other people, the group, the institution or the social structure. Professionals may resist the spread of self-advocacy. For instance, research by Mind and self-advocacy groups raised the need for the establishment of self-help groups for people who wish to reduce or monitor the doses of their own medication or perhaps withdraw from major tranquillizers. But, as the authors of the report note, resources to run such groups

are unlikely to become available in the foreseeable future. Resources are controlled by professionals who are likely to be hostile to their patients changing or modifying their treatment on their own initiative. (Rogers et al., 1993, p. 134)

practice study

A disabled person wishes to join an ongoing adult education programme in management and finds it permeated with disablist assumptions at the structural, group, interpersonal and individual levels.

commentary

If non-disabled people outnumber disabled people in the programme, if the tutor does not practise disability awareness, there is even more need for the individual to be prepared and able to address the issues. This same consciousness-raising process needs to extend to our own thoughts and feelings.

There is a need for many practitioners to engage the assistance of a consultant, supervisor or mentor to examine, for example, how to remain self-aware about areas of oppression and aspects where our thoughts and feelings are not in touch with each other. Knowing and feeling is a holistic act central to empowerment in practice. This is easy to skate over, but difficult to realize in practice. People need resources for consultation consistent with their individual circumstances. The fact that this implies that women, black people and disabled people are paired in consultant–consultee relationships, where required by the worker, should be regarded as an aspect of the worker's rights, and not diagnosed as a sign of personal weakness or difficulty.

Tackling aspects of inequality

Such inequalities as exist in one's situation may not always be obvious. For example, discrimination may lead to disabled people, or women, being excluded from certain activities by other people in group settings, simply by the way non-disabled people and men are favoured by a facilitator in a discussion group. Research points to the tendency for men in group learning situations to receive more than their fair share of attention, and to behave more assertively than women. It is important for women to prepare themselves to challenge such imbalances (Phillipson, 1992, pp. 44–5). The responsibility should not be put on women to attend to the gendering of learning situations. But it is a prerequisite that women develop techniques of self-empowerment that will enable them to tackle such issues. Key skills in this regard include gender awareness and assertiveness, including the challenging of routines and language that are disempowering.

Using assertiveness, self-actualization and personal growth

The domain of self-empowerment draws in part on insights from psychology and social psychology concerning self-development to maximize personal growth and human potential. It is based on the assumption that people themselves can make a decisive contribution to the self-set goal of realizing their own potential and making the most of relationships with other people. One example is the growing field of assertiveness training, which people may undertake in their own time, or which may form part of an in-house training programme. The *Dictionary of Social Work* defines assertiveness as 'behaviours and thoughts that have at their root a concern to establish interests or rights either of oneself or of others' (Thomas and Pierson, 1995, p. 27). Some literature on self-help and assertion in the early 1980s may be criticized for its emphasis on the aggressive, even macho image it espoused (Lindenfield, 1986). Later publications focus more on self-realization and techniques that avoid confrontation and enable the individual to acquire expertise in facilitating other people in developing their own potential. The assertive person enables others to achieve self-realization.

Reflection

Reflection – thinking about the action – is a repeated, if discontinuous process. It involves taking snapshots, describing and interpreting to oneself or others, while in the midst of practice (Schön, 1991, pp. 276–8).

Using reflection and reflexivity

The concept of reflective practice can be applied not only in the human services but also in the disciplines of social science and humanities, which provide the knowledge base underpinning their practice. Reflective practice increasingly provides a rationale for both research in these disciplines and the education and training of practitioners in, for example, social work. Being self-aware and self-critical are intrinsic to self-empowerment and these are furthered by being reflexive (Payne et al., 2002, pp. 1–12). Reflexivity (Table 4.4) feeds into the ideas about self-empowerment we have discussed above. Clearly, there is a division between those aspects of our experience that relate to our practice as social workers and those that lie more within our personal development. This does not mean that personal and professional development are separate, but simply reflects the reality that, in books of this kind, our professional development tends to receive more attention than the personal aspects of development. This is unfortunate because, as the literature on occupational health and such topics as 'burnout' and stress indicate, the worker as a whole person requires investment; it is short-sighted for employers to exploit staff without attention to the non-managerial supervision, consultation, support and development opportunities that they require.

Table 4.4 Reflexivity and self-empowerment

Reflexivity	Self-empowerment
Reflexivity involves those areas of ourselves – values, knowledge, thinking, feeling, sensitivity, self-awareness – which, formally speaking, lie outside our professional work	Self-empowerment is the reflexive dimensions of empowerment To say what self-empowerment does is easier than to say what it is
We use these feelings and self-knowledge to help us understand, critically reflect and act in response to the information we receive	We equip ourselves with the knowledge, skills and resources to identify, interpret and achieve control over aspects of our personal and professional development

People who have been excluded and are disempowered can make the transition to being empowered, by empowering themselves. Kabeer (1999), examining work with women, identifies three dimensions as crucial to this process, which can apply more broadly: resources, agency and achievements (Table 4.5).

Table 4.5 Dimensions of choice in empowerment

Dimension	What it entails
Resources	Current access and future claims to material, social and human resources
Agency	Extent of power to make decisions rather than being manipulated, deceived or excluded
Achievement	How far people are benefiting in terms of well-being

Using perspective transformation

A feature of useful approaches is that they tend to be passed on from one person to another. Thus, the notion of perspective transformation, which Phillipson illustrates below, is based on Freire's process of conscientization (see Chapter 3) and has been used by Jack Mezirow (1983, pp. 124–7). Phillipson's comments are worth quoting at length (1992, p. 46):

> Mezirow's ideas spring from working with women in re-entry into learning programmes, in which they came to question and see afresh their previously held beliefs about the 'proper' roles of women. By a process of sharing and trying out different options and behaving, they came to new ways of seeing and acting, a process that Freire call 'conscientization'.

> Mezirow details 10 stages involved in perspective transformation starting with a disorienting dilemma, moving on to self-examination, and through a 'critical assessment of personally internalised role assumptions and a sense of alienation from traditional role expectations' to trying new roles and behaving differently. While Mezirow's model was refined during working with women returners, the model is equally useful for working with men. Many men are discomfited by some of the traditional expectations of masculinity, and perspective transformation offers a route to unlearning, re-framing and change that men can work on together.

Two further examples from Mezirow referred to by Phillipson illustrate some dilemmas of perspective transformation that might be a starting point for discussing practice issues. First, there is the example of the male student who learned of the research on the sexual division of labour in group discussions; acquiring this knowledge poses him with a dilemma concerning how much and when he should speak (Phillipson, 1992, p. 46). We expand the second example into a practice study with commentary.

practice study

A practitioner is told by both his female partner and his daughter that he often does not listen, yet he sees himself as a sympathetic and intelligent listener. This feedback from his family makes him question his own sense of himself and his skills as a practitioner; he isn't sure what kind of listening they're talking about (Phillipson, 1992, p. 46).

commentary

If empowerment involves an equality-based practice, then it is inadmissible to engage in self-empowerment at another person's expense. In other words, 'good' self-empowerment should, in theory, empower other people. In practice, that may not be inevitable. It involves the development of areas of expertise, with the purpose of self-realization and personal fulfilment, but not at the expense of other people. Dilemmas and contradictions may arise. A balance should be struck between one person's empowerment and another person's disempowerment.

Discussing dilemmas such as these, unravelling the power relationships rooted in professional and institutionalized ideologies that we have absorbed (for example about talking and listening), then trying out different ways of behaving could pave the way for the more challenging dilemmas that social work practice reveals, for example about child sexual abuse (Phillipson, 1992, pp. 46–7).

Conclusion

This chapter has shown that self-empowerment is not the monopoly of the professional and that self-empowerment involves attempting to infuse anti-oppressive practices throughout the process of empowerment in action. It is at least a working hypothesis, if not an unambiguous conclusion, that a person who feels disempowered will find it more difficult than a person who feels empowered to work with other people towards their own empowerment. But at the heart of self-empowerment, involving the worker, colleagues and service users among others, is the need to transcend the simplistic mechanical notion of self-empowerment as the precursor of empowerment of other people. If empowerment is not to replicate and multiply the oppressiveness of the societal and professional contexts that it inhabits, it needs to be employed with due attention to the mutuality of exchanges between people, in their respective sites of self-empowerment. There is no conceptual boundary between self-empowerment and other related activities such as co-counselling and self-help groups. Thus, although separated, for the purposes of structuring this book, from the topic of empowering other individuals that now follows, the concepts inherent in this chapter cannot be disentangled from those in the succeeding chapters.

putting it into practice

Activity 1

List the main stages of self-empowerment.

Activity 2

Identify the main barriers to self-empowerment.

Activity 3

Specify the main approaches and techniques you would draw on to achieve self-empowerment.

Further reading

Beresford, P. and Croft, S. (1993) *Citizen Involvement: A Practical Guide for Change*, Basingstoke, BASW/Macmillan – now Palgrave Macmillan. A useful handbook for people wanting to become more involved, focusing on the resources, techniques and steps involved in increasing one's participation.

Freire, P. (1972, reprinted 1986) *Pedagogy of the Oppressed*, Harmondsworth, Penguin. A ground-breaking book, which introduces concepts such as conscientization, providing the foundation for empowering practice in education, social work and many related fields.

Payne, M., Adams, R. and Dominelli, L. (2002) 'On Being Critical in Social Work', in R. Adams, L. Dominelli and M. Payne (eds) *Critical Practice in Social Work*, Basingstoke, Palgrave Macmillan, pp. 1–12. A useful reflective chapter on how a social worker may develop as a critical practitioner.

Useful website

www.seishindo.org. One of a huge variety of websites and publications dealing with self-empowerment and the related fields of personal growth and self-improvement.

5 | Empowering individuals

In work with service users, I was aware that Josie (not her real name) had the capacity to make a valuable contribution to the work of many local, regional and even national organizations. The barriers to this lay first of all in her own restricted view of her expertise and her lack of confidence. Over a two-year period, I saw how our invitations to her to join us at meetings led to her gaining confidence. Between all of us – agency staff, other service users and Josie – we managed the tension between reinforcing her dependence and making available the resources for her to empower herself. We gave her support and she attended what, in effect, were personal and skills development meetings. She began to contribute occasional comments. Eventually, she became a regular participant, capable of making her own independent critical contributions, based on her own experiences and judgements. Her growing assertiveness acted as a spur to other members of the group. Her contributions began to affect the course of the events she attended. She began to take up with local service providers, for herself and her partner, those aspects of the services she regarded as inadequate and was delighted to be able to achieve some improvements.

Introduction

The focus of this chapter highlights the central paradox of empowering individuals – namely, that it involves the practitioner in doing other people's empowerment for, or preferably with, them. Clearly, in social work, such work needs to take the fullest account of the experiences of carers and service users and, where possible, work directly with the views and preferences they express.

While some of the work that social workers do takes place with and within families, organizations and community groups, interaction between individuals forms a more basic, although different, ingredient of work with people. Before practitioners can work effectively to empower groups, they need to understand how to empower individuals. Thomas and Velthouse (1990) produced a multidimensional model of psychological empowerment, predicting three outcomes of empowerment: improved personal effectiveness, satisfaction at work and reduced strain due to work. Spreitzer et al. (1997) identified four dimensions of empowerment of significance to the individual: meaning, competence, self-determination and impact. Empowerment involves the key roles of social workers and potentially represents an added dimension in all of them. Much of the literature takes for granted that individual people will not have to overcome major obstacles, in becoming involved in self-empowerment, empowering groups, networks and community organizations. In fact, traditional social work ignores either deliberately or by default the disempowerment implicit in people's everyday circumstances. Workers tend to expect the person to adjust to the normality of things as they are, rather than to join in a reframing of them, perhaps as a struggle against oppression. Members of the public may be invited to join 'citizens' juries' to comment in an ad hoc way on particular policies or services, with no continuity or direct route to having a say in decisions or directly influencing policies.

Complexity of empowering work with individuals

Social work that has the goal of empowering individuals is invariably not straightforward. One of the main factors to consider is the knock-on effects of empowering one person, on other people with whom they interact. Here is an example illustrating the complexity that can arise in such a situation.

practice study

Raissa and her 12-year-old daughter Noni have sought help from social services following threats and physical violence to Noni at the hands of Raissa's male partner, Tom. Raissa and Tom were unemployed, living in rented accommodation in a dilapidated property in the most poverty-stricken district of the town. The first contact Raissa had with social workers left her bemused. She felt under scrutiny as a possible abuser and worried that Noni was about to be removed to protect her from both adults. Within a short while, this position changed. The social worker acted to ensure that Tom left the family home for the time being to stay with his brother. The social worker began to work with Raissa and Noni to assess the situation.

commentary

The worker recognized several types of complexity in the situation:

- power imbalances within the family – between Raissa and her partner, between the adults and Noni – and between family members and the social worker
- an inherent contradiction between the social work goals of empowering family members and protecting Noni, the child, and Raissa, her mother, from harm
- significant levels of discrimination and disadvantage experienced by family members.

The worker clarified the relationship between Raissa and her partner, who was not Noni's biological father, discovering that Raissa did not want anything more to do with him. The social worker used four general aims of empowering practice drawn from Boushel and Farmer (1996, pp. 98–9) as the basis for negotiating more specific goals with Raissa and Noni. These general aims were:

- to meet the needs of child and adult family members
- to respect the rights of children and adults
- to take proper account of the views and feelings of children and adults and others with whom they have contact
- to reduce and counteract discrimination and disadvantage encountered by family members.

Identifying barriers to empowerment

We move now to identify barriers to carers and service users becoming empowered through greater participation in the organization, as identified by research into participation initiatives in social care and social services. Barriers are identifiable in two areas:

1. in the experience and situation of people who use services and carers
2. in the territory of service providers, professionals and other people holding power.

Barriers from the viewpoint of people using services

In a survey across England in 2005, the following barriers were identified by people who use services:

- a lack of access to knowledge and resources that would enable people to become empowered
- a lack of skills such as how to survive, manage and get the best out of meetings and organizations
- a lack of confidence in dealing with professionals and office staff (Adams et al., 2005).

Before 2000, there was a dearth of evaluative research in the UK concerning the empowerment of individuals – adults, children and families who use social work and social care services. Since that date, this situation has improved somewhat. It is apparent from this research that the levels of participation and empowerment of carers and people who use services, both adult and children, remain relatively low (Carr, 2004a). This is true even for disabled people, who are among the more active among carers and people who use services (Barnes et al., 2003, p. 5). There are two general reasons for this:

1. The general resistance of organizations providing services.
2. The fact that the lives of carers and people who use services are often so pressured that they are unable, or unwilling, to participate.

Barriers to participation and empowerment remain stubbornly present across all categories of people. The findings of a critical review of the literature on children's participation include:

1. Negative attitudes of those children who have tried taking part and became disillusioned because it felt tokenistic.
2. Too little time devoted to setting up participation, leading to failure.
3. Lack of appropriate methods of participating and a lack of integration between these and established structures, thereby creating the feeling that they are tokenistic.
4. Lack of information being given to those participating, including a lack of feedback on where, and how, their views have been used (Danso et al., 2003, p. 8).

Disabled people's evaluations of their experiences, for example, identify the following additional barriers: a lack of time for meaningful discussion; a lack of access to senior staff; and too much regulation of the participation of the people using services (Barnes et al., 2003, p. 21). These findings tend to confirm the feeling of those taking part that despite policies and procedures stating they should be involved, many people still feel that managers and practitioners do not listen to them (Danso et al., 2003, p. 8).

Social factors: structural inequalities

The barriers to empowerment may reflect those inequalities associated with ageism, racism, sexism, 'classism', disablism and other dimensions that contribute to people's oppression. Classism may be ignored amid the flurry of activity around the prominent 'isms'. Lerner (1979) wrote of the 'surplus powerlessness' of the working classes in developed countries. Lerner used this term to describe the psychological burden that oppressed people carry with them, which, if not challenged and modified, acts as a script for their future actions.

Psychological factors: disempowerment, helplessness

Empowering individual people draws extensively on psychological theories of empowerment, especially on the psychology of powerlessness. Examples of the significant developments, particularly in the USA, of psychological strategies – specifically cognitive-behavioural – aimed at empowering people by enabling them to feel in control were provided by Baistow in 1994 (Rappaport, 1984; Swift and Levin, 1987; Wallerstein, 1992; Zimmerman and Rappaport, 1988). Baistow (1994, p. 39) notes that such approaches may provide opportunities for professionals to enhance, rather than reduce, their regulatory control of service users' lives, through such approaches to user empowerment.

We can look in more detail at the psychology of individual empowerment through the work of Barber. Barber (1991, p. 38) has identified two critical moments in the development of powerlessness, or the psychological state of helplessness: exposure to uncontrollability, and the attitude that it would be useless to respond. These theories resonate with research into not so much why people protest as why, given the ongoing existence of many factors conducive to dissatisfaction, people do not engage in collective protest more often (Adams, 1991, p. 9).

Barber (1991, pp. 32–3) refers to the application to people of Seligman's (1975) behavioural studies of dogs to illustrate the development of 'learned helplessness'. Learned helplessness is the state of mind that leaves people unable to see the point of engaging with a new task in view of a previous experience of failure, not necessarily in an identical situation, but sometimes in one with only some similarities. If unchallenged, 'the helpless individual will virtually give up and lie down' (Barber, 1991, p. 33). A further feature of learned helplessness which concerned Lerner was that even if 'helpless' people managed to achieve things, they seemed to be unable to perceive that it was their efforts which led to positive outcomes, tending to explain them in terms of factors external to themselves. Lerner regarded this theory as helping to explain why some of the left-wing activists did not capitalize on their successes in the 1960s and 70s (Lerner, 1979, p. 19, quoted in Barber, 1991, p. 34). According to Seligman (1975), learned helplessness may have the negative effect of producing paralysing rather than motivating fear in people, similar to the apathy experienced when people are depressed.

Overcoming barriers to empowerment

We can identify a range of ways of working with people to enable barriers to empowerment to be overcome (Table 5.1). The strength of empowering work with individuals is that it can enable people to engage directly with issues of change. Its weakness is that it can leave people floundering, without a way of linking their personal empowerment with wider organizational, community and social goals for empowerment. Barber (1991, p. 41) views the goal of empowering individuals as enabling them to become more self-directive and assertive, and to develop an optimism that engaging in collective work with others is likely to lead to constructive outcomes. Nelson et al. (2001) use the experiences of mental health survivors to identify empowering factors contributing to their recovery at micro- (interpersonal), mezzo- (group and organizational) and macro- (policy) levels. As Nairne and Smith (1984) note in their account of how women tend to share their experiences of depression, much benefit and mutual support can come from the blurring of boundaries between work with individuals and with groups. Baistow (1994) has correctly identified the weaknesses of attempting to deal with the psychologically based approaches to empowerment separately from group and community-based empowerment, as though these levels are best left mutually segregated. It is as though the empowered person and the empowered group and/or community fuse without the need for further work or explanation. Both Solomon and Freire have tussled with this problem and proposed how empowering work with individuals may be carried out.

Table 5.1 Ways of overcoming barriers to empowering individuals

Approach	Examples of what it entails
Gaining skills	Skills needed in telephoning, talking computers (e.g. emailing), meeting with people individually and in meetings, writing letters
Building confidence	Making contributions in meetings, making first contact with people, coping with uncertainties
Negotiating resources	Booking rooms, filling in applications for funding
Advocacy and self-advocacy	Speaking up for self and for other people, being assertive
Awareness-raising	Developing awareness in self and others of issues such as shared problems of poverty and exclusion
Networking	Contacting people, sharing information and experiences, building trust and working relationships, developing common strategies
Taking collective action	Identifying issues, deciding on how to tackle an issue, carrying out a strategy, reviewing and evaluating what has been done

Solomon

Solomon rooted her pioneering ideas about empowering individuals in the movements for social justice and social change in the USA in the 1960s. She underlines the paradox of the practitioner with power attempting to empower the person to self-empower. She recognizes that advocacy on behalf of the person who has been exposed to intense negative valuations may lead to the perception of the practitioner as doing something either because the worker does not want the person to do it or because the worker believes the person is not competent to do it (Solomon, 1976, p. 26). She argues that, at the heart of the process of empowerment, the practitioner needs to tackle this by showing an understanding of the 'dynamics of powerlessness and its consequences' in order to develop practice skills in empowerment (Solomon, 1976, p. 26). This entails one or more of the following, in helping the person:

● to perceive him or herself as a causal agent in solving his or her own problems
● to regard the practitioner as having usable knowledge and skills
● to see the practitioner as a partner or collaborator in problem-solving
● to perceive the multifaceted power structure with various levels of commitment to the status quo and so open to influence (Solomon, 1976, p. 26).

. Solomon points out that just because people see themselves as causal forces does not deny the multiple factors contributing to change. That is, individuals are not the sole cause of their problems, so the problems cannot be solved merely by a change in the self. This takes us away from the medical model of identifying a cause, that is, a germ, which can be killed and the disease killed (Solomon, 1976, p. 27).

Freire

Freire's work shows how consciousness-raising has the potential to transform personal awareness, and the world, by forging links between personal empowerment and people's circumstances. In contrast with Seligman's ultimately restricting theory, Freire's contribution lies in the extraordinary vision of positive strategies linking individual empowerment with social change. Conscientization brings together both the psychological processes and the structural context within which the interaction between the worker and the person is located. The basis for this approach is the assumption that social as well as psychological insights into the causes and surmounting of oppression are essential to an understanding of the process of empowerment. The work of Freire (1986) provides a key reference point, building on his experiences in Brazil of poverty and hunger in the Great Depression of the early 1930s. The entire thrust of Freire's work on consciousness-raising and empowerment was informed by his basic analysis that the individual's state of mind – the psychological dimension of the process of empowerment – was the priority to be tackled. Freire was concerned to engage in a process of consciousness-raising with poor people, to the point where they could overcome their economic, cultural, intellectual and emotional oppression and challenge their dependence and powerlessness. This concept, to which he applied the term 'conscientization', means 'learning to perceive social, political, and economic contradictions, and to take action against the oppressive elements of reality' (Freire, 1986, p. 15). Freire uses everyday terms in a special way to capture the essence of the process of overcoming oppression and empowering people. Thus, the heart of the process is dialogue between people:

> the encounter in which the united reflection and action of the dialoguers are addressed to the world which is to be transformed and humanized, this dialogue cannot be reduced to the act of one person's

'depositing' ideas in another, nor can it become a simple exchange of ideas to be 'consumed' by the participants in the discussion ... Because dialogue is an encounter among men who name the world, it must not be a situation where some men name on behalf of others. It is an act of creation; it must not serve as a crafty instrument for the domination of one man by another. (Freire, 1986, pp. 61–2)

Dialogue, education and criticality go hand in hand: 'Only dialogue, which requires critical thinking, is also capable of generating critical thinking. Without dialogue there is no communication, and without communication there can be no true education' (Friere, 1986, p. 65). Again, 'true dialogue cannot exist unless it involves critical thinking' (p. 64). In order to achieve dialogue, people require words:

But the word is more than just an instrument which makes dialogue possible; accordingly, we must seek its constituent elements. Within the word we find two dimensions, reflection and action, in such radical interaction that if one is sacrificed – even in part – the other immediately suffers. There is no true word that is not at the same time a praxis. Thus, to speak a true word is to transform the world. (Freire, 1986, p. 60)

Freire (1986, p. 73) envisages praxis as the continuing means by which people 'create history and become historical-social beings'. This involves replacing domination, 'the fundamental theme of our epoch', with liberation. He views this as a humanizing process involving the elimination of oppression, transcending those situations that reduce people to things (p. 75). The key to action links critical reflection with investigation. This is an educational process of a deepening historical awareness of people's situations. As people become aware of the conditions of their existence, they acquire the ability to intervene and change it (Freire, 1986, pp. 80–1). Freire is wary of attempts to reduce the complex process of educating and conscientization:

Manipulation, sloganizing, 'depositing', regimentation, and prescription cannot be components of revolutionary praxis, precisely because they are components of the praxis of domination. In order to dominate, the dominator has no choice but to deny true praxis to the people, deny them the right to say their own word and think their own thoughts. He cannot act dialogically; for him to do so would mean either that he had relinquished his power to dominate and joined the cause of the oppressed, or that he had lost that power through miscalculation ... It is absolutely essential that the oppressed participate in the revolutionary process with an increased awareness of their role as Subjects of the transformation. If they are drawn into the process as ambiguous beings, partly themselves and partly the oppressors housed within them – and if they come to power still embodying that ambiguity imposed on them by the situation of oppression – it is my contention that they will merely imagine they have reached power. Their existential duality may even facilitate the rise of a sectarian climate leading to the installation of bureaucracies which undermine the revolution ... They may aspire to revolution as a means of domination, rather than as a road to liberation. (Freire, 1986, pp. 97–8)

Empowering individuals in practice

Empowering work with children and families

Two general points can be made about empowering work with children and families:

1. There is a tension between empowerment and protection in social work with children and families. It is difficult to imagine circumstances where all family members will benefit from the empowerment of one member. More often, one person's empowerment means another person's disempowerment. For example, parental involvement does not necessarily lead to greater children's involvement.

2. Following from the previous point, it is important not to deal with the individual child in isolation from parents, the family and the wider environment. Research into empowering social work with parents and children identified as psychologically disturbed indicates the value of a multi-level approach (Scheel and Rieckmann, 1998).

---

example

Take the example of Gemma, who is unwilling to visit her grandmother in residential care. The task is not how to persuade her, but how to find out what is inhibiting her from going. In the event, a conversation with Gemma established that last time she had visited, she had caught sight of a box in the manager's office and thought it was a coffin. Her fear of this was compounded when she saw an old lady asleep in her chair and thought she was dead and would soon be put in the box. The social worker visited the home before Gemma's next visit. On Gemma's next visit, the manager left the box in the hall so that Gemma could see it only contained laundry. Efforts were made by staff and family members to present the environment of the home as more child-friendly, Gemma's hesitance about visiting disappeared and she felt empowered to play the piano for her grandmother and other residents on a following visit.

The goal of working in partnership with parents in pre-school settings such as playgroups and nurseries has been well-established in Britain since the 1980s (Pugh et al., 1987). Pugh and De Ath (1989, p. 33) define partnership as working with a shared sense of purpose, mutual respect and a willingness to negotiate. This is distinct from empowering people through enhancing their particip-ation, since adults and children play a minor part in decision-making yet may still be regarded as working as partners.

Empowering work with children and families is best seen in a continuum of power relationships, spanning different family members. Overall, we can observe that partnership and participation approaches in work with children and families are complex and demanding to practise. Empowerment cannot be shared evenly across a family with multiple difficulties, especially when interven-tion is required in one aspect and support or therapy in another, as when a family member is under investigation for abuse. Also, during the work, some family members, such as the father, may exclude themselves from the situation, thereby making inclusive working difficult or impossible.

The development of family support services and partnership approaches is likely to have a significant effect on the relationships between practitioners and users. Lupton and Nixon (1999) review research into the outcomes of the family group conference in empow-ering practice and in general these seem to be no worse than tradit-ional social work methods. Similar tensions arise in family group conferences, generally initiated and led by professionals and some-times required by procedures, as in other areas of empowerment – that it is somewhat dishonest to push family members into participating, using the argument that it is empowering them. Professionals cannot have their cake and eat it. If people are to empower themselves, they have the right to do this in the way they choose. Practitioners cannot then do their empowering for them. For example, Peled et al. (2000)

have researched how physically abused women who choose to remain with their abusers construct their circumstances so as to balance their needs and rights in an empowering way.

Working with disabled people

The basis of empowering work with disabled people is the social model of disability (Oliver, 1990), which argues that people with physical impairments are disabled by the structural and social barriers embedded in society, organizations and institutions around them. Taylor (1999) illustrates how the social model of disability can be used to show how deaf and hard of hearing people from ethnic minority communities manage their circumstances and challenge their isolation in an empowering way. It is necessary to support the struggles of disabled people for their rights, rather than perpetuating their situation as dependent people who need care (Morris, 1997).

Participatory research can be used to enhance practice with disabled people, for example drawing on photographic methods (Aldridge, 2007). Oral and life history research (these methods both involving taking careful biographical accounts of people's lives as the basis for analysis) can be used as an empowering way of doing research with people with learning difficulties (Atkinson, 2004). Work in groups with people with learning disabilities has been researched relatively rarely. A participatory study of the process of group empowerment involving a self-help group of people with spinal cord injury drew the following conclusions (Stewart and Bhagwanjee, 1999):

1. participants made gains in self-reliance and empowerment
2. the group shifted from being professionally led to being service user led
3. the role of the practitioner leading the group changed from facilitator to consultant by invitation of the group.

practice study

Rhoda is a member of a disabled people's group. She is unable to work following a stroke and has applied for a personal assistant. Her sister Tina, who lives 30 miles away, is trying to persuade her to take care services instead, on the grounds that employing a personal assistant using direct payments will be stressful for her. The social worker takes on the job of finding a less stressful way of achieving this.

commentary

The social worker locates a private, not for profit, organization that acts as the broker for disabled people wishing to employ personal assistants without the personal responsibility of carrying out the employer's duties. This enables Rhoda to continue to reject the 'care' model that she sees as keeping her dependent and to adopt the 'rights' model that gives her rights as an independent person. She sees her future as an independent person as a civil right for which disabled people have campaigned. A year later, with the support of the broker organization, Rhoda is able to start her own business working with that same organization to bring other disabled people into employing personal assistants. Rhoda says that, for the first time in her life, she feels like a 'real person' who is making her own contribution to the community.

Working with older people

The challenges of empowering work with older people are increasingly being written up, in home care (Francis and Netten, 2004; Patmore, 2001), intermediate care (Andrews et al., 2004) and work with dementia, which poses particular tensions between empowerment and safeguarding (Bamford and Bruce, 2000; Brannelly, 2006; Cantley et al., 2005; Cheston et al., 2000; Proctor, 2001). Thursz et al. (1995) have brought an international perspective to empowering work with older people, focusing on Denmark, the Dominican Republic, Ireland, India, Japan, Mexico, Pakistan, South Africa, the UK and the US. Research indicates that there is considerable variation in the meaning of growing older within and between different societies and evidence-based practice can be rooted in an empowering process (Heslop, 2002, p. 1):

1. Directly involving older people in carrying out their own analysis of their situation.
2. Recognizing and using their knowledge of advocacy and making decisions.
3. Engaging them in the participatory process of gathering information.
4. Going beyond this especially to involve poor and marginalized people in policy and service development.
5. Enabling them to participate in planning, carrying out and disseminating research and so directly communicate their circumstances to decision-makers and practitioners.

6. Linking these issues they voice to broader policy developments.
7. Incorporating their evidence about needs in interventions and economic and social development targets.

Kam (2002), at the City University of Hong Kong, illustrates how various factors – the attitudes and working styles of practitioners, use of medical or controlling models of practice, denying opportunities to participate, restricting choices and rationing resources – can contribute to disempowerment. Sixsmith and Boneham (2003) explore how older men, whose deteriorating health affects their participation in work, can gain some compensatory empowerment from increasing informal community activities, developing their capacity to build social networks. Research into the care needs of families of oncology patients in palliative care in New South Wales indicates that they felt most empowered by their need for information at crucial stages being met (Wilkes et al., 2000).

practice study

Working with Rose who is 68 and living in sheltered housing, the social worker is aware that for several years she has been treated as dependent. The worker is focusing on empowering Rose. Rose has the ambition of moving out of sheltered housing and living in her own flat again. The social worker knows that Rose is too vulnerable in physical terms to do this. Her goal is to try to reconcile Rose with her present circumstances while empowering her as far as possible.

commentary

The social worker is aware of the necessity to avoid patronizing Rose, manipulating her or simply ignoring her wishes. The five stages of this work are:

- to encourage Rose to talk about her ambition in more detail
- to find ways of enabling her to explore the viability of this
- to become aware of its shortcomings and impracticality through her own exploration
- to accept the reality of this, and let go of her old dreams
- to adjust to her present life in sheltered housing.

Working through these with Rose is time-consuming and somewhat painful for Rose, because she needs to adjust to the consequences of her own ageing and accept what she has lost as well as gained in growing older. To achieve this, the worker

- builds Rose's confidence in interacting with people
- helps her to develop her social skills of meeting people and going on social outings with them.

Ultimately, this empowers Rose and ironically promotes her independence from her unrealistic dreams and enables her to assess the positive opportunities of life in sheltered housing – such as increased feelings of safety and decreased isolation – and make the best of them. She experiences the positive aspects of disengaging with her former life, maintains her self-esteem and makes the transition to sheltered housing as a social change and not a social decline.

Working with people with mental health problems

Linhorst (2006) illustrates how empowering work can be carried out with people with severe mental illnesses. The research instruments used to research empowerment of mental health service users may be constructed by users themselves (Rogers et al., 1997). We may view mental illness from three perspectives: physical, social and psychosocial. The recovery approach is empowering in its assumptions and methods, as we can see in the following situation.

practice study

Winston was diagnosed 12 years ago as schizophrenic and has spent periods of time in mental hospitals. His social worker has introduced him to a group that meets regularly to explore the benefits of the recovery approach, in the hope that he may be able to gain control of his day-to-day life (Deegan, 1997).

commentary

Winston joins the recovery group. Over a period of time, Winston manages to shift from holding a 'cure' view of his schizophrenia to having a 'recovery' view. This means that he stops feeling a failure because his symptoms have not disappeared in a complete cure and begins to gain satisfaction from the fact that his symptoms are under control and, little by little, he can regain his previous, 'normal' pattern of life. He starts to talk about the recovery approach with his friends and relatives. Whereas previously Winston's failure to achieve a complete cure was emphasized by the attitudes of professionals, now he feels empowered by being on the journey to recovery. After a year, he is able to resume work, on a part-time basis.

The example below of empowerment through self-advocacy crystallizes the challenge to traditional practice.

example

Ken is a 21-year-old man with a learning disability. Customarily he sat silent while his mother spoke to the practitioner about him. Now he has become a self-advocate, he is not only learning the skills of speaking up for himself, but dramatically changing his relationships – notably power relations – with those around him. This involves the worker and his mother sharing power with him and changing their attitudes towards him and towards each other.

Empowering approaches to work with individuals

Heron has divided work with individuals into two categories: authoritative and facilitative (Table 5.2). Authoritative work – prescriptive, informative and confronting – involves the more overt exercise of control; facilitative work – cathartic, catalytic and supportive – is less overtly directive (Heron, 1990). Heron calls the first three authoritative because they are more hierarchical and involve the practitioner taking responsibility on behalf of the person. The facilitative interventions are less hierarchical and involve the practitioner enabling people to become more autonomous and take responsibility for themselves. Heron's analysis is across different professional contexts, including medicine, nursing, social work, business management and counselling, teaching in secondary and higher education, policing and youth and community work. Its value, from the point of view of empowerment, is in distinguishing those social work activities that may be less amenable to empowerment (the first three) from those that lend themselves more readily to empowerment (the second three).

Table 5.2 More and less empowering approaches to work with individuals

Nature of work	Authoritative Less empowering	Facilitative More empowering
	Maintaining professional control, power, professional distance	Sharing or handing over power; encouraging independence
Examples	**Prescriptive** Directing what people do, e.g. enforcing court order and applying the law	**Cathartic; facilitative** Enabling people to express feelings, e.g. work with bereaved person
	Informative Giving people information, e.g. offering people access to knowledge about services	**Catalytic** Enabling the person to engage in self-discovery, self-directed living, and problem-solving, e.g. discharging painful emotions of loss
	Confrontational Facing people with an aspect of their assumptions or behaviour, e.g. challenging their attitudes, perhaps through modelling or group pressure	**Supportive; catalytic** (i.e. enabling interaction) Affirming a person's worth, building self-confidence and empowerment
	Intervening (e.g. cognitive-behavioural therapy)	**Advocacy and self-advocacy** Speaking up for people; enabling them to speak up for themselves

Source: based on Heron, 1990

Heron argues that while the six elements are independent of each other, in that there is a sense in which each cannot be reduced to the form of any other, they overlap significantly in certain respects. For example, information-giving may be confronting and prescription may be catalytic (Heron, 1990, p. 7). Incidentally, we have made intervention, which Heron regards as underlying many elements, explicit and have added advocacy to the facilitative activities.

Counselling

The practice of counselling is intrinsically empowering (McWhirter, 1997). Thompson gives the example of the use of counselling and other similar methods to boost a disabled person's self-confidence, and advocacy to promote her or his status as a citizen. This contrasts with their starting situation:

> disenfranchised by marginalization, isolation and dehumanization – at a personal level through prejudice and misdirected pity; at a cultural

level through negative stereotypes and values; at a structural level through a society dominated by capitalist notions of 'survival of the fittest' and charity for those who are 'handicapped' from competing. (Thompson, 1993, p. 127)

Advocacy

This includes a range of activities from citizen advocacy to advocacy by the worker. There are several types of advocacy: individual; citizen; self-advocacy by carers; professional; and collective advocacy for change affecting a category or group of people. Individual advocacy for or with people is vulnerable to the charge that it compromises their autonomy and independence as empowered persons.

example

One of the most apt illustrations of collective advocacy is Survivors Speak Out, an organization in the field of mental health. It was formed in Britain in 1986 'to promote awareness of the real possibility of recipient action and to improve personal contact and the flow of information between individuals and groups' (Lawson, 1991, p. 73). Survivors' groups such as Survivors Speak Out include former patients, such as people who have been in mental hospitals, and have spread through many Western countries in recent years. Some have well-established networks of contact people, furthered in some cases by magazines or newsletters. Such groups exist in stark contrast with the lack of democracy and participation by patients in mental health facilities (Brandon and Brandon, 1991, p. 143). In Survivors Speak Out, both 'systems survivors' and 'allies' are working together in this organization to develop self-advocacy (Survivors Speak Out, Newsheet, 1988). Research into protest movements in the penal system in Britain and the USA and into protests in the schooling system in Britain (Adams, 1991, 1994) indicates that it is unrealistic to expect that organizations, which are led by survivors and are likely to be critical of professionals, will automatically succeed in empowering their members. Such initiatives require a good deal of planning and adequate resources.

Conclusion

In summary, the development of an empowering practice leads to a rich array of opportunities for people, away from dependence at one extreme and oppressiveness at the other, towards contributing to services, and perhaps transforming them (Figure 5.1). There are tensions between these, of course, and the practitioner needs to manage these.

The variety and complexity of cases makes empowering practice even more demanding when some family members require an authoritative, interventionist approach and others need support, so it is clear that a 'one size fits all' approach is not effective.

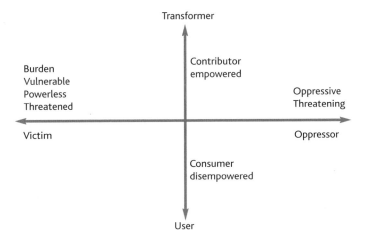

Figure 5.1 Tensions of empowering roles in work with individuals

putting it into practice

Activity 1

Specify the main barriers to be overcome in empowering work with individuals.

Activity 2

List the main ways in which you would work to overcome barriers to empowering individuals.

Activity 3

Describe the main stages of individual empowerment.

Further reading

Beresford, P. (1999) 'Making Participation Possible: Movements of Disabled People and Psychiatric System Survivors', in T. Jordan and A. Lent (eds) *Storming the Millennium: The New Politics of Change*, London, Lawrence & Wishart. A useful article reminding us of the significance of activism by disabled people and survivors of mental health.

Braye, S. and Preston-Shoot, M. (1995) *Empowering Practice in Social Care*, Buckingham, Open University Press. A practical text covering aspects of theory and practice in social care empowerment.

Heller, T., Reynolds, J., Gomm, R. et al. (eds) (1996) *Mental Health Matters: A Reader*, Basingtoke, Macmillan – now Palgrave Macmillan, pp. 215–66. A collection of short articles, extracts and chapters covering a wide range of mental health issues, including empowering experiences of those receiving mental health services.

Lupton, C. and Nixon, P. (1999) *Empowering Practice? A Critical Appraisal of the Family Group Conference Approach*, Bristol, Policy Press. An independent and critical study of claims that the family group approach empowers children and families.

Meetham, K. (1995) 'Empowerment and Community Care for Older People', in N. Nelso and S. Wright (eds) *Power and Participatory Development: Theory and Practice*, London, Intermediate Technology Publications, pp. 133–43. Provides examples of older people becoming empowered.

Thomas, N. (2000) *Children, Family and the State: Decision-making and Child Participation*, Basingstoke, Macmillan – now Palgrave Macmillan. A study of children's participation in social work that locates practice in the wider context of childhood.

Wilkinson, H. (ed.) (2002) *The Perspectives of People with Dementia: Research Methods and Motivations*, London, Jessica Kingsley. Illustrations of the experience of dementia, with implications for empowering practice with older people.

Useful website

www.helpage.org HelpAge International provides examples of older people taking action to empower themselves and influence others.

6 | Empowering groups

I met founding members of a county-wide 'forum' that was set up and run for several years by service users and carers across one county in the north of England. This provided a meeting place for service users and carers to express views, share debate and seek services to meet their needs, contribute to their independence and achieve a better quality of life. As well as securing personal services for individuals, the forum increasingly acted as a voice on the quality of service planning and delivery. The forum's activities expanded to include the county-wide meetings, the committee that ran the forum and the regular meetings with health and social services to discuss aspects of policy and practice. Primary advantages of this service user and carer-led group included enabling services to be: based on more accurate assessments; person centred and focused on actual need; better coordinated through using budgets more effectively throughout the county; and more effectively evaluated using direct feedback from people. Additional benefits to members included social benefits such as reduced isolation and rewards of meeting people, mutual support, better services and positive activities for isolated, lonely and depressed people.

Introduction

Social workers may not do a lot of work within groups, but many will work with groups. A huge amount of empowerment takes place in group settings, sometimes set up by practitioners, at other times run completely independently of them. The above example is of a group run quite independently of professionals. The practice study below is of a therapy group run by professionals. Do the vast variety of such groups that set out to empower people share any common characteristics? Can we identify any guidelines for practitioners wanting to work with them? This chapter tackles both questions and finds that, broadly speaking, the answer to both questions is 'Yes'. We need to be realistic about what groups can and cannot achieve. They can provide support for the individual, reduce the risk of isolation, and offer a context in which personal skills can be developed and practised and a means by which an individual, whose consciousness has been raised, can work towards fulfilling heightened personal expectations.

practice study

Empowering therapeutic work with children and young people

Tomi and Tania are two refugee children with no surviving relatives, who live in a town in northern England. They were quiet and withdrawn at school and in their foster home and were losing weight. For months they refused all attempts to induce them to talk about their feelings, circumstances or background. Their social worker tried to ward off such attempts and persuaded them to attend a number of informal sessions run by workers using a range of art, drama and music therapy approaches. Within a few weeks, they had begun to participate, were forming friendships with other children, performing better at school and becoming more communicative and less apparently depressed at home.

commentary

Therapeutic group approaches such as drama therapy are inherently empowering. Groups provide settings where action approaches maximizing the participation of group members and/or work involving creativity and originality can be developed. They can target particular issues such as violence against women (Wood and Middleham, 1992), work with young people in schools or within the juvenile justice system, those facing life-threatening illnesses, and abused, autistic, long-term fostered and adopted children (Bannister and Huntington, 2002). Empowering approaches to drama therapy can be used in work with young people (Chesner and Hahn, 2001). Plummer (2001) gives practical illustrations of how work in groups with children, enabling them to express themselves imaginatively in words and pictures, can be fun as well as therapeutic. Such approaches are inherently empowering. They often focus on the use of the whole self, permitting the group member to remain in control, incorporating and absorbing approaches and skills then letting go and performing. They encourage a continual process of reflection and performing or acting (not necessarily in the sense of just acting a part, but with the added meaning of engaging in action). In such ways, the person may experience the empowering sensation of integrating doing and being, thinking and feeling, reflection and action.

Mullender and Ward (1991, p. 12) assert that 'groupwork can be immensely powerful if it is affiliated to a purpose which explicitly rejects the "splintering" of the public and private, of person and society'. Yet, as Baistow (1994, p. 36) observes, the idea of groupwork as an empowering strategy to counter oppression is based on a view 'of the "problem" as being implicitly amenable to psychological solutions. In this case the proposed solution is groupwork, in another, counselling.' One limitation of self-help or user-led groups arises from the potential conflict between the anti-oppressive principles that Mullender and Ward (1991) claim as their basis and the oppressive activities in which group members might engage. Should the practitioner facilitator intervene, thereby disempowering other members? Page (1992, p. 92) sees the tangible achievements of Mullender and Ward's approach as likely to be extremely modest, and greater for the practitioner facilitators and educators than for other group members, unless the diverse perspectives of group members can be translated into more unified and realizable demands, via a coherent overarching strategy addressing the goal of collective consciousness-raising (Page, 1992, p. 90). Empowered groups may give their members a positive experience, but probably will not tackle wider problems arising from poverty, joblessness, poor housing, inadequate health and social care services and so on.

Features of empowering groups

Any group can be disempowering or empowering. The key question is what leads to these outcomes. Rather than attempt to encompass the entire range of groupwork, the rest of this chapter considers self-help and user-led groups. User-led and carer-led groups form a distinct category of self-help groups and, of course, not all self-help groups are led by carers or people who use services.

Self-help groups

Katz and Bender's definition of self-help as a group activity is a good starting point. They say that self-help groups are:

voluntary, small group structures for mutual aid in the accomplishment of a specific purpose. They are usually formed by peers who have come together for mutual assistance in satisfying a common need, overcoming a common handicap or life-disrupting problem, and bringing about a desired social and/or personal change. (Katz and Bender, 1976, p. 9)

User-led and carer-led groups

Many commentators use the term 'user-led group' to cover all forms of groupwork where the members directly govern what happens in the group. Groups run by carers as well as groups run by people who use services are covered by this. This field is beset by problems of what to call people. Authors such as Mullender and Ward have tended to refer to 'users'. Mullender and Ward (1991) provide a conceptualization of user-led groupwork, which they term 'self-directed groupwork'. The model of self-directed groupwork they set out in their book grows out of the experience of workers and service users across the human services and is intended to apply to a range of professions, disciplines, settings and user groups. Self-directed groupwork corresponds to the process of self-help described towards the end of this chapter. It focuses primarily on consciousness-raising and empowerment of group members. This involves the two major activities of analysis and action. Group members, in this case users, are supported in the early stages, the workers building the group with users as partners. This is to enable users to 'set the norms for the group, define and analyse the problems and set the goals' (Mullender and Ward, 1991, p. 18). Subsequently, users may move repeatedly through the sequence of clarifying problems and goals and taking action, as they take charge of the process with growing confidence. Finally, the users take over the group to the extent that the workers move into the background and may leave altogether.

Varieties of self-help and user-led groups

One of the features of the field of self-help and user-led groups is the great variety of practice. Some groups adopt a therapeutic mode, others are based on consciousness-raising. Some are led, or facilitated, by a practitioner, such as a social worker. Others, such as self-directed groups, have designed into their framework a process whereby the worker starts by playing a key role as facilitator and progressively moves to a marginal, or even a non-participant, position. This corresponds to the three basic types of relationship between practitioners and service users outlined below, depending on whether such groups are integral to, facilitated by or autonomous from the practitioners.

Relationships between social workers and self-help/user-led groups

Table 6.1 shows how the three types of relationship between social work and self-help or user-led activity may be distinguished from each other, in terms of the degree of resourcing, leadership and support that comes from the professional organization (which we are assuming here is normally a social work organization) and the nature of the relationship between the practitioner and the self-help/user-led activity.

Using the analogy of driving, in the integral situation, the worker owns the car and is in the driving seat; in the facilitated situation, the worker accompanies the self-helper who is driving; while in the autonomous situation, the self-helper/service user owns the car and drives it independently of professional help.

Table 6.1 Relationship between social work and self-help activity

Category of self-help	Resourced by organization	Led and managed by professional	Supported by professional	Example of how professional relates to self-help
Integral	Much or all	Direct	Regular	Innovates and makes activity available as part of service
Facilitated	Some	Indirect	Intermittent	Stimulates activity
Autonomous	None	None	None	Refers people to and imports learning from existing activity

Integral self-help

It will be evident from Table 6.1 that this is the most paradoxical type of relationship, since self-help activities apparently are rooted in the social work agency and yet exemplify the purposes and goals of self-help. This relationship involves activity promoted, supported and directly led by practitioners in a social work organization that largely or wholly sponsors the self-help. Gartner and Riessman (1977, p. 71) comment that the major health organizations are now sponsoring self-help clubs (for example the American Cancer Society supports the laryngotomy, mastectomy and ostomy groups, and at a convention, the American Heart Association recommended that its state affiliates encourage and promote the establishment of stroke clubs).

At first sight, it looks as though integral self-help is a simple contradiction in terms. Integral self-help is difficult to reconcile with the simple statement that self-help necessarily is independent of all outside funding. What is more crucial, perhaps, is the need to clarify the relationship between integral self-helpers and practitioners. Many are prepared to admit that professional guidance may play a legitimate part in self-help activity, although the structure and mode of operation must be under members' control. Examples of integral self-help include settings such as the independence unit in the social work facility, often using the word 'self-help' in its title, in which residents or service users involved in daycare are responsible for programming their own activities. They also include self-help groups organized and resourced entirely within a social work agency, but nevertheless run on self-help lines.

Facilitated self-help

This type of relationship occurs where social workers take enabling action to bring people together or create a climate for activity in some other way. It involves activity in which practitioners provide some support and a degree of indirect leadership. Examples of such work come especially from areas of social work such as mental health, where a degree of professional knowledge, skills or resources at the preparatory or early stages of self-help can make the crucial difference between the survival or non-survival of an activity. It has been observed that people experiencing depression often find it hard to take the plunge and initiate a self-help group without some prac-titioner input in the form of knowledge, skills and resources (Lindenfield and Adams, 1984).

Autonomous self-help

Some self-help can be distinguished from other forms of helping in that people help themselves without recourse to practitioners. That is, in the process of self-help, they are not treated, given therapy, counselled or otherwise put into the situation of clients of social workers. This form of self-help is initiated, organized, resourced and run entirely independently of professionals, and here the distance between the social worker and self-help can be seen most clearly. Yet, in some senses, this sharpens the need for some articulation of that relationship itself. Again, as in the case of integral self-help, it seems at first glance as though this category of self-help has nothing to do with social work practice. But quite commonly, because of their subject matter, the issues they raise, as well as how their connections with social work are made, autonomous self-help activities deserve particular attention. Autonomous self-help includes 'anonymous groups', survivors' groups, groups resisting stigma, such as those in the disability movement, and consciousness-raising groups.

Some common features of self-help and user-led groups

We see in Table 6.2 some common features of self-help and user-led groups. One difficulty with Killilea's description is that it implies that activities focus on reinforcing desired behaviour and change for individual participants. Clearly, self-help occurs at different levels and focuses on other aspects besides people's problems. A complication in the context of empowerment is the fact that while social work and self-help are complementary in some respects, in others, self-help may function as an alternative to, or is actually in conflict with, professional values.

Among self-help and user-led health groups, we can distinguish those providing direct services from those concerned with ancillary activities such as research, education or campaigning activities. The latter are more likely to be more well established and secure, while the former are more loosely organized, informal and with small or non-existent operating budgets (Tracy and Gussow, 1976, p. 382). Five kinds of self-help activity may be identified:

- therapeutic
- social
- educational
- research
- community action.

A shared feature of all these kinds of self-help is the way people involved in a given situation experience the problems and issues with which they are grappling.

Table 6.2 Features of self-help and user-led groups

Author	Features of self-help and user-led groups
Moeller (1983, p. 69)	All members are equal in status Each makes decisions for herself or himself The group is responsible for its own decisions Each member joins because of her or his own problems Group proceedings are confidential Participation is free
Knight and Hayes (1981, Ch. 2)	Voluntary activity Members having shared problems Meetings for mutual benefit Sharing of the roles of helper and helped Constructive action towards shared goals Groups run by members Groups existing without outside funding
Killilea (1976, pp. 67–73)	Members sharing a common experience Mutual help and support The helping of peers by those normally on the receiving end of help themselves Differential association by which people who wish to change decide to join groups in which existing members reinforce the desired behaviour Collective willpower and belief in the group's values emphasizing the fact that change is within members' capacities Information about which experiences and changes are likely to be encountered by a member of a group Use of activities as a constructive occurrence that members share in pursuing planned goals

Scope of self-help and user-led groups

The vast field of self-help and user-led groups is constantly changing, which makes it difficult to pin down their essential characteristics. Groups are coming into existence and disappearing all the time. They vary from groups focusing on problems or issues, through self-development to consciousness-raising (Table 6.3).

Table 6.3 Scope of self-help and user-led groups

Type of group	Example
Problem and issue focused	Therapy groups, anonymous groups
Self-development	Integrity groups, health groups
Consciousness-raising	Survivors' groups, self-advocacy groups

Problem and issue focused

Problem- and issue-focused activities range from people's efforts to help themselves and each other with health problems such as eating disorders or substance abuse, to mental health problems such as depression and phobias and social problems such as loneliness. They include service user groups such as anonymous groups, relatives' and carers' groups, therapy groups and groups for people experiencing stigma. The growth of groups such as Sexual Compulsives Anonymous, Excessives Anonymous, Sex Anonymous (in New York), Sex and Love Addicts Anonymous (in San Francisco, Los Angeles and Boston) (Altman, 1986, p. 159) illustrates a growing movement towards self-help with what are perceived as sexual problems.

Anonymous groups

There is an ever-expanding list of groups modelling themselves on Alcoholics Anonymous (AA), the largest, most well known and probably the oldest of them all. They include Cancer Anonymous, Checks Anonymous, Convicts Anonymous, Crooks Anonymous, Delinquents Anonymous, Disturbed Children Anonymous, Divorcees Anonymous, Dropouts Anonymous, Fatties Anonymous, Gamblers Anonymous, Migraines Anonymous, Mothers Anonymous, Narcotics Anonymous, Neurotics Anonymous, Parents Anonymous, Parents of Youth in Trouble Anonymous, Recidivists Anonymous, Relatives Anonymous, Retirees Anonymous, Rich Kids Anonymous, Schizophrenics Anonymous, Sexual Child Abusers Anonymous, Skin Anonymous, Smokers Anonymous, Stutterers Anonymous, Suicide Anonymous and Youth Anonymous (Gartner and Riessman, 1977, p. 25).

Well-established groups such as AA tend to have clearly specified principles covering their meetings and rules for members. AA has a number of principles that are relatively unchanged since its founding in 1935, many of which are also found in other anonymous groups, including:

> the focus on behaviour; the attention to symptoms; the importance of the role of the group and the value of the knowledge and experience of the 'oldtimers' [long-time members]; and the viewing of the problem [alcoholism] as chronic [the alcoholic is viewed as never being cured]. (Gartner and Riessman, 1977, p. 25)

The controlling tendencies of Alcoholics Anonymous – mutual surveillance by members and public concern about, if not actual punishment of, backsliders – are found in many other anonymous groups. Such groups invariably are concerned with working within accepted societal norms to change the behaviour of individuals. In AA, the individual is expected to be guided by the Twelve Steps and the Twelve Traditions, which express the principles on which the groups are run.

The fact that the ideology of AA has found its way into several of the other larger anonymous organizations is not surprising, because Gamblers Anonymous, Narcotics Anonymous and Neurotics Anonymous were founded by members of AA and have accepted the Twelve Steps and the Twelve Traditions on which their work is based (Gartner and Riessman, 1977, pp. 29–31).

Carer-led groups

Many groups have been set up to deal with the special circumstances and difficulties that can arise for people who are living with somebody with a need or problem. For example, in community care, self-help groups offer an indirect form of support for those with needs or problems, through the help given directly to the carer, who may be a friend or relative of the cared-for person.

The groups may run in partnership with an existing group that caters directly for the person experiencing the problem. An example is Al-Anon, for relatives and friends of someone with a drink problem, who may be a member of an AA group. The nature of this sort of support group, sometimes called a 'living-with group', is greatly affected by the extent of dependence on the carer of the person with the problem. The carer of an elderly confused relative who is doubly incontinent, for example, may have to cope with a much greater intensity of round-the-clock involvement in the task and the impact on her or him may be much greater.

The living-with group quite often caters for members trying to cope with people who share similar conditions. Initial contact with such a group is likely to provide the newcomer with the reassurance of meeting someone who previously has faced similar problems. It will probably also provide her or him with much needed information about the condition, from the standpoint of the carer. Thus, parents who get together because they have children suffering from the same illness may share experiences, from their first awareness that something was wrong, to the present day.

Self-help therapy groups

There is a huge variety of self-help groups with a therapeutic orientation. However, it is in the area of feminist therapy groups that some of the most exciting, and paradoxical, features of self-help can be seen. Feminist therapy reflects the influence of feminism on psychotherapy and, unsurprisingly, its principal focus is on the impact of sexism on the problems of individual women. Importantly, the attention is paid to sexism as one aspect of the social structure (Howell, 1981, p. 512). To that extent, feminist therapy, no less than much psychotherapy, acknowledges the social dimension of problems that may otherwise seem to be located purely within the individual.

The feminist therapy group may be represented as one type of consciousness-raising. But to the extent that consciousness-raising is concerned with social and political – or at any rate extra-psychic – change, the activity of therapy may be absent from it altogether (Howell, 1981, p. 510). With regard to feminist therapy groups, a more subtle and challenging issue emerges. If we accept that fundamental to the feminist viewpoint is the preoccupation with the socially based rather than individually based explanation of a person's symptoms, then the likelihood is that the feminist will regard as suspect any hint that the causes of a problem lie in individual pathology. Thus we may find that feminist therapy that rejects psychodynamic discussion of the origins of, and responses to, problems resembles consciousness-raising, since it is likely to assert the need for social change and political action.

Groups for people who are 'hard to reach' or 'seldom heard'

'Hard to reach' is a phrase that agencies and professionals are more likely to use to label this area, whereas 'seldom heard' is the term more likely to be preferred by people themselves. The most obvious examples are people who take drugs or have problems of alcohol use, but the list also includes offenders, older people who are vulnerable and carers for people.

Groups for people who are stigmatized and excluded

Groups for people who are stigmatized and excluded may also be regarded as 'seldom heard'. There are many groups aiming to improve the circumstances of people experiencing stigma. In the early politicization of HIV/AIDS, there was a hardening of attitudes towards the victim of the condition, which for a time heightened the moralistic tone of official responses. But the self-help groups and organizations that grew in response to HIV/AIDS differ from AA. Whereas AA itself has taken on some of the moral values of society in relation to drink problems, self-help HIV/AIDS groups, if anything, set themselves against such moralistic attitudes.

In the US, Gay Men's Health Crisis (GMHC), a well-known self-help organization, was founded in 1981 by 40 men whose friends or lovers had HIV/AIDS. Although its members sought services to help them, they soon found that they had to take action to help themselves (Altman, 1986, p. 84). In 1982, the HIV/AIDS Foundation developed from its base in California into a national organization, involved in educational and lobbying activities (Altman, 1986, p. 88). In general, in countries where gay organizations flourish and have strong links with government, HIV/AIDS self-help has tended to develop around them. This has happened in Canada, Denmark and the Netherlands. In Britain, after Terrence Higgins died from HIV/AIDS, the Terrence Higgins Trust (THT) was founded in 1982, modelled largely on the GMHC. Gay organizations have mobilized and grown in strength around health issues such as HIV/AIDS, in much the same way that many feminist groups have focused upon issues concerned with women's health. In Africa and Asia especially, there is growing concern about how to counteract the spread of HIV/AIDS through the general population.

Self-development

Self-development includes a wide variety of activities with an educational, social and personal development focus, including peer self-help psychotherapy groups and integrity groups that have spread widely throughout the US. It also includes a great range of gender-associated health groups in Britain.

Peer self-help psychotherapy groups

Peer self-help psychotherapy groups may or may not be affiliated to the national network of the same name, and their local practices, such as frequency of meeting, vary widely. Their focus also varies, from quite major shared problems of addiction or neurosis to the general area of personal development. It has been noted that these groups are not without a number of the difficulties that beset self-help groups generally: the development of cliques; disruption to group activities by individual members who are feeling upset or disturbed; exploitation of the lonely and distressed by predatory group members; and the reinforcement of problems by an overemphasis on problems and bad experiences in meetings (Hurvitz, 1974, p. 93).

Integrity groups

Integrity groups exemplify the way some such activities cross the boundary between problem-focusing and self-development. Integrity groups operate in the US and illustrate a well-established and structured approach to self-help in mental health. The groups run according to detailed guidelines that are open enough to allow a variety of practice. Members have to commit themselves to three principles: honesty, responsibility and involvement in group proceedings.

Gender-associated groups

Although the women's movement is particularly visible and influential in the field of self-help and health, this is not to suggest that the issues of gender should be addressed only in that area. Clearly, gender issues affect the entire field of self-help. Although women self-helpers may be described as benefiting from the support offered by a group, this is an experience that many men also seek. Increasingly, gender-based groups tackle men's issues, including fatherhood and different perspectives on different masculinities.

The nature of gender-linked groups has been influenced by feminism and the way that the women's movement has highlighted the oppression of women in general – in the workplace, the home, education, leisure and other activities. It also confronts gender inequalities in the practice of professionals such as doctors, teachers and social workers. It is unavoidable that challenges by women to the masculine biases in the study of culture and society (Rowbotham et al., 1980, p. 55), and in the power relations reflected in them, tend to be reflected by the illustrations here of women's groups. This should not be regarded complacently as inevitable or proper, but as one sign of male power over the everyday construction of knowledge of self-help and empowerment.

Gender-associated groups illustrate the impossibility of segregating self-help activities concerned with problems of self-development from the concerns of consciousness-raising. Women's groups include those concerned with health, therapy and consciousness-raising. However, some female writers distinguish Women's Liberation groups from therapy groups, by the fact that the latter promote solutions to the problems of individual women, while the former are based on the principle that solutions for individual women depend first on changes in the conditions in which all women live their lives (Zweig, 1971, p. 161).

People with mental illnesses

Empowering strategies and techniques offer people experiencing mental health problems, such as depression, ways of improving their coping skills, self-confidence and self-esteem and may lead to them assuming greater control over their own lives, as we now show.

practice study

Belle was a sufferer from a severe anxiety disorder. For years she lived alone and stayed at home, unable to face shopping or employed work because of her agoraphobia. The worker from the community mental health resource team was able to provide her with transport to attend a self-help group in a day centre. Over a two-year period, she abandoned anti-anxiety medication and took on first a voluntary, then a paid position in the canteen at the centre, and in time was able to walk the short distance to and from home, in the company of other group members. Eventually, she acted as a helper for a new group member suffering from agoraphobia.

commentary

This example shows how group support can enable a person progressively to gain in confidence and self-esteem, to the point where it is possible to make the transition from being helped to being the helper. It also demonstrates the relevance of empowerment as a therapeutic tool in mental health work.

Health groups

Health groups may be viewed by members as educating them out of their socialization in professionally dominated situations. Groups may set out to reveal ways in which the health professions shelter behind displays of practitioner knowledge and skill. Such groups tend to contradict the consumerism of market-based community care. They represent a public approach to health rather than a private contract to cure (Chamberlain, 1981, p. 155). Groups may thus be able to resist dominant social attitudes and may act politically to tackle health issues.

Women's health groups are concerned more broadly with the struggle for autonomy, the right to choose, make decisions and exercise control over what happens to their bodies. Women's health groups typically comprise eight or nine members meeting regularly to exchange experiences and knowledge about their bodies, feelings, attitudes and problems. While members discuss some matters of particular concern to women, such as pregnancy, menstruation and some cancers, they may also be concerned with more general health issues. Women's health groups may be based on holistic principles, having regard to a person's needs in relation to the entire environment.

Consciousness-raising

The essential elements of consciousness-raising (CR) in the self-help field that are worth noting at this stage include their critical stance in relation to the services which people receive, and the innovative and (from the viewpoint of the bureaucrat) often untidy and unruly character of groups and organizations. Yet, this is the vital, energizing and creative force that gives this area of self-help so much of its momentum, from which social workers have so much to learn and gain. CR may focus on benefit to the individual, but in such settings as women's health groups or community action groups, it may take on a social change character. To the extent that feminist therapy reflects the influence of feminism on psychotherapy, the concern of such groups is partly focused on problems and partly focused on sexism as one aspect of the social structure (Howell, 1981, p. 512). Self-help groups involving women cover a wide range of areas, from specific gynaecological topics to general health or CR. However, Marieskind's (1984, p. 28) point that most are primarily educational and concerned with enabling individuals to realize their potential should not deflect our attention from the tensions between problem- and issue-focused activities and those associated with CR.

Survivors' groups

Survivors' groups form a powerful and growing force in the field of mental health reform. But in the fields of mental health and disability, professionals and carers still may disempower people by doing their participating and self-helping for them. One illustration of the upsurge of consumer-led self-advocacy is the growth of organized survivors' groups. Survivors' groups have spread throughout the developed countries and include former patients, such as people who have been in mental hospitals. Some have well-established networks of contact people, furthered in some cases by magazines or newsletters. For example, the networking organization Survivors Speak Out (see Chapter 5) helps individuals and groups to keep in touch with each other and encourages self-advocacy. Another example is the development of groups by and for women who have experienced sexual and other forms of abuse.

Self-advocacy

Self-advocacy is particularly important in disability and mental health. Cooperatives for people with physical and mental disabilities, linked with self-advocacy, are becoming more common as people seek more imaginative ways of promoting self-advocacy among those experiencing a range of disabilities. These latter developments reflect attempts to move towards the democratization of social work services and have helped to give social workers the impetus to explore ways of working alongside consumer groups in the health and social services. This is partly as a result of the growing strength of consumer-led movements generally. One consequence has been a trend towards some professionals acknowledging that many people have the capacity to do things for themselves, but need empowering in order to achieve them.

Processes of group-based empowerment

Three stages are common to many self-help and user-led groups: initiation, sustaining and moving on. Caution needs to be exercised, however, about how rigidly the general analysis of stages can be applied to particular groups.

Initiation

Initiation or entry entails starting an activity or breaking into an existing one. A variety of significant elements may be associated with the start of the process, to do with the preparations an individual makes, such as admitting that an issue or problem has reached the point where something needs to be done about it. At this point, the person may desire to join a group or find someone with whom to share the experience. During this period, a new group may be set up, or an agreement may be reached between a new member and an existing group, about how the group may be useful and what she or he may bring to it.

Several factors are involved in the process of initiating group-based empowerment and ensuring its effective continuance, either for a limited period or on an open-ended basis. These include the following: finding enough group members; finding a place to meet; guaranteeing adequate support; recruiting helpers; and achieving 'legitimacy' or credibility. The more autonomous the group, the less relevant will be the support of various professionals and agencies in efforts to establish its credibility.

Sustaining

Sustaining includes a self-sustaining element. This may be:

- problem centred
- socialization or growth centred
- self-development or training centred
- consciousness-raising or social action centred.

We can be more specific. For instance, in the problem-centred and problem-solving areas, the focus may be upon change. Change may be anticipated at different levels and is not confined to interpersonal change. It may involve conversion or healing, what Sarbin and Alder (1971, p. 606) call 'the annihilation and reconstruction of the self'. Or, less melodramatically, a certain behaviour may cease and another behaviour take its place. Conversion may be stimulated by trigger mechanisms, or the use of a structure such as the public confession, which forms a part of many problem-centred self-help groups. This happens in a good many of the anonymous groups modelled on AA, but it may be present also in the personal statement required of a member of a consciousness-raising group. Healing, or some other form of help, may be made available to an individual by other members of the group by means of mechanisms such as acceptance. Acceptance may sound akin to forgiveness, although, as happens in AA groups, healing may lie a long way from the self-reliance or mutual aid of other groups, since in AA, responsibility for healing and forgiveness is held by God as the ultimate, extra-group authority. Again, the cost of cure may be seen in quasi-religious terms to involve some act of penance, as may happen in AA. The member may be expected to go through the disempowering experience of baring his or her soul to the group, in the struggle towards the empowerment of gaining control over the drink problem.

Self-help or user-led groups need to involve sufficient participants to enable the programme to proceed. The effectiveness of the involvement of participants depends on how well activities are managed. Group meetings in particular need effective leaders. On the whole, a democratic style of leadership is preferable to authoritarian or laissez-faire approaches. Some people argue that larger groups benefit from having two or more leaders working together, but Preston-Shoot (1987, Ch. 4) considers this too simplistic and examines the conditions under which it would be appropriate.

It is tidy, but misleading, to assume that user-led and self-help groups' activities correspond with the total of members' self-help and self-care. It is quite common to find members developing relationships within their group, which generate a variety of extra-group activities. In informal, social, leisure and other areas, relationships, projects and friendships develop out of meetings, sustain them and are sustained by them.

It is a short step from this process to consider the notion that groups may be open ended rather than time limited. In contrast with many contract-linked, therapeutic areas of a more formal or traditional nature, self-help or user-led activities generally do not have the same concern with limited involvement in the helping process. By the same token, members of a group may not set their sights so much on total cure or release from problems as the outcome of activities, as on the week-by-week management of those problems as the group proceeds. In other words, membership of a particular group may become a way of life.

Associated with this broadening of relationships between group members is the issue of confidentiality. Some self-help or user-led groups actually have rules forbidding members to discuss business relating to the group outside the meetings. This underlines the need for participants to clarify the boundaries of their relationships with, and responsibilities to, each other.

Moving on

In the further, possibly final, stage, an individual may either end involvement with the group or move on to other activities, for example helping other people, or starting other, similar groups. It is a mistake to see this as necessarily following conversion, since there are circumstances where a person repeatedly moves from one to the other and back again, or the two processes of helping others and being helped may proceed simultaneously. Finally, of course, a person may simply leave the group, or may look outside the group and even advertise the positive impact of the experience by recruiting others, or the person may leave the activity to start a fresh one.

People in different situations encounter very different issues as they go through the process of group-based empowerment. Thus, members of WeightWatchers may be able to share their successes proudly with others, whereas members of more stigmatized groups may feel driven to be more circumspect. In the latter case, members of AA may share similar problems of reacceptance by others, such as some former mental patients. In the past, AA has tried to counter this by using the allergy concept of alcoholism, which assumes that people develop drink problems because of a physiological predisposition over which they have no control. In this way, AA members could be viewed as sick rather than as mentally ill or blameworthy. One consequence could be that the presumption that the drinker is merely an allergic victim of alcohol may lead simply to the eventual release of the non-drinker from the deviant label of 'alcoholic'. Paradoxically, the outcome could be that problem drinking becomes seen as behaviour over which some people have no control, so they use this as an excuse to cease trying to combat it.

In contrast, the experience of a CR group is likely to be more overtly empowering, by being more educationally than problem focused:

> A CR group decides to look at the topic of education. From the discussion of their personal experiences the women learn that many of them were interested in the sciences but were not encouraged to pursue their interest. They go on to look at how the fields of science are dominated by men who were actively encouraged at school to continue their education. The women learn something about the limits imposed by sex-role stereotyping in education. (Donnan and Lenton, 1985, p. 17)

It is important to be able to recognize the stage reached in a particular group empowerment initiative. These have been conceptualized in different ways, as Table 6.4 shows. However, there is much similarity between them.

The key processes of initiation, self-movement and proselytizing, for example, relate to the practical stages of beginning, maintaining and ending through which all groups pass. Some writers have produced detailed checklists of the stages that groups go through. In general, the more specific and detailed the checklist, the more caution has to be exercised when applying it to the vast range of specific situations. However, our simple framework discussed above fits quite well with most of these. In their model of self-directed groupwork, Mullender and Ward (1991, pp. 18–19) detail five major stages, which they break down into twelve steps. Lee's (2001, p. 308) chart of the twelve stages of the process of empowering groupwork is similar (Table 6.4). However, the variety of practice does not lend itself to rigid categorizations. On this, Mullender and Ward (1991, pp. 18–19) caution that:

> we would not suggest that what actually happens in practice is as neatly tied and labelled as such an account may imply, nor that

anyone should try to force reality to conform to the stages and steps of the model. One way of conceptualizing the framework is as a grid, upon which can be placed all our ideas and actions in a piece of work, thus enabling us to see them in relation one to another, rather than in a linear progression.

Table 6.4 Stages of group empowerment

Mullender and Ward (1991, pp. 18–19)	Adams (1990, pp. 52–75, 2006, pp. 97–9)	Lee (2001, pp. 308–50)
	Initiation	*Beginning phase of work*
Stage A: Workers take stock Step 1 Assembling the team Step 2 Establishing support Step 3 Agreeing empowerment principles *Stage B: Group takes off* Step 4 Open planning	Starting an activity	1. Meeting and taking stock of group 2. Formation of group 3. Defining empowerment goals together 4. Choosing theme to begin with
	Sustaining	*The work phase*
Stage C: Group prepares for action Step 5 Group identifies problems, sets agenda Step 6 Group asks why these problems Step 7 Group targets changes, prioritizes tasks *Stage D: Group takes action* Step 8 Group carries out agreed actions *Stage E: Group takes over* Step 9 Group reviews Step 10 Group identifies new issues Step 11 Group links different issues Step 12 Group decides what next	(self-movement: self-development and learning) Doing the work *Moving on* (ending or proselytizing) Concluding the group, or taking on wider activities	5. Using social work skills to develop mutual aid power of group 6. Worker encourages members to pose challenging questions 7. Group members asked to share feelings and analyse on personal, institutional and system levels 8. Group develops tools for raising consciousness 9. As the tools are questioned, the group consciousness becomes more critical 10. Group develops options for action personally, institutionally and politically 11. Group members take action 12. Group reflection on action continues until members decide action is complete

Conclusion

This chapter has examined evidence from research and practice that helps to clarify what is involved in setting up and running empowering groups and the practice issues for social workers who want to become involved in them. The huge variety of such groups makes it impossible to be prescriptive about the detail of the processes groups go through, but we have drawn some general pointers from a wide range of research and practice.

---

putting it into practice

Activity 1

Make a list of what you regard as the more common features of self-help and user-led groups.

Activity 2

Give examples of the different types of self-help and user-led groups.

Activity 3

Describe what you regard as the main stages of group-based empowerment.

Further reading

Lee, J.A.B. (2001) *The Empowerment Approach to Social Work Practice: Building the Beloved Community* (2nd edn) New York, Columbia University Press, pp. 290–350. Offers a detailed illustration of the process of group empowerment.

Mullender, A. and Ward, D. (1991) *Self-directed Groupwork: Users Take Action for Empowerment*, London, Whiting & Birch. Pages 18–54 provide a useful guide to the principles and stages of groupwork in which service users take various leading roles.

Whitaker, D.S. (1985) *Using Groups to Help People*, London, Tavistock/Routledge. A thorough and easily read guide to the stages of groupwork, with the emphasis on therapeutic and social work groups.

7 | Empowering organizations

The organization delivering social work services, as viewed from the vantage point of staff, is very different to the organization as experienced by its customers, clients or users. This is crucial when it comes to empowering them. I was working on a research project with a voluntary childcare organization, aiming to discover how parents and children using a drop-in centre on a large housing estate found out about it. Was it through the information campaigns and publicity from the drop-in centre? The findings of the research were surprising to staff in the organization. Practically every newcomer heard about the centre 'on the grapevine' of 'gossip' between parents on the housing estate. Views about the centre, the quality of services and the staff were passed on from person to person, rather than extracted from any material supplied by the organization. On the other hand, the parents had no direct involvement in running the childcare organization, which stayed 'outside' the centre and made most of its decisions about the future running of the centre from this position, independent of staff running the centre, at two steps removed from the face-to-face practice with parents and children.

Introduction

This chapter explores the factors that act for and against practitioners doing empowering work and being empowered in the different organizations where they practise. We are concerned not with the broad span of the organization's work but only with those aspects of direct relevance to empowerment of practitioners and those with whom they work.

Factors affecting empowerment of people in organizations

In order for the organizations managing the delivery of local services to be empowered and empowering, two aspects need to be trans-formed: the way local government or governance is viewed, and the role of the citizen. In the UK, some changes are taking place in ideas and practices and it is these we examine in this chapter. Undoubtedly, the organizations that deliver services are changing to reflect the increasing prominence of policies promoting a view of citizenship which is almost synonymous with greater citizen involvement. At the same time, local government is becoming less of a monopoly by corporate public sector organizations and more a series of partner-ships with a multiplicity of independent service providers in the private and voluntary sectors. In other words, there has been a shift from local government to local governance. Let us examine briefly the meanings of these words citizenship and governance.

Changing meanings of governance and citizenship

Participative governance

The style of governance of the organization affects how participation by people is regarded by professionals. What do we mean by gover-nance? In essence, **governance** means how policy is sustained in practice. Newman (2005, p. 101) defines governance as 'the setting, application and enforcement of the rules of the game in a way that enhances legitimacy in the public realm'. She acknowledges that the advantage of moving towards participative governance is that it enhances the legitimacy of government institutions (Newman, 2005, p. 119). However, she also points out that as power is devolved, the issue of how to decide which matters are the realm of public deter-mination and which are private choices by individual people is exposed more sharply rather than resolved (Newman, 2005, p. 119).

Newman (2005, p. 120) refers to Habermas (1989), who proposes a way forward for the public sphere, which he regards as eroded by the rise of the mass media (which he calls 'commodification') and the interweaving of public and private spheres (which he calls 'femi-nization'). A way past the consequent legitimation crisis is the repoliticization of the public sphere by enabling people to take part in what Habermas refers to as 'communicative interaction' (Newman 2005, p. 120).

Johansson and Hvinden (2005, p. 115) distinguish the republican from the socio-liberal forms of citizenship and governance. The socio-liberal form involves trying to develop ways of involving people in so-called 'hard to reach' or seldom heard groups, including those regarded as 'excluded', and giving support to self-help groups, carer and service user associations. The republican form aims at broader popular participation in policy and decision-making. It emphasizes the freedom of choice of the individual, participation and self-initiated activity without forgetting obligations and responsibilities. It crosses boundaries between and around categories such as 'self-help group' and 'user group' and engages citizens as partners in running public agencies (Johansson and Hvinden, 2005, p. 114).

Citizenship

The exact form of citizenship affects how participation is seen from the citizen's point of view. **Citizenship** refers to the status of citizens, with its related rights, privileges, powers, duties and responsibilities of social, political and community involvement and participation. Johansson and Nvinden (2005, p. 105) distinguish three models or forms of citizenship – socio-liberal, libertarian and republican – which are likely to be combined in periods of change to enable new relationships between the individual and the state (Table 7.1). The socio-liberal form of citizenship rests on the assumption that there should be an agreement or contract between the individual and the state, following the principle that all individuals should have equal rights (such as the right to care, protection and economic security) and obligations (such as carrying out paid work and caring for oneself and other adult and child dependants), enjoying a fair balance between these (Johansson and Nvinden, 2005, p. 108). Of course, it may be difficult for individuals and the state to agree on what that fair balance should be for everybody. On the whole, a shift towards a view of more active citizenship tends to accompany a trend towards more demands being made on the citizen. The libertarian form of citizenship also rests on the idea of a contract between the individual and the state. There is acceptance of the principle that the state imposes certain fundamental rights on behalf of the individual, but at the same time, the state does not take responsibility for what is deemed to be the private responsibility of the individual for ensuring his or her own health and welfare. This means that the individual is more of a citizen-consumer, with the right to choose, but the responsibility for earning that choice, in terms of seeking paid employment, investing towards a pension and insuring against risks such as unemployment and ill-health (Johansson and Nvinden, 2005, p. 109). The republican form of citizenship rests on the assumption that people can and should enjoy significant civil, political and social rights that give them the freedom and capacity to participate as active citizens. This participation is seen as empowering them to the point where they can significantly affect decisions about the future nature of society (Johansson and Nvinden, 2005, p. 110).

Table 7.1 Forms of citizenship, participation and empowerment

Form of citizenship	What it entails
Socio-liberal 'entitled citizen'	Agreement between person and state All people have equal rights and obligations Fair balance between rights and obligations
Libertarian 'citizen-consumer'	Agreement between person and state People have rights, but state does not take responsibility for personal health and welfare
Republican 'active citizen'	People have significant civil and political rights People have freedom and capacity to participate, which empowers them to influence decisions about policy and society

Within the republican stream of ideas, Johansson and Nvinden identify three distinct brands of republican ideas: communitarian, deliberative and radical citizenship. Communitarian citizenship prioritizes what are seen as traditional values, for example expressed through preserving and supporting the family. Deliberative citizenship, in contrast, does not propose a view about the ideal society but relies on individual citizens to debate rationally among themselves. The optimistic assumption is that, given freedom, people will transform their individual wishes into a negotiated, general, social good. Radical citizenship regards the deliberative approach as too restricted, governed by procedures and segregated from the social and political context. The term 'active citizenship' may be used to refer to circumstances where the individual takes part. However, Johansson and Hvinden (2005, p. 112) regard participation as a process of negotiation and even conflict, as citizens struggle in various informal, formal, interpersonal, group and organizational arenas to get their views across and influence decisions.

We have established that different forms of governance of an organization affect participation by people in its operation. What can research tell us about the effectiveness of initiatives aiming to empower citizens by enhancing their participation in organizations? The general message from research is that a piecemeal approach to this is less effective than a whole system approach. This entails giving major attention to the organization and working through a series of stages: auditing existing policy and practice; devising goals for empowering people; clarifying how these goals are to be met; and working with staff to reach the goals. In the first part of this chapter, we highlight the main factors likely to act as barriers to empowering organizations and in the second part we consider ways of overcoming them.

Factors militating against empowerment in organizations

Complexity of local government and governance

The processes and procedures for financing, administering, managing and delivering services are extremely complex. The local government of services has widened to include a proliferation of partnerships and contractors in the independent – that is, private and voluntary – sector, to the extent that it is more realistic to refer to local governance rather than local government. One consequence of devolving responsibility for delivering services to localities and neighbourhoods and 'outsourcing' is replacing the monolithic supply of everything from the centre with a multiplicity of partnerships with private and voluntary agencies. This may lead to a fragmentation of provision, which may discourage agencies from moving in that direction.

Bureaucracy and managerialism

The management of local authorities is, in the descriptive rather than pejorative sense of the word, a bureaucracy. The word 'bureaucracy' was used by the sociologist Max Weber (1997) to describe the way in which the office functions in an industrialized society, where a host of complex tasks require hierarchical arrangements, the division of labour and procedures to guide staff to be specified in a detailed way. Thus, in the century or so since Weber wrote, bureaucracy in local government, as in other large organizations, has become associated with rigid rather than flexible and creative ways of administering and delivering local services. Clearly, these do not correspond with the image of a local government that responds to the wishes and demands of citizens. Management systems that enter the territory of the professional and provide a layer of regulation over and above professional supervision are referred to as 'managerialist' (Clarke et al., 1994) and as meeting the needs of the organization rather than being accountable to the wishes and needs of the 'client', that is, service user or carer.

Discrimination

Many organizations disempower people and discriminate against particular groups, such as women, black and disabled people. Barnes and Bowl (2001, p. 165) argue that organizations committed to promoting greater participation by users of services need to develop more comprehensive empowerment strategies. This is not a straight-forward matter, because we do not live our lives detached from the wider community and social context. Askheim (2003) argues that Rogerian approaches to counselling, for example, may make the person feel empowered, but they cannot be expected to challenge discriminatory structures in the person's life. It is unavoidable that power will still be associated with dominant meanings in this setting. Its effectiveness will be policed, in effect, by structures, hierarchies, committees, groups and individuals with authority, wielding power. The practitioner who is trying to empower the person, as well as the patient, client or service user, almost certainly will remain part of a subordinate group, who may even be in a majority in numerical terms, but will not prevail in terms of power. An altogether constrasting problem is that noted by the author, anecdotally, in older people's forums, where it is possible for one or two people with particular experiences to dominate the group and be the 'loudest shouters' who get their way, rather than representing local community interests.

According to Carr, the most commonly referred to barriers are as follows: a lack of embedded policy and practice; professional and organizational resistance; and issues associated with power (Carr, 2004b). Let us take these in turn.

Lack of embedded participation in policy and practice

It is difficult for the organization to become empowering in the absence of specific policies and practices that lend themselves to this. It is noticeably easier to subscribe to a list of general principles than to work through the process of turning them into strategies and policies that we then proceed to implement. The more complex the organization, the more it is essential for the strategy and the policy that follows it to be embedded in different departments, that is, owned by people working in all parts of the organization.

Professional and organizational resistance

Staff in the organization, and particularly those who are less convinced of the need for change, are likely to use the lack of policies and procedures underpinning change as a justification for maintaining the status quo. Large organizations with a multiplicity of staff in different roles, including a diversity of professional roles, are likely to experience more difficulty in making rapid and wide-ranging changes. Independently of Carr's work, one fear expressed by local authority managers examining the viability of empowerment through the devolution of services is that the more power people have, the more they will drive up the costs of services by demanding more and better quality services (Wilkinson, 2004, p. 18).

Power issues

Carr (2004b) draws attention to a range of factors in connection with concerns about power-sharing, which we can summarize as revolving around the continuing gulf between the structural power of staff and the relative powerlessness of citizens. Talking through power issues does not make them go away. All we can do is recognize them, reflect critically on them and continue to work at empowering policy and practice in the organization. It is not realistic to expect that empowering work with an individual or group within an organization or institution will totally change the nature of the organization.

Tackling barriers

It is important to accept that there is no quick and simple way of creating a more empowered and empowering organization to deliver local social care services. Means of empowering people through the organization may be direct or indirect. Direct means include ways of democratizing the organization. Indirect means include other measures such as decentralization, in which an element of democratization is not necessary. Wide consultation is generally held to be helpful, to precede the implementation of any scheme. This should include all the identified **stakeholders** – people with an interest in, or power to influence, a policy, project, organization, service or activity – if the changes are to be endorsed and supported by the widest possible constituency of interests, groups and individuals. There may be a need for continued induction and staff development to ensure that new, democratized ways of working are endorsed by new employees and that ongoing issues are tackled with the existing workforce as they arise, rather than being left to fester and create confusion and conflict.

Wilkinson (2004, pp. 20–2) has noted several factors raised by local authority staff at a seminar on devolving governance to area committees and neighbourhood management, drawing attention to four features required for an integrated model of decentralization of services: flexibility in the process of sharing control; localized models that are matched to the needs of each area; clarity of structure and purpose; and systematic arrangements for long-term participation.

finding models for localized democracy

There have been many attempts to introduce greater democracy into the workplace, some based on staff development and adult education principles (Dew, 1997), others on different models of organizational democracy (Manville and Ober, 2003). In industry, there is a long history of democratization of the workplace and the question is how much of this experience has lessons that can be transferred into the public services. In summary:

1. Decentralization of services accompanied by the complexities of devolving budgets may be skewed by the issues of costs and resources. It is important to change the culture of the workplace so that the empowerment of all stakeholders becomes viable. This is a fundamental requirement, at least as important as efforts to decentralize.
2. Flexibility and a willingness to change on the part of staff are required.
3. It is important not to try to manage the changes too precipitously, so that all staff, for example, have the chance to talk through the implications. A more democratized organization will affect different grades and levels of staff differently. For example, the truism that one person's empowerment may be another person's disempowerment applies just as much in the organization as in social work with families.

Research and theorizing on empowering organizations

Is research and theorizing able to indicate to us which organizational forms are potentially more empowering? Given the vast range of organizations, it is impossible to create one template that fits them all. Burns and Stalker (1961) distinguish between mechanistic and organic organizations, the former being more suitable for stable conditions and displaying a greater reliance on control of staff, hierarchical management, obedience to superiors, and attributing greater significance to local rather than generalized or cosmopolitan knowledge. In contrast, the organic organization is less hierarchical, information and control can be decentralized and located at any point, and networking and multidirectional communication are as important as top-down communication to reinforce control. A related idea is that of the learning organization, which matches many of the characteristics of the organic organization. Gould and Baldwin (2004) borrow the term **learning organization** to refer to an organization geared to rapid changes in working practices that enable it to tackle many issues and problems. Organizational change involves staff becoming accustomed to instability and uncertainty as 'normal'. Schön's Reith lectures on the loss of the stable state were subsequently published in his book *Beyond the Stable State* (Schön, 1973), in which he argued that people delude themselves when they organize their lives and work around the assumption that this or that current reorganization is only creating temporary disruption. The reality is that there is no permanent stable state and we should expect continuous change and transformation. The implications for organizations are that in order to survive and remain effective, they need to become capable of continually transforming themselves. Many of the characteristics Schön highlights – networking and flexibility – are similar to those of the organic organization. Schön (1973, pp. 28–9) writes about organizations becoming learning systems in order to transform themselves. A learning organization may remain an ideal, in the sense that Pedler et al. (1996, p. 1) conceive the entire organization as making possible learning by all its members and continuously transforming itself.

Building a shared culture in the workplace

It is important to recognize that while staff represent a concentrated interest, service users and carers are a dispersed interest, in the sense that staff work together and have opportunities to build up a shared culture in the workplace, whereas service users and carers seldom meet unless special arrangements are made to bring them together. There is a need for capacity building with individuals (see Chapter 5) and communities (see Chapter 8) in order to enable them to take part. Active participation requires that members of the public feel they can assert their views with local authority employees – managers and practitioners – and elected councillors (Wilkinson, 2004, p. 24). Practitioners have a vital role in ensuring that empowerment works for staff, for people who use services and for carers. This extends to ensuring that democratization of the organization is representative and effective. Representative arrangements will need to include particularly targeting people who are excluded at present, those who are 'hard to reach' or 'seldom heard'.

The experience of the Living Options in Practice (1992) project suggests ways of identifying service users and carers and working with them. Such work is akin to community work. It uses local community resources and networks as locations for practitioners, service users and carers and other people to meet and exchange information. This emphasizes how essential it is to involve local voluntary groups and organizations coordinating the voluntary sector, established self-help groups, carers' groups and user groups and individual service users and carers. All of these can act as sources of further information and contacts. Local purchasing and providing health and social care/social work agencies will need networking also. Those involved in the work will need to clarify what it involves as early as possible, and specify how it is to be monitored and evaluated.

Tackling structural power and discrimination

As part of the agenda of tackling power issues in the organization, it is necessary to challenge discrimination and reduce inequalities. Research demonstrates the need to rectify gender imbalances in the management of health and welfare organizations in many Western countries, including the UK (Orme, 2001), exemplified by the fact that whereas women are the main users and providers of services, they play only a marginal part in the management of social services. Changes in policy, legislation and working practices governed by principles of empowerment are viewed as key strategies by which to address this problem area (SSI, 1991, p. 55).

On the other land, the problem may be addressed by empowering reticulists. Knight and Hayes (1981, p. 50) describe these as young, middle-class, articulate and socially and politically committed people. However, they admit that while such people may succeed in initiating groups, this may perpetuate the elitist tendency for such people to retain leadership of activities that ideally might have been owned and run by poor and deprived people (Knight and Hayes, 1981, p. 79). **Reticulists**, according to our definition, are people who are committed to achieving change through their skills in crossing organizational and professional boundaries, strengthening existing networks and forming new networks with individuals and groups. They are likely to have more success in empowering people who are seldom heard.

Teams, partnerships and networking

Teams and partnerships are a focus for empowering work, where many organizations work collaboratively across professional and organizational boundaries. Networking may be effective where organizations can develop into learning systems with the capacity to transform themselves.

Involvement in local community or wider issues comes more easily to some groups than others. Some groups may be more used to taking up issues than others, for example by becoming involved in activities that raise community awareness, through some form of information-gathering locally or an educational campaign concerning a health issue. As time passes, some groups or organizations develop outside activities to the point where their resources begin to stimulate the growth of other helping activities in the community. While some groups, notably consciousness-raising groups, have this more or less built into their aims, others may move towards it slowly and with difficulty. Those involved may need the encouragement of a ready-provided rationale. Three justifications can be given:

1. Those who have met to help themselves and each other have already demonstrated their commitment and motivation and may have reached the point where they would be stimulated by, and help others through, a wider focus for their efforts.
2. Groups need to avoid becoming insular and should benefit from keeping in touch with local developments.
3. Groups may find it fruitful to encourage and support other people who are interested in self-help but have not yet taken the plunge (Lindenfield and Adams, 1984, p. 94).

But the growth of a formal organization is not dependent on outside activities. They are used here as an example of typical developments that would produce pressure towards it. We move on to consider the nature of those formal organizations that are empowering, to see if we can be more specific about their characteristics.

Characteristics of empowering organizations

We can see in Table 7.2 some contrasting features of traditional and empowering organizations. In many ways, the informal arrangements in the organization are more likely to be empowering. It is noticeable that more empowering organizations enable people to work within and with them more flexibly, creatively and imaginatively.

Table 7.2 Traditional and empowering organizations

Characteristic	Traditional organization	Empowering organization
Mission	Maintaining the organization	Benefiting people (staff and users)
Goals	Fulfilling organizational requirements	Meeting people's needs
System	Closed	Open
Boundaries	Working within closed boundaries	Boundary abolishing, blurring, crossing
Accessibility	Restricted	Unrestricted
Culture	Defensive Rule-following	Critical; self-awareness Creativity; innovation
Most important person	Chief executive	Service user/carer
Membership	Staff and 'others'	Inclusive (users, carers, including 'seldom heard')
Roles	Rigid roles	Flexible roles
Primary accountability	To line managers	To peers/service users
Management style	Hierarchical Maintaining status quo	Democratic
Attitudes to change initiatives	Relatively non-receptive	Initiating and responsive
Communication from below	Mainly top down; responses	Multidirectional; horizontal, upward, diagonal
Rewards	Staff paid, users voluntary	All contributors rewarded; salaries, fees, expenses
Relationships	Restricted to formal lines of accountability	Informal relations contribute to agenda for change
Power	Concentrated among senior staff	Dispersed; shared by all staff and users

Culture change in the organization

The more traditional organization needs to undergo a culture change, to become more open to participation by people who use services and carers. We use the term 'culture change' to indicate that this would require systemic change in the way the organization works, in this instance, towards becoming more participatory. The development of a participatory culture has been explored by Kirby et al. (2003a, 2003b). Typically, a **participatory culture** is one where participation is central and fundamental to the functioning of the organization. Change from traditional working to becoming participatory is likely to involve a major staff development programme. A learning organization in the process of change towards a more participatory way of working is likely to need to develop an infra-structure to support staff. An **infrastructure** is the systems, proce-dures and processes for supporting staff in their work. The task of bringing about change in a learning organization is no less difficult and painful than for individual learners. The features of a learning organization are indicated in Table 7.3.

Table 7.3 Features of a learning organization

Feature	Characteristics
Change	Enables staff to change their working practices
Learning	Creates an environment where staff can both learn and work
Exchange	Provides people with the necessary knowledge and skills to enable individual, group and organizational change to take place
Innovation	Encourages innovations by staff
Experiment	Supports staff in experimenting with new ways of working
Risk-taking	Furthers a 'no blame' culture at work, where staff are encouraged to take risks

Let us be more specific about what we mean by the culture of the organization. We can identify five components of the culture of the organization (Table 7.4). It follows that in order to change the culture, we would need to change the values, norms, organizational systems, means of peer support and the general climate in the organ-ization. Many people would say this is an impossible task. However, there are three main incentives:

1. 'Policy drivers' pushing the organization towards being more responsive to clients, consumers and users of its services.
2. Professional incentives for staff.
3. The extent to which service users and carers have the motivation and capacity to become positive participants.

This raises the question of how sympathetic the organizational culture is towards participation. Kirby et al. (2003a, 2003b) distin-guish three main types of organizational culture that could be said to be participatory: consultation focused, participation focused and people focused. We have added change focused to this, producing four types (Table 7.5), which we now examine in turn.

Table 7.4 Features of the culture of the organization

Component of organizational culture	Characteristics
Values	The beliefs of people in the organization about what they should and should not do
Norms	Widely accepted codes of practice in the organization's everyday work, regulating such areas as procedures for paying expenses to people who participate
Organizational systems for supporting people	Human resources and personnel functions, e.g. recruiting and inducting new staff, communications and arrangements for rewarding and paying people
Peer support	Formal and informal means by which staff relate to each other, interact and support each other
Organizational climate	General 'feel' of the workplace, how friendly, relaxed or tense it is

Table 7.5 Four types of participatory organizational culture

Type of culture	Characteristics
Consultation focused	Taking advice from people who use services and carers One-off consultations rather than continuous participation
Participation focused	Decisions made on basis of ongoing involvement Boundaries around participation set by organization staff Focus of participation determined and run by organization staff
People focused	Starting from experiences and perceptions of individuals who use services and carers Some work of the organization shaped in the light of these views
Change focused	Starting from experiences and perceptions of people who use services and carers Much work of the organization can be influenced by them, including structural changes

Consultation-focused organizations

Consultation-focused organizations gather the views of people who use services and carers, but retain control over the decision-making process and do not involve them in this. Consultation may, on one hand, be tokenistic, but, on the other hand, it may be set up so as to enable people's views to be taken seriously. It is possible to use regular, repeated consultations as a way of keeping the organization in touch with people's thoughts and feelings.

Participation-focused organizations

Participation-focused organizations take their commitment to people who use services and carers beyond consulting, by enabling them to join the decision-making process. This may happen to a significant extent. It is common, though, for the staff to retain control of the process. Also, it is usual for the staff to determine the areas of the organization's work in which participation is considered appropriate.

People-focused organizations

The people or person focus enables the views of the individual carer or person using services to be taken into account. The culture of the organization enables this view to be considered in some aspects of the organization's work. The boundaries around this include:

- only the views of individuals are considered
- only some of the work of the organization is available for scrutiny, influence and change.

Change-focused organizations

The change-focused organization is primarily concerned with bringing about organizational change through the views of people. Whereas the people or person focus is on change, it is change at the individual level only. The change focus acknowledges this. Its features include:

1. Specifically enabling people who use services and carers to express their views collectively as well as individually.
2. Enabling people who participate to exercise power, so as to influence and change most or, some would say, in ideal circumstances, all aspects of the work of the organization.

Conclusion

This chapter has examined some of the main barriers to empowerment and some of the ways in which these may be tackled. It has paid particular attention to the means by which organizations may become more organic, and more responsive to pressures to involve carers and people who use services. The more successful social welfare organizations are at becoming empowering, the more likely they are to maintain their capacity as learning organizations, ensuring the inward flow of knowledge and experience that contributes to the quality of their services.

putting it into practice

Activity 1

Describe in your own words what you see as the culture of participation in your organization.

Activity 2

Identify the most appropriate type of participatory culture for your organization.

Activity 3

List the values you regard as underpinning the culture of participation in your organization.

further reading

Adams, R., Dixon, G., Henderson, T. et al. (2005) *A Strategy for Bringing about Participation by Service Users in the Work of Skills for Care*, Middlesbrough, University of Teesside. An England-wide survey of experiences of people who use services and carers, followed by practical recommendations on how to tackle barriers to enabling them to participate in the organization.

Barnes, C. and Mercer, G. (1999) *Independent Futures: Creating User-led Disability Services in a Disabling Society*, Bristol, Policy Press, pp. 71–121. Research dealing with the barriers to effective participation by disabled people and ways of overcoming them.

Blackburn, J. and Holland, J. (1998) *Who Changes? Institutionalizing Participation in Development*, London, Intermediate Technology Publications. Chapter 16 of this intriguing collection of studies from different countries discusses lessons learned from participatory approaches in bringing about organizational change from participatory rhetoric to participatory reality.

Hardina, D., Middleton, J., Montana, S. et al. (2006) *An Empowering Approach to Managing Social Service Organizations*, New York, Springer Tackles theoretical and practical aspects of empowering organizations.

Netting, F.E., Kettner, P.M. and McMurtry, S.L. (2003) *Social Work Macro Practice* (3rd edn) New York, Allyn & Bacon. Useful discussion of many relevant aspects of bringing about change and empowerment of people in social work organizations.

Wilcox, D. (1994) *A Guide to Effective Participation*, York, Joseph Rowntree Foundation. Written in a simple, direct style, it outlines practical ways of developing participation by people.

8 | Empowering communities and political systems

In work for a voluntary childcare agency in the north of England, we encountered one group of young people on a council housing estate with limited play facilities, who were excluded from most recreation facilities, including youth clubs, on account of their disruptive behaviour. We sat with them and asked them what, in an ideal world, they would like to happen. They listed things we could not directly change, or which would take much longer to influence, such as they way they viewed school, what they were taught and how it was taught. They also talked about how people treated them and how it felt to be labelled as 'bad', so that whenever fresh trouble occurred on the housing estate, they were the first people the police called on. We took action to work more closely with the local school, by one of us meeting the school counsellor, which led, after a while, to us being invited regularly to meetings between the counsellor and teaching staff. We also invited the community police officer to meet us with the young people and see some of the positive work they were doing. There was one local aspect of life in their community they identified that we thought we could help with: their complaint that there was nowhere to play and when they played on the street, residents constantly complained. We went with them to the run-down playground, with its old, inadequate play equipment that was hardly used. We asked what they would like to see and they described, in effect, an adventure playground. We set about with them to develop an adventure playground. They helped us to negotiate with local councillors and gain their support. They came with us on trips to a yard where old telephone poles were stored and we begged a large number from the proprietor. They worked with us to design and build the adventure playground, which became a focus for children's recreation on the estate (Adams, 1981, pp. 230–1).

Introduction

This chapter considers approaches to empowering work with and within community groups and political systems. How can the worker act so as to empower people in these settings? Such work contains an essential element of individual and group-based activity, so many of the points made in earlier chapters about work with individuals and groups apply here. Conditions in formal organizations are very different to community settings, where the work may be with community associations or incipient self-help organizations. But in whatever setting, community and political empowerment will be marginalized and probably useless unless that empowerment becomes institutionalized and part of the fabric of the community or political system. In practical situations, communities and political systems cannot be separated, but to enable us to examine a range of issues and examples in this chapter, we shall deal with them separately and in turn.

Empowering communities

What do we mean by 'community'?

The term 'community' has a variety of meanings, including the following:

- a relatively small and cohesive geographical locality such as a neighbourhood or housing estate
- a social network of people, linked by a common interest or sense of identity, such as a supporters club for a sports team
- a physical space such as a factory and nearby houses for the workers.

As Jackson notes (2004, p. 3), definitions of 'community' in terms of physical location risk underestimating the importance of residents' involvement and participation.

Variety of empowering work with communities

This is not a chapter about community work, although there is an overlap between empowering work with communities and community work. Not all the work with communities we describe below could be described as 'community work'. We define **community work** as working with people in communities on goals they define to enable them to achieve them. There probably will always be an empowering element in work with communities that is less driven by people themselves and includes the component of being devised and resourced from outside the local community. Community empowerment spans the continuum from state-sponsored initiatives (Watt et al., 2000) to those initiated by local non-professionals themselves, which are autonomous, that is, independent of agencies and professionals (see Table 6.1). It is crucial that empowering work in and with communities should extend to disadvantaged, marginalized and socially excluded people and should be participative. This means it is work with people that involves approaches which engage with them, elicit their wishes, facilitate them formulating their own goals, address their needs, inequalities and/or disadvantages, and enable them to achieve their goals. This is recognized as desirable, across the field of health and social welfare. For example, Chiu's (2004, p. 3) participatory community health educator model, underpinned by the twin principles of empowerment and participation, aims to improve the health of people in ethnic minorities by engaging them in a three-stage participatory process:

1. Identifying needs, jointly with them.
2. Developing methods of health intervention, with their active participation.
3. Implementing and evaluating, with the support of stakeholders, and feeding back into further action through stage 1.

Mutual aid and community empowerment

Mutual aid and collective self-help responses to social problems can offer a variety of viable models for empowering communities. The creation of methods of small savings may be the beginnings of self-empowerment, through people preserving self-respect. In this connection, friendly societies, the history of which goes back to before the Industrial Revolution, are respectable sources of mutual support for people of limited means. For example, the author's father donated one penny a week throughout his working life to the Hampshire Friendly Society, with a view to covering the cost of funeral expenses. The cooperative movement has generated many similar schemes. Credit unions, another long-established institution, are also adapting to changing circumstances and local conditions and still meet people's needs. Burns et al. (2004, pp. 131–47) have examined the concepts and nature of community self-help in some detail, demonstrating how the mutual aid aspects of self-help offer the potential for its community benefits to offer a mainstream resource, rather than simply a means of individuals helping themselves.

example

Asian Resource Centre

A well-established example of a self-help organization functioning largely autonomously from social services agencies was the Asian Resource Centre (ARC) in Birmingham, which came about through a grassroots initiative by people involved in a multicultural centre called Action Centre. Workers involved at that time noted the need for a centre specifically designed to meet the needs of Asian people. The ARC was located in a street of shops in Handsworth and acted as a community centre for the Asian community:

> working in the relevant languages with a deep understanding of the religious and cultural aspirations of the people it serves. The services are provided through advice work at the Centre, running appropriate projects like the Asian Elders, Women's Welfare Rights, Housing Welfare etc., and by providing resources and practical help in such areas as immigration, nationality and anti-sexism. The Centre produces leaflets, pamphlets in Asian languages and acts as a pressure group to statutory services. It provides educational and training facilities for the local community, voluntary and statutory agencies. The Centre is staffed by Asian workers and managed by elected representatives of the Asian community. (Asian Resource Centre, 1987)

The aims of the ARC were stated as follows:

> to identify and analyse the cultural and the social system placed upon particularly disadvantaged sections of the Asian community within the neighbourhood and elsewhere, and also identify its general and specific needs; to initiate, participate and assist in projects designed to protect their civil and human rights, to encourage freedom of cultural expression and encourage all Asians to reassert their cultural identity, self confidence and pride. (Asian Resource Centre, 1987)

The management committee of the ARC comprised eighteen people, including ten members elected by open vote at the annual general meeting, five who were coopted for their particular skills and two councillors who represented the local authority. Its seven full-time workers were funded by the Inner City Partnership Programme, the housing authority, the social services department, Cadbury Trust and other donations and funds. An effort was made to maintain a balanced staff team, reflecting Bengali, Pakistani and Punjabi (Indian) interests, in its broad range of community-oriented activities.

> The ARC exemplified the autonomous sector of self-help, in that it came into being as a result of the awareness of groups in the community that their needs were not being met by professionals and who were motivated to generate a community initiative to that end.

Consciousness-raising and empowerment

Some forms of empowering work with communities are regarded as social and political education and this means workers 'set out to empower the communities they work with to question dominant assumptions – in Freire's terms to get the oppressor out of their own heads' (Mayo, 2000, p. 6). This involves empowering people 'to analyse the sources of their problems for themselves, to explore their own needs and develop their own strategies' (Mayo, 2000, p. 6). The example at the start of this chapter hovers on the boundary between prioritizing needs and prioritizing rights. As was noted at the time, the emphasis on participation and self-help within the project, like the shift towards community projects, was 'consistent with a move towards a "rights" approach and away from a "needs" approach' (Adams, 1981, p. 241). Freire regards personal consciousness-raising as the key to social transformation. Such ideas have applications in many different settings, including adult education, economic development, social education, participatory research, literacy, health education, sport, recreation, cultural and community programmes and projects in the crafts, arts and different media, such as drama, mime, song and dance (Mayo, 2000, pp. 7–8). In Western and developing countries alike, community development work plays an increasingly important role in urban and rural regeneration programmes and in strategies designed to combat social exclusion, although as Bar-On and Prinsen (1999) point out, all too often community initiatives proceed without an awareness of the potential benefits of participatory approaches such as participatory rural appraisal and participatory action research (McTaggart, 1999).

> **example**
>
> The South Tyrone Empowerment Programme in Northern Ireland is a community development initiative aiming to promote inclusion and community participation. It offers emergency accommodation,

measures to combat homelessness, helping young fathers to become more involved in their children's lives, interpreter services through more than 200 interpreters and translation services in more than 30 languages as well as giving support to migrant workers. The migrant support work includes community capacity development, individual language support, training and translation services.

Features of community empowerment

Community empowerment can take place at a variety of levels and can be controlled in different ways by different groups and interests. In Table 8.1, we categorize different types of community activity according to whether they are controlled by the authorities or by people themselves.

Table 8.1 Features of community empowerment

Type of action	Control	
	by local people	by the authorities
Community development	Neighbourhood action groups	Regeneration projects
Mutual help	Credit unions	Anti-poverty programmes
Self-expression	Arts cooperatives	Government-funded community arts

Community arts

Carnivals, initiatives to promote tourism, the transformation of former docklands into marinas, in such diverse parts of England as Bristol, Liverpool, Salford and Hull, and the creation of sporting occasions around the building of a new stadium or complex have many economic and social benefits, but also may reinforce divisions and perpetuate unemployment, homelessness, disempowerment and depression, as other parts of urban and rural landscapes suffer prolonged deterioration. Community arts and community craft cooperatives in Derry, Northern Ireland are examples of constructive community empowerment expressing the richness and vitality of local costumes, music and culture. At the end of the 1980s, a group of women previously on a temporary employment creation scheme developed the Templemore Craft Cooperative. They used their knowledge and sewing skills to make Irish dance costumes, but despite initial success, the cooperative eventually collapsed through lack of government-led business support and skills and capital investment. This specific failure, however, does not lessen the contribution that such initiatives can make to people's employability, through developing their skills and confidence (Mayo, 2000, pp. 128–30).

Education and community action

The Youth Empowerment Partnership Programme (www.yepp-community.org) was set up in 1991 by the Network of European Foundations and aimed at youth and community empowerment. It now extends from Brazil to European countries including Italy, Germany, Sweden, Belgium and Ireland. Kol Kore (A Voice is Calling) is a national, non-partisan student organization linked with volunteer events at universities in Israel with the aim of community and social action.

Community empowerment and tackling structural social problems

At their best, such community initiatives are empowering, but at their weakest, they may divert public attention from wider and more deep-rooted structural social problems of unrest, polarization between social groups and the persistence of social exclusion (Mohan and Stokke, 2000). Funding agencies, in effect, may determine which community empowerment initiatives proceed, no matter what the stated goals may be. Partnerships and networks between countries are increasingly common. Schemes such as the Millennium Dome in London are paralleled by many local authority initiatives, in that they are heavily controlled by political, managerial and business interests and local people have relatively little influence over their nature and outcomes. Their top-down nature distances them from the empowering goals of the community worker. Collaborative empowerment functions more effectively when participating people are enabled to develop a mechanism for meeting together, sharing experiences and developing a common strategy to tackle their problems.

A feature of the New Entity for Social Action (NESA) in India is the Nyaya Sangamam or People's Movement forum, which is the focus for making decisions. This is one of many empowerment initiatives aiming to tackle socioeconomic inequalities, poverty, illiteracy and the consequences of the caste system for an estimated 240 million dalits (people who are considered 'untouchable', 'outcastes' from the caste system and eligible only for the most menial jobs). The NESA is a human rights-based organization aiming to empower dalits and it works with over 5 million people through its 46 constituent agencies in Karnataka, Kerala and Tamil Nadu. Other initiatives tackle the diversity of the population, but significantly, the overwhelming majority focus on women as a major oppressed group and potentially as the main agents of change. For example, Solidarity Action for Youth Women's Empowerment combines educational opportunities, leadership and decision-making training, self-esteem and political participation for women. It aims to enable women to progress from poverty and participate more fully in community decision-making.

example

SPARC is an NGO set up in 1984 in collaboration with the National Slum Dwellers' Federation and Mahila Milan (which means 'Women Together' in Hindi) to work with the pavement dwellers and slum dwellers of India. It has spread from Nepal to 27 cities and more than 10,000 families. The approach of SPARC is to enable pavement dwellers to form 'micro-savings' groups that can oversee the design and building of their houses. Women, at the centre of the family as a unit, make a crucial contribution to the empower- ment process through Mahila Milan. At the start, opportunities are provided for women pavement dwellers to meet and share exper- iences. From this, leaders – about one to each 15 houses – are identified, the savings scheme is set up along with committees to oversee negotiating with the authorities, buying materials and construction. A participatory approach is taken to having a say in the design of individual houses and the group as a whole. The entire process is community based, initiated, led and focused.

The development of collective empowering activity is a contested area. To take one area as an example, the impulse for collective social protest, which is often regarded as having reached its peak in the late 1960s in Western societies, appears to be in decline (see, for example, the conclusions of Bagguley's study (1991, p. 139) on political movements of unemployed people). But in Britain during the early 1990s, the anti-poll tax riots and protests against new motorway developments, blood sports and the export of live animals to Continental Europe are a few examples that contradict such a conclusion. Again, as research into the history of protests by pupils (Adams, 1991) and prison riots (Adams, 1994) demonstrates, the incidence of protest may form a hidden history, not least when it involves oppressed groups or when it does not suit management to have incidents exposed to public or media scrutiny. Furthermore, such protest activity may be regarded as illegitimate by some and justifiable by others. So, the opportunities still remain for people to achieve self-realization through empowering activity of various anti-oppressive kinds, whether or not involving overt protest.

Empowering social work through communities has the potential to combat multiple oppressions, which, as Thompson (1993, p. 122) observes, may be interlocking and mutually reinforcing. The list of guidelines for white workers about working in non-racist ways, prepared by Twelvetrees (1991, p. 150) and influenced by Ohri et al. (1982), could be adapted to apply to other aspects of oppression such as discrimination against people on the grounds of disability, age or sexuality:

- Recognize that racism is a reality throughout British society.
- Understand that racism is a white problem.
- All of us need to find non-racist ways of working.
- Recognize that you collude with racism.
- Monitor whether the group or organization in which you are involved is acting in a racist way.
- Your primary role is to challenge white racism (supporting black self-help is secondary).
- Do not confuse having relationships with black people with anti-racism.
- Encourage other workers to work together to combat racism.
- Familiarize yourself with issues of concern to the black community.

Empowerment and exclusion

It is important to make the link between the above list and the broader issues of working with excluded people. We define **exclusion** as the lack of participation in, and segregation from, the mainstream of social and economic life of individuals, groups and communities. It includes discrimination of various kinds and poverty, but is not restricted to them. For instance, the following example of working with excluded people confronts the breadth of individual, social, political and spiritual aspects in which the caste system is rooted. In Nepal, the three-year Dalit Empowerment and Inclusion Project is designed and run by a consortium of six leading dalit organizations, with a budget of more than £1 million. It aims to empower the 15 per cent of Nepal's population who are dalits and include them in the mainstream of society.

Community capacity building

We have referred in passing several times to community capacity building (CCB), which is a core component in many initiatives aiming at community empowerment. CCB is a multifaceted concept. **Community capacity building** can be defined as the means by which communities build on their existing knowledge, skills and expertise and develop so as to meet the needs and priorities perceived as necessary by community members. There is overlap between community development and CCB, in that the goals of both are similar, although according to Atkinson and Willis (2006), they differ in their process, CCB relying more for its impetus on skills and resources from outside the community in question.

---

example

In Israel, the Mossawa Center, an advocacy centre for Arab citizens, promotes equality for Arab/Palestinian citizens of Israel while preserving their rights as Palestinians, and also works for gender equality of Palestinian women. Its methods of work include a focus on the empowerment of people through advocacy, capacity building, community work and campaigning. The capacity building project of the Mossawa Center aims to empower Arab local councils, work with heads of education departments and work with women's groups and communities, which are poor and otherwise unrecognized. This latter work includes Mossawa professionals being at the disposal of local groups and communities to research needs, such as family and health needs, and enable them to advocate successfully for funds to establish such services as family health clinics.

The Agency for Co-operation and Research in Development (ACORD, 2002, p. 8), drawing on experience in Okavango, a subdistrict of Botswana, distinguishes between strategic capacity building, which aims to meet the mission of the local community-based organization (CBO), and practical capacity building, which aims to meet the objectives of the CBO. In relation to capacity building to counter the impact of climate change, Cissé et al. (n.d., p. 1), based in Dakar, Senegal, in sub-Saharan Africa, argue that before beginning a programme of capacity building, the first priority is the setting up of an institutional framework that will provide an infrastructure of relationships between the different partner agencies and organizations and enable concerted action to take place. The middle ground of institutionally based and individually focused community capacity building is occupied by many initiatives and organizations. For example, the Refugee Women's Association in London builds the capacity of small refugee women's organizations so that they can help and empower individual women in their communities. The association has European funding and many years' experience of working in partnership with other European organizations. Among other items, it runs courses on applying for funding, setting up and running organizations and involving volunteers and users of services (www.refugeewomen.org/news/capbuild.htm, accessed 25.11.06).

Another positive direction in which people may move is towards more overt community action. Twelvetrees (1991) and Henderson and Thomas (1980, pp. 148–86) have commented on the stages involved in the process of community work. Twelvetrees (1991, pp. 35–6) identifies nine stages in work with community groups (Table 8.2).

Table 8.2 Stages of work with community groups

Stage	What each stage entails
1. Contacting	Getting in touch with people and analysing needs
2. Identifying needs	Bringing people together, helping them to identify needs and developing the will to meet those needs
3. Clarifying goals	Helping people to understand what will need to be done for those needs to be met
4. Setting objectives	Working with people to adopt objectives
5. Organizing	Creating a suitable organization to this end
6. Detailed planning	Helping people to form a plan of action, breaking down broad goals into smaller objectives and tasks
7. Carrying out tasks	Helping people to allocate and carry out the consequent tasks
8. Modifying objectives	Helping them to feed back and evaluate results of the action and adopt fresh objectives in the light of this
9. Repeating cycle	Enabling them to take on the repetition of stages 3 to 8, whereupon the worker withdraws to a servicing role

Involving communities in designing 'preventive' environments

There is a move towards planners, architects and designers empowering communities to take part in developing existing and new buildings and services. Individuals and groups who use services may give their views, as part of a positive process of community involvement in the development of better designed and planned human services. Involvement may be minimal, for example one-off consultation; it may be viewed negatively as a way of minimizing adverse public reactions once plans are agreed and development starts; or it may be tackled as a positive means of public participation. The role of social workers in facilitating participation by service users should not just be tokenistic, as part of the public relations task, but a significant contribution to empowering people to improve health and social care environments.

The design of buildings can contribute to prevention, treatment and care. A well-developed research literature (more than 700 reputable research studies worldwide) underpins evidence-based design studies, with key indicators including the benefits to well-being of quieter buildings, improved safety through reduced risk of airborne infections, greater numbers of conveniently located hand rub dispensers and sinks to reduce contact-spread infections, single rather than multi-bedrooms to reduce infections, better layouts of facilities to reduce staff fatigue and improve efficiency, more daylight and 'rooms with a view' to reduce depression, stress and sensations of pain and improve emotional well-being (Ulrich, 2006).

Research has been carried out in the US into how people in low-income minority ethnic communities build on their capacity to improve their physical environment (Saegert and Winkel, 1996). The process of empowerment was researched in housing cooperatives at four levels:

1. The psychological level: extent to which the individual feels empowered
2. The group level: extent to which cooperative activities affect living conditions and the ownership of the cooperative
3. The quality of life level: extent to which the quality of life in the building was judged to have improved
4. The community participation level: extent to which participation in civic activities increased.

Empowering political systems

Individual empowerment is a four-lane highway leading out into a desert unless it is made part of a wider process of change in governance and political systems. As evidence for this statement, we shall take research into one key element, micro-savings by women as part of a micro-financing initiative to enable them to buy goods and services in the community. Micro-finance involves people saving and borrowing tiny amounts of money and, individually or collectively, accumulating enough resources to make capital purchases of, for example, land or property that will improve their living conditions and enable them to sustain themselves and their families through productive agriculture. Linda Mayoux (2000) has reviewed the evidence for the growing practice of using micro-finance as a strategy to combat poverty and bring about sustainability. She concludes that while it is true that women and children benefit from micro-credit and are more reliable than men at repayments, empowerment and sustainability do not follow automatically from micro-finance initiatives. There need to be other improvements so that, for example, women's savings can be spent productively and fed into the process of planned development, or micro-finance 'is unlikely to make more than a limited contribution to empowerment' (Mayoux, 2000, p. 4).

In order to appreciate the strengths and potential of community empowerment, we need to explore common ground between different communities and societies and make links between the local setting and global political and policy realities. The Department for International Development (DFID) in the UK published a White Paper on international development in 1997 (DFID, 1997), which proposed to halve the proportion of people living in extreme poverty by 2015 and noted the particular need to strengthen the participation of poorer people in developing countries and the need for human rights and women's organizations, NGOs, cooperatives and trade unions to increase their contribution to 'giving poor people a greater voice' (DFID, 1997, p. 103). The DFID (2000) followed this with a publication aimed at achieving the government's ambitious international development targets, including the goal of empowering women and eventually eliminating world poverty. In this process, the empowerment of women is regarded as an essential precondition to the DFID's core targets of eliminating world poverty and upholding human rights (DFID, 2000, p. 26). Educating girls and eliminating gender inequalities in schooling are viewed as essential to achieving these aims. Grassroots community development and 'fundamental changes in policy, laws and attitudes will be required' (DFID, 2000, p. 8) to achieve the linked goals of women's empowerment and gender equality (pp. 29–30). In order to achieve these goals, we need to understand how ideas about community development are affected by the way we conceptualize citizenship and governance (considered in Chapter 7).

It is helpful to consider the relationship between ideas about inclusion and empowerment policy and social work practice, in the light of the social contract and social compact models of inclusion and stakeholding considered by Askonas and Stewart (2000, pp. 60–2). They consider the extent to which the dominance of the social contract model of inclusion in Britain at the turn of the twenty-first century strengthens empowerment through the operation of market principles and forces. The unrestricted operation of the market reduces inequalities in the provision of services, but this is achieved at the expense of concentrating power among those who determine how other stakeholders deploy their stakes. In contrast, the social compact model of inclusion depends on the concept of participation. The authors observe that, ironically, on the one hand, social justice may be achieved at the expense of involving people as empowered participants in the process; on the other hand, a participative practice may finish up celebrating the process of living the good life in the diversity of different communities and interests, while each holds to its version of the good life and excludes others. As Askonas and Stewart put it, in a postmodern conception, diverse communities, by their very nature, emphasize a politics of valuing difference rather than a politics of eliminating inequality. This is represented in Table 8.3. In the top left of Table 8.3, social exclusion coincides with a lack of participatory democracy. In the top right, the social contract model dominates. In the bottom left, the social compact model dominates. In the bottom right is the transcendent ideal, which prioritizes both justice and participation and, therefore, aims to achieve the empowering society.

Table 8.3 Justice and participation in the empowering society

Disempowerment Exclusive/unjust/ disempowering	**Social contract** Inclusive/just/disempowering (emphasis on achieving justice in society for different people)
Social compact Exclusive/unjust/ empowering, participating	**Fully empowered** Inclusive/just/empowering (emphasis on process: in community and living the good life)

Empowering policies

Let us return to consider empowering policies and practices in the wider political system. The DFID makes the important point that both grassroots empowerment through community development and policy and legal change are necessary to transform people's lives. This goes far beyond governments giving aid and development grants between countries:

> However, it is not donor action in itself that will bring about lasting change, but the actions of governments and, most importantly, women and men themselves which will bring about the fundamental transformations the goal of gender equality demands. (DFID, 2000, p. 29)

This transformation depends on 10 objectives being achieved:

1. Promoting equality in international rights for women and men
2. Achieving economic opportunities and job opportunities
3. Reducing gender inequalities in education and health
4. Promoting more equal participation by women in decision-making and leadership at all levels
5. Improving personal security for women and reducing gender-based violence
6. Improving mechanisms to enable women to advance in government and civil society
7. Promoting women's equality in law and ending discrimination in access to justice
8. Reducing stereotyping based on gender and changing social attitudes so as to favour women
9. Developing gender-aware management of the environment and protecting natural resources
10. Making progress in upholding girls' and boys' rights in keeping with the UN *Convention on the Rights of the Child* (DFID, 2000, pp. 29–30).

A huge body of research and critical commentary repeatedly makes similar points of women's experiences of inequalities and consequent disempowerment in all continents of the world, although to a greater extent in the developing countries. We can generalize from this experience to the experience of men and women, girls and boys. Where opportunities for empowerment are identified, the barriers that perpetuate disempowerment often fall into two predictable categories:

1. The nature of policies and laws
2. The extent to which adults and children have rights of access to relevant knowledge, skills and resources.

A good example of initiatives tackling the latter are projects such as the African Information Society Initiative, which aims to further the development of infrastructures for information and communication in Africa so as to encourage socioeconomic development. This can be done using information and communications technology (ICT), through computers and the internet. The problem, however, may be perpetuated where powerful interests prevent the necessary policy and legislative changes. Ruth Ochieng's article, in the launch issue of the online journal of the African Gender Institute, shows how the potentially empowering features of ICT to offer individuals and groups knowledge and the chance to interact can be blocked by restricting people's access to relevant technology. She argues that knowledge readily available to other people may be denied to women through 'deeply entrenched structural and political hierarchies', which exercise 'control over knowledge in the ICT process' and 'the impact of different forms of policy-making' (Ochieng, 2002, p. 3). What is needed are integrated programmes of empowerment. An example of such a programme is the Indira Mahila Yojana initiative of Kerala in southwest India, which has become the Integrated Women's Empowerment Programme. The significance of this is that it aims to tackle women's empowerment holistically, by improving confidence and awareness of women's status in society, health, education, nutrition, hygiene, sanitation, legal rights, economic advancement, savings habits and access to micro-credit and involvement in local planning and other services and departments.

Some organizations, such as the Hamlet Trust, work to empower service users and NGOs to enable people to contribute to policy, for example in the field of mental health (Bureau and Shears, 2007). The purpose of the Living Options in Practice (1992) project was to facilitate the setting up of comprehensive local services for adults with severe physical and sensory disabilities and to enable service users to participate significantly in assessing the needs for planning, implementing, monitoring and evaluating the services. A practitioner appointed across the different provider agencies and purchaser authorities was engaged in this process. The following were the seven major areas of work (Living Options in Practice, 1992):

1. Making initial contact with disabled people

2. Arranging and carrying out consultation meetings and other events
3. Ensuring that information reached disabled people
4. Setting up and maintaining groups of service users
5. Ensuring joint working between professionals and service users
6. Organizing appropriate training to enable people to make full use of the process
7. Securing ongoing funding for the user group of disabled people.

There is a danger that linking words like 'empowerment', 'community', 'participatory' and 'development' will be assumed to be sufficient to tackle poverty and inequality and will be sufficient to change the world. Marilyn Waring (2004), from Massey University New Zealand, cautions against a cosy view of community development. We can summarize two points from her important writing:

1. Partnerships between government and other organizations and poor people need to work to achieve not only their economic and social benefits but also their civil and political benefits. This is about their human rights not being ignored or diluted into ideas like 'citizenship' and 'governance' (Waring, 2004, pp. 5–6).
2. Genuine participatory development by poor, powerless people will always be about working from the grassroots upwards. This is time-consuming and always vulnerable to takeovers by powerful organizations and official bodies, sometimes in the name of development (Waring, 2004, p. 4).

Community profiles

Community profiles are a participatory way of carrying out community-based initiatives (Burton, 1993; Hawtin et al., 1994). A **community profile** may be defined as an assessment of need that is mapped with the participation of local people, at the level of the community in which they live. Involving the community is participatory and collaborative, and we can see in Table 8.4 how the process of community profiling is both participatory and empowering.

Five particular points can be highlighted from this process:

1. Be sure to seek advice from local agency managers before beginning.
2. Ensure any necessary clearances are obtained regarding ethical research.
3. Make sure informed consent is gained from the subjects of the

community profile, that is, those from whom information is gathered.

4. Make sure the location of any group meetings for data collection is considered carefully in advance. Neutral territory may be preferred, but some people prefer to meet on their own territory.
5. Ensure that ground rules for the conduct of any group meetings are drawn up, made clear and agreed by all participants in advance.

Table 8.4 Stages of carrying out a community profile

Stage	What is entailed
Beginning	1. Beginning: meeting group members
Preparing	2. Preparing
	3. Selecting methods of gathering information
	4. Deciding on the unit of analysis
	5. Specifying the information to be collected
	6. Seeking advice and ethical clearance
	7. Designing research tools, e.g. questionnaire and interview schedule
Carrying out	8. Piloting the tools
	9. Carrying out the data collection with group members
Analysing findings	10. Assembling findings
	11. Analysing and producing reports – verbal and written
	12. Feeding back results to group members
Using findings	13. Deciding with group members how to use results
	14. Evaluating the community profile

Conclusion

Community empowerment, like community development, cannot be disengaged from the political systems that either resource it or segregate it from real political and social power. Empowerment is not merely a 'good' like other economic assets, or a skill to be tacked onto other social work skills in working with people, in isolation from the contexts of both the worker and the service user. Empowerment as a process is as important as empowerment as a product. Viewed in these terms, empowerment is a theorized approach to participatory inclusion and social justice, rather than a technique merely enabling the individual to benefit. The ideal is an empowering society, committed to both the process and outcomes of empowering citizens and practitioners. It is not sufficient to work with individuals, out of their group, family, organizational, social, political and economic context. Empowering practice needs to engage with the social and political as well as with the personal dimensions of people's lives, so that empowerment practice engages with inclusion, participation and social justice.

putting it into practice

Activity 1
Describe the different levels at which community empowerment may take place and give illustrations.

Activity 2
List ways in which community empowering work may combat various forms of discrimination and oppression.

Activity 3
Describe the main features, advantages and processes of community profiling.

Further reading

Barnes, M. and Bowl, R. (2001) *Taking Over the Asylum: Empowerment and Mental Health,* Basingstoke, Palgrave – now Palgrave Macmillan. Chapters 3, 5 and 7 in particular discuss policies, practices and new directions in movements towards empowering people in mental health, including through 'new social movements'.

Burton, P. (1993) *Community Profiling: A Guide to Identifying Local Needs,* Bristol, SAUS. A practice guide to carrying out a community profile.

Community Development Foundation (2000) *Achieving Better Community Development Handbook: A Framework for Evaluating Community Development,* London, Community Development Foundation. Examines practical issues for the evaluation of community development initiatives.

Craig, G. and Mayo, M. (eds) (1995) *Community Empowerment,* London, Zed Books. A stimulating collection of essays illustrating the diversity of community empowerment.

Guijt, I. and Shah, M.K. (eds) (1998) *The Myth of Community: Gender Issues in Participatory Development*, London, Intermediate Technology Publications. Chapters 1 and 2 examine the potential and limitations of participation through development initiatives, although many other chapters are also useful.

Hawtin, M., Hughes, G. and Percy-Smith, J. (1994) *Community Profiling: Auditing Social Needs*, Buckingham, Open University Press. A useful guide to what is involved in carrying out a community profile.

Jacobs, S. and Popple, K. (eds) (1994) *Community Work in the 1990s*, Nottingham, Spokesman. A relevant examination of community work trends and practices up to the early 1990s.

Ledwith, M. (1997) *Community Development: A Critical Approach*, Bristol, Policy Press. Pages 9–29 contain a useful discussion of the policy context of community empowerment initiatives.

9 | Empowering research

I was adviser to some research that had the goal of equipping people who use services to evaluate their own services. In the process, I learned how difficult it is to engage with this process without succumbing to the temptation to take over. It was difficult to remind the researcher not to prepare a proposal in advance of the first meeting. This felt as though it violated a principle of efficiency. As the project developed, I found it hard to hear about people struggling with tasks and to caution the researcher not to say 'don't worry, I'll do that for you.' I had some useful feedback that while I thought I was behaving in an empowering way, my body language suggested otherwise. My colleague could guess what I was thinking even though I wasn't saying it and had some hard questions to ask me about my ethical commitment to the task. From this, I learned that commitment to an empowering approach to research is far more complex than subscribing to some headlines of 'dos and don'ts'. I need to be committed to every detail of the text. I also need to examine my approach holistically and not just what I say. This experience reminded me that practising reflectively is as much associated with a state of being as it is with carrying out a series of things that need doing.

Introduction

This chapter deals with how we adopt an empowering approach to carrying out social work research. It would be a mistake to regard this as a largely technical chapter. Research is probably never 'just' a matter of learning and applying techniques. Stewart (2003, p. 2) reminds us that it always depends on the chosen methodology, value base and interests (to whom accountable) of the researcher.

Let us start by clarifying the basis for research. Why do research into social work? There are many different reasons, and different kinds of research will be appropriate, depending on the goals. However, our focus in this chapter is doing research that empowers and we are narrowing our interest to research into practice. There are three major justifications for practitioners to become involved in research into their practice:

1. As a contribution to their critically reflective practice.
2. As a means of achieving systematic feedback on the quality of practice.
3. To increase the evidence base for their own, and other people's, improved practice.

Without such research, social work practice lacks the evidence base to give it credibility. Empowering research by whoever does it, practitioners, service users or carers themselves, or researchers from 'outside', is crucial to empowering social work. This chapter examines how to do this research in an empowering way. It provides clarification on adopting different approaches and some guidelines on how to carry out research in an empowering way.

Difficulties of finding out whether participation is making a difference

One of the central features of empowering research, as we shall see, is the meaningful involvement – that is, participation – of the people who are its subjects – that is, from whom the data is collected – in carrying out the research. There are three reasons (Doel et al., 2007, p. 32) why it is difficult to find out whether participation is making a difference to people's lives:

1. In order to make this judgement, we have to ascertain what different people regard as a sufficient difference to satisfy them.
2. There may be pressure from the agencies funding research to gain some immediate feedback from research. Research in the short term will not pick up changes occurring in the medium and long term.
3. There may be such barriers against participation that success may be relative, in that it consists of a slowing of the negative outcomes or a lack of further deterioration in the circumstances, rather than an outright or immediate improvement.

It is important, however, to recognize that how research is carried out can carry just as forceful a message as what it finds out.

What makes research empowering?

Research is empowering when it involves the people who are the subjects in actually planning and carrying out the research. It is easy to be accused of either doing this in a token way or compromising the research. Research that is empowering must manage the tension between the two extremes of, on one hand, not involving people sufficiently and, on the other hand, overinvolving them. If they are underinvolved, the research becomes tokenistic; if they are overinvolved, the research goals may be compromised. This raises not just practical – that is, method – questions, but also theoretical – that is, methodological – questions and questions of research ethics. These methodological and practical aspects have been written about at length (Barnes and Mercer, 1997; Fetterman, 2000; Fetterman and Wandersman, 2004). Faulkener (2004, p. 3), writing about the ethics of survivor-based research, notes:

> empowerment means adopting an agenda for change ... ensuring that service users' voices are heard through the research and challenging attitudes about people with a mental illness diagnosis. It also has significant implications for the way in which research participants are treated and involved during the research process.

practice study

In the 1980s, I was in the middle of an evaluative research project, in which the agency had posed some straightforward questions and asked me to find out the views of the people who used a service for adults with children. Towards the end, when I had collected the data and was writing the report for feeding back to staff, a new manager arrived in the agency and stated that the research should have been planned and carried out so as to involve the users of the service from the outset. The first draft of the report would have to be shared with the users before it was submitted to the agency. The report was not written in language that was accessible to the users and the process of sharing it, while interesting and a learning situation, raised many questions we had not considered before the start. There was no opportunity to do this now and reframe the research. The time and resources allocated to it were almost used up. I vowed I would never make this mistake again, but it was too late for this situation and most of the people involved in it.

commentary

A common feature of research into practice is the lack of attention given to thinking through the way it is carried out, before engaging in it. Sometimes, evaluation is invested with too much significance, especially when managers try to impose it as a tool to brush up the quality of practice. Thorpe (1993, p. xv) notes that the pressure for quality, in the education sector and private enterprise, may lead to evaluation being redesignated as quality assurance. Research may be imposed on practitioners and/or service users from line managers, or from outside the work setting. Thus, they may receive a request, or an instruction, to cooperate with a visiting interviewer and may have little or no control over the design, execution, analysis, or subsequent use of the data being collected about their practice. If this approach leaves practitioners feeling disempowered, it is easy to imagine how service users feel when they are on the receiving end of this approach to data collection. Frequently, research is remembered after the action has begun or, even worse, at the end, when attempts may be made rather belatedly to 'build some research into what we're doing', rather than developing it from the planning stage of the social work activity. It is also ethically wrong and practically impossible to start some research and later decide to involve some of the service users who are its subjects.

Empowering research is likely to have the first of the following goals and probably at least one of the others:

1. Bringing in service users and carers as partners from the outset in research to discover their needs.
2. Raising professional and public awareness of the needs of practitioners, people using services and carers.
3. Contributing to a process of empowering vulnerable, excluded and otherwise 'seldom heard' people experiencing particular difficulties – such as disabled people and people with mental health problems – by exploring and perhaps highlighting their circumstances and problems.
4. Critically appraising particular aspects of practice with people, using a range of survey and case study (that is, practice example) approaches.

It is increasingly recognized that subjects who contribute significantly to the research should be rewarded accordingly, by paying them fees and reimbursing expenses (INVOLVE, 2006). This is not a prerequisite of empowering research. More fundamentally, perhaps, empowering research requires that the subjects – whether these are carers, service users or other members of the public – should share control with the practitioners carrying out the research (Turner and Beresford, 2005).

Approaches to empowering research

Six approaches to empowering research are considered here: reflection-in-action, action research, participatory action research, new paradigm research, participatory research and interactive holistic research (Table 9.1). This is not an exhaustive or comprehensive list, but it represents the major currents of empowering research.

Table 9.1 Empowering research: authors and approaches

Author	Research approach
Schön, D.	Reflection-in-action
Lewin, K. Moreno, J. Stenhouse, L.	Action research
Wadsworth, Y. McTaggart, R.	Participatory action research
Reason, P. Rowan, J.	New paradigm research
Marsden, D. Oakley, P. Holland, J. Blackburn, J. Chambers, R.	Participatory research
Cunningham, I.	Interactive holistic research

Reflection-in-action

Research commonly begins with the practitioner asking one or more questions about the practice. Schön envisages the reflective practitioner as a quasi-researcher. As he describes it, the process of reflective practice is essentially a process of research. Schön (1991, pp. 141–53) uses terms that amount to the practitioner experimenting through the process of reflective action. He maintains that reflection-in-action must involve experiment, through the rigour of evaluating the entire process of reflecting on examples of action and reframing them. This is likely to involve problem-setting and tackling a number of questions (Table 9.2).

Table 9.2 Reflection-in-action

Element	How it is put into effect
Experimental process	Repeated sequence of reflecting on examples of action, reframing them, reflecting later, and so on
Focusing on element	Questions which follow
Identifying problem	What is the problem or question we have to tackle or answer?
Specifying method	How do we go about this?
Speculating on outcomes	What, if anything, will come from this?
Questioning added value	What will we gain from this?
Confirming theoretical rigour	Will what we gain be coherent in theories and practice?
Checking out values	Will what we gain be consistent with our values?
Determining the extent	Will we keep the reflection going?
Deciding further actions	What will we do next?

As Schön envisages it, this process differs fundamentally from traditional approaches to research, which involve hypothesis-testing or controlled experiments. Schön points out that reflection-in-action violates the basic conditions of controlled experiments, which require the researcher to maintain a distance from the behaviour observed, but is no less rigorous, since the practitioner continually tests, modifies and retests theories and hypotheses embedded in the action, reframing as necessary, in order to confirm the hypothesis or explore it further. Schön's reflection-in-action is not traditional research, but neither is it necessarily empowering. It closely resembles action research, which we examine below.

Both of the above-mentioned features of traditional evaluative research – hypothesis-testing and controlled experiments – are diametrically opposed to the viewpoint of this chapter, since empowering evaluation must involve the major stakeholders, including service users, from its earliest stage. We can now respond to the question, 'what makes research empowering?', by setting out three guidelines for empowering research practice.

Empowering research:

1. is likely to involve the participants, whether workers, service users, carers, or all of these, as co-producers and/or participants in managing and carrying it out themselves, as self-managed research.
2. should endeavour to collaborate with, and thus empower, the service user – the major stakeholder most vulnerable to exclusion

from key aspects of the process. This is part of what Freire means by the dialogic activity, referred to in Chapter 5.
3. is likely to involve the researcher engaging with and interacting with the phenomena observed, but is no less rigorous, since the practitioner continually tests, modifies and retests theories and hypotheses embedded in the action, reframing as necessary, in order to confirm the hypothesis or explore it further.

In order to make the link with the roots of Schön's reflection-in-action, we need to go back half a century to action research.

Action research

Action research is often linked with participatory research (Table 9.3), because it links the research with the social action that grows from its findings and conclusions, rather than just with more theory and more publications by academics. Kurt Lewin (1890–1947), a social psychologist, is generally regarded as having 'invented' action research in the first half of the twentieth century, in his attempts to develop research methods that could harness the energies of the subjects of research to undertake applied research into their problems, such as poverty and deprivation (Lewin, 1948). Many different variants of it have developed over more than half a century.

From the point of view of this chapter on empowering research, it is important not to focus on action research as though it is simply a research technique or method. It can only be regarded as empowering when it is accompanied by a commitment to

● engaging the cooperation of the people who are its subjects
● empowering them to collaborate in the research
● identifying and understanding the factors contributing to their problem.

Three distinct approaches to action research have been identified (Masters, 1995): technical, mutual and enhancement. We can summarize these as follows:

1. *Technical:* This is based on a scientific approach to problem-solving. The researcher as expert identifies the problem and a specific way of tackling it and works with the person to carry this out.
2. *Mutual:* This is based on the researcher and the person meeting and identifying the problem together. They negotiate a way of tackling the problem and the researcher carries it out.

3. *Enhancement:* This is an emancipatory action research approach, based on the researcher and the person working together in a way that empowers the person, so as to identify and work at the problem while carrying out the research together.

Table 9.3 Action research and participatory action research

	Action research	Participatory action research
Origins	Work of Kurt Lewin (1890–1947), social psychologist, in early twentieth century	Work of social educational researchers from 1980s, e.g. Wadsworth and McTaggart
What is it?	An approach to research that can contribute to reducing social conflict	An approach aiming to promote change in social practice
Assumption	People are more likely to follow up and act on decisions to which they have contributed	People can improve social practice by taking part in researching it
Basic principle	Action research relies on group decision-making to gain the cooperation of the subjects	Participatory action research is collaborative, in that those whose actions are researched are involved in the research and in improving the outcomes from research
Process	The action research process is cyclical	PAR involves a continuous spiral of processes

Identifying starting point

Reflecting ——————→ Revised starting point

Planning

Gathering information

Revised plan

Gathering more information

And so on until the goal is met

Participatory action research

It is logical that participatory action research (PAR) is used in social work, but it is also necessary to use it critically (Healy, 2001), not least to ensure that it empowers rather than controls its subjects – the people who use services. The following summary of the components of PAR is based on McTaggart's 16 tenets of PAR (1989):

- improving social practice by changing it
- a political process
- involving critical analysis
- starting with small cycles
- starting with small groups
- based on authentic participation
- collaborative
- rooted in a self-critical community
- a systematic learning process
- involving people objectifying their experiences
- involving people theorizing their practice.

New paradigm research

New paradigm and participatory research share significant differences from traditional research, as Table 9.4 shows. Participatory research blurs the traditional division of position and function between researcher and subject. Its two aims are to:

1. Gain new knowledge and understanding.
2. Achieve change in people's circumstances.

Table 9.4 New paradigm and participatory research

Key questions	Traditional answers	Participatory research answers
For whom are we doing it?	Professionals, universities, service providing agencies, managers	Service users, pressure groups
Who controls the appraisal?	Researchers, service providers, universities, funding organizations	Service users, carers, general public, members of local community
At what stage are people who use services and carers involved?	Only when asked questions, as subjects	Throughout the entire process from funding, through deciding goals, methods and carrying out, analysing, writing the report and spreading and deciding what to do with the findings

New paradigm research is the label used by Reason and Rowan, in their writing from the early 1980s. This referred to the fact that the researchers recruited people who were the subjects of research as co-researchers or collaborators. The term 'collaborative research' was also used to refer to this approach (Table 9.4) (Reason, 1994; Reason and Rowan, 1981).

Participatory research

Participatory research may be put forward not only as a research method but as a different research paradigm. The theoretical basis for participatory research is the social construction of meanings and knowledge and its purpose is twofold:

1. To extend knowledge and understanding.
2. To use these to create change.

The view of the Centre for Popular Education and Participatory Research is that participatory research is integrated research and education, with the aim of leading to a more equitable society. Others in the development field argue that the most productive methodology for evaluation is likely to be participatory (Holland and Blackburn, 1998; Marsden and Oakley, 1990), collaborative or new paradigm research (Reason, 1994; Reason and Rowan, 1981). Chambers (1997) has used participatory rural appraisal as a means of empowering people in developing countries. In the developing world, participatory research tends to be linked with community work and empowerment through economic development (Carr et al., 1996), social development programmes (Barker et al., 2000; Blackburn and Holland, 1998; Guijt and Shah, 1998; Slocum et al., 1995), or community-based organizations.

Without undermining the undoubted virtues of participatory methods, it is necessary to bear in mind that they are not necessarily equipped to tackle the wider, structural questions of policy that affect poverty and exclusion in society (Stewart and Wang, 2003). Stewart (2003) makes four further points:

1. Participatory research methods are contested, which means that the case for them is not agreed by everyone.
2. One problem is to decide who should participate. Why should only poor, excluded people be heard? There are other stakeholders.
3. Research should include evaluation of the donors (funders and initiators) of the research as well as the recipients.
4. Recognizing all the complications, the bottom line is that the

starting point of any research, however participatory, should be to assess the extent to which the conditions of the worst off people have been improved.

Interactive holistic research

Appraisal is a means of empowering both service users and social workers. It should not be used to perpetuate the oppression of those in whose interests it is allegedly carried out. Cunningham (1994, pp. 164–7) provides a helpful list of principles to guide what he calls 'interactive holistic research'. It is collaborative, dialogic, experiential, action based and contextualizing (Table 9.5).

Table 9.5 Interactive holistic research

Principle	What it entails
Collaborative	Joint pursuit of the appraisal by a group of people
Dialogic	Interaction between two people the basis for data collection
Experiential	Focus on direct experience of the person and/or worker
Action based	Action research is the central focus of the process
Contextualizing	Process of putting the action into context

Empowering qualitative methodology

There are overlaps between empowering research and the use of qualitative methodology. It is likely that where practitioners and/or service users are doing the research themselves alongside other responsibilities, one or more qualitative methodologies will be used, on its own or, in rare cases, in conjunction with quantitative, statistically based methods. **Qualitative methodology** can be defined as the collection and analysis of non-quantitative data, using non-traditional research methods, which may be based on assumptions from the critical social sciences that the researcher can become a research instrument through subjective involvement in the research process. Qualitative methods may include participant observation, ethnography, case studies, or critical appraisal (Lofland and Lofland, 1984).

Critical appraisal by case study

Case studies are a particular form of qualitative methodology and the arguments for this approach are put strongly by Patton (1982, p. 219).

A case study covers both formative and summative studies of empowering activities. The preference for this is based partly on grounds of time and other resource constraints that are likely to rule out more full-blooded approaches to evaluation. However, there is a real danger that research of this kind could intimidate service users and put them into a relatively passive and powerless situation, or, in other words, disempower them (Table 9.6).

Table 9.6 Critical appraisal by case study

Features	What each feature involves
Qualitative methodology	Relies mainly on qualitative rather than quantitative methods of data-gathering
Flexible process	Is flexible, in that research questions, goals and hypotheses can be altered as the study proceeds
Unstructured information-gathering	Among more structured data collection, likely to involve the researcher in some kind of relatively unstructured data collection, e.g. observation
Reflexive method	Necessitates the researcher being reflexive, that is, using her or his own reactions to a situation as a source of data, further reflection and evaluative activity
Process orientation	Is geared to understanding the process of the activity rather than simply drawing conclusions after it has finished

Key et al. (1976, pp. 10–11) distinguish two approaches:

- hard line: relying more on the notions of scientific evaluation that we might encounter in the business world or the natural sciences
- soft line: more concerned with impressionistic, subjective or experience-based findings.

We suggest that terms like 'case study' and 'critical appraisal' are preferable to 'evaluation'. Critical appraisal is more flexible than Schön's idea of experiment, which implies a preformed framework for research and action. We need to use a more flexible approach. Some commentators use the term 'critical appraisal' (see Key et al., 1976, pp. 44–6 for a fine description of this term) to describe a more flexible and realistic approach to evaluation, which does not downgrade its essential contribution to practice, and the development of practice theory, or theory through practice. By this means, evaluation has the potential to benefit service users as well as cultivate criticality in reflective practitioners.

The term 'appraisal' describes the attempt to give people answers to questions they pose about what they are doing, how they are doing it and how 'well' they are doing it. On the whole, the sort of appraisal those involved in empowerment will encounter is concerned with the present or the immediate past rather than the future. That is, the most common question to which an answer will be sought by means of appraisal is: 'how have we been doing in this activity.' But the equally important sequel should be 'what does this mean?' and then, 'what do we do now?'

The research process

We now go into more detail regarding the task of researching and how we intend to go about it. There are five main stages to consider (Table 9.7): clarifying the research task, preparing for the research, carrying out the research, producing and using the research and evaluating the research. Steel (2004) has edited and updated the second edition of some briefing notes of research evidence geared towards practice, available from INVOLVE, a national advisory group funded by the Department of Health (www.invo.org.uk).

Table 9.7 Stages of carrying out empowering research

Stage	What each stage entails
Clarifying the research task	Clarifying goals jointly with people from whom data is to be collected
Preparing for the research	Planning the schedule of the research, deciding who should do what, ensuring adequate resources of time, skills and money Deciding how to sample, from whom data should be sought. Confirming ethical standards have been met
Carrying out the research	Carrying out the data collection, ensuring this is done rigorously and respecting the participatory principles of the appraisal Carrying out the analysis of the data, jointly with the people from whom data is sought
Producing and using the research	Writing the report of the appraisal, jointly with the people from whom data is sought
Evaluating the research	Evaluating the extent to which all stakeholders in the appraisal regard it as having met its goals

Clarifying the task

We have to start by asking what the rationale is for appraising a particular empowering activity. Is it absolutely essential for some purpose, desirable or merely contemplated out of interest? This begins before the research has started and continues throughout. In settings where the activities change direction and character, or where qualitative methodology is used, the person doing the research needs to be accustomed constantly to putting the entire research process under scrutiny and being prepared to shift objectives, change the emphasis and area of data collection, and rethink the analysis and projected outcomes. At the more bread-and-butter level, the process of reflection needs to focus on the data gathered.

Preparing

Generally there is a point where those involved in the research feel able to make some practical plans and draw up some kind of programme. In the light of the previous paragraph, it is clear that while this needs to be firm enough to enable effective progress to be made, it should be sufficiently flexible to cope with any necessary changes.

Carrying out

Carrying out involves translating the programme into action and making sure some kind of limits are set to the study. This latter point is important because there is a great temptation to devise research that is too grand ever to be achieved. The task needs to be kept manageable. To this end, it is important to set some realistic deadlines for each stage of the process, and stick to them.

The procedure of carrying out a quantitative study may make it possible to separate out these stages fairly clearly. But in qualitative research, there is usually no clear point at which the collection of evidence ceases and the analysis begins. Often what happens is that the process of analysis begins as soon as the researcher starts to pick over the evidence and draw some preliminary conclusions, to be fed back into further attempts to gather evidence. This is a continual process, so further reflection, reprogramming and data collection may continue right to the end of the study.

In the final phase, there is always the need to consider what will happen if the outcome of the research is not a happy ending. For instance, research of women's consciousness-raising groups has highlighted the divergence between them and other helping groups, in respect of their impact on women's problems. A striking contrast exists between the reduction of symptoms achieved in psychotherapy and the lack of impact on people's symptoms in consciousness-raising groups. Rather than the emphasis in consciousness-raising groups being upon a specific outcome, their impact may be evident in members' general increased self-esteem and self-worth (Howell, 1981).

Producing and using the research

When producing and using the research, the stakeholders – service users, social workers, managers and others – will all need to play their proper part. If all has gone reasonably well, although not necessarily according to plan as we have seen above, there will be something to report back to others. This is an important stage. The products of the research may be in the form of PowerPoint presentations or a written report. It is important, where possible, to produce a finished report. Far too often, the results of research stay in someone's filing cabinet as 'that brilliant study I will write up some day when there is time'. Provided the above cautions have been heeded, the scope of the study was kept modest and the deadlines have been adhered to, the main skill required now is the assertiveness and confidence actually to commit oneself to sharing the results with others, either in written form or face-to-face meetings. How it is done is not as important as ensuring that it happens.

The needs of most activities are likely to be met best by a series of different sorts of products at different times for different purposes and audiences. A plan based on that tactic would seem more suitable than the idea of a single mammoth work, produced years after everybody who was connected with the activity has long gone (or, more likely by that stage, perpetually in a state of revision and never finally published at all).

Feeding back the findings needs to involve service users as centrally as it did when the preparations for the appraisal were being made. Absolutely essential to this process, of course, is the issue of who owns the appraisal document, what control the service users have over its content, and what their power is to negotiate changes in it, or even veto statements with which they may disagree.

Now we have reached the end of the process of carrying out the research, Table 9.8 provides a checklist of questions summarizing the process described above.

Table 9.8 Checklist of questions in carrying out the research

Clarifying what the research is about

What kind of appraisal is sought?

Is there evidence in advance to justify starting an empowering activity?
Are local conditions such that an empowering activity is feasible?
Are there enough potential service users in this field in this locality?

What activities are going on?

What is the story of empowerment in action, in this particular setting?
What needs to be done in order to improve this programme of empowerment?

What is being appraised?

Is the subject of appraisal a short-lived activity that took place some weeks or
months ago, on which retrospective information is sought?
Is it current, or planned at some time in the near future?
Is it a newly established or a well-established group, with a single, local base or a
national network of federated groups?

Preparing for the research

What sources of information are sought?

Will a single individual or group activity be used as a source, or a sample of these?
Will one kind of source be sought, or a variety of sources?

How much information should we collect?

Three points need to be made about carrying out the appraisal:

1. We should pose one or a few key questions that the appraisal will address and
   collect only such information as will contribute to answering these.
2. We should not collect too much data. It will only clutter up the filing cabinet and,
   eventually, long after we have failed to use it, find its way into the rubbish basket.
3. We should keep in mind the need to write a short, concise report and collect
   evidence to this end, and not for the sake of collecting it.

What evidence will be collected?

When will it be done?

Over what period will it be done?

Will the appraisal be carried out over a short term, say two weeks, or over a long
period, such as five years?

Possible products of research

Will the outcome of appraisal be used simply for personal reflection?
Will it lead to the sharing of experiences only among participants in the
empowering activity?
Will some form of report be written, summarizing the findings of the appraisal?
For which audience will it be written?
Will the appraisal be used by professionals, service users, students or the general
reader?
Will the product be a formal summary of survey findings or questionnaire results,
or a case study in the form of thumbnail sketches?
To what extent will the product be tailored to the requirements of some external
demand, such as the need to justify continued funding?
Will this mean that the product is more of a public relations exercise than an
objective, critical study?

Evaluating the research

We need to ensure after the final stage that all the people participating in the research have the opportunity to comment on the extent
to which it has met its goals.

---

example

The evaluation of community empowerment on the Castle Vale
estate near Birmingham, England was a partnership between the
School of Public Policy at the University of Birmingham and the
Castle Vale Housing Action Trust (CVHAT) and is a good example
of participatory research into an empowerment project. The aim
was to evaluate the effectiveness of the resident empowerment
strategy of CVHAT in its regeneration work and review progress
towards the formal winding up and succession of the HAT. Significant progress in both areas was found, more than a quarter of the
respondents to a 'vox pop' (literally 'voice of the people', often
carried out on the street) survey saying they had been involved
personally in contributing to improvements on the estate (Beazley
and Smith, 2004, p. 52). Some residents felt resident involvement
was limited and that residents had only had the scope to influence
certain aspects of the regeneration programme (Beazley and Smith,
2004, p. 52). The tensions between the ideal of full participation by
all stakeholders, including researchers and residents, and the realities of different skills being held by different participants are illustrated by the fact that while residents did take part in training in
research methods (Beazley and Smith, 2004, p. 7), clearly there
were some skills in research management, analysis and report
writing that would be more appropriately used by university staff.
On the title page of the evaluation report, the research was
claimed to be led by the residents (Beazley and Smith, 2004, p. 1),
but in reality it appears that a community research team was
formed and while the university staff managed the research
process, most of the data was gathered by the residents (Beazley
and Smith, 2004, p. 3).

We need to ask whether the researchers have built in formal measures for the appraisal itself to be evaluated and what provision there
is for the service users to contribute their own (perhaps anonymous)
candid comments on the researchers and the research. This is the

moment of truth, in which the success or failure of the research is known and the power relationships between participants in an empowering activity may be laid bare.

We can approach empowering research in a different way, by considering how a range of factors are brought to bear on the subject. Table 9.9 summarizes these.

Table 9.9 Researching aspects of empowerment

| Factors affecting empowerment | Extent of empowerment | | |
	Does the person have choices?	Does the person use choices?	Does the person achieve choices?
1. Personal agency (resources)	Have I the resources to be empowered?	Have I used the available resources?	Have I achieved what the resources allow?
Psychological	Can I feel empowered?	Am I using this?	Am I achieving my potential?
Informational	Have I the information?	Am I using it?	Have I achieved it?
Organizational	Do organizations give me choices?	Am I using these choices?	Have I achieved what is available?
Material	Do the material resources give me choices?	Have I used them?	What have I achieved using them?
Social	Do other social factors give me freedom?	Which of these freedoms do I use?	Which of these freedoms have I achieved?
Financial	What financial independence have I?	How do I benefit from financial independence?	Have I achieved this independence? In what ways?
Relationships	In which relationships do I have choices?	In which relationships do I use my choices?	In which relationships do I achieve choices?
2. Opportunity Legislation	Am I legally able?	Am I using this power?	What have I achieved?
Procedures	Do the procedures give me choices?	Am I using these?	What have I gained?
Societal norms	Do these allow me choice?	Am I using these?	What have I achieved?

Alsop and Heinsohn (2005, p. 4) provide three criteria, used in Table 9.9, by which to evaluate the 'degree' to which empowerment is achieved, that is, the outcomes, in terms of:

1. Whether a person has choices.
2. Whether a person uses those choices.
3. The extent to which the person achieves those choices.

These three outcomes clarify the two factors affecting individual empowerment:

1. *Personal agency* – put simply, the power to act. This is made up of psychological, informational, organizational, material, social, financial and human resources.
2. *Opportunity* – the opportunities a person has are affected by legislation, procedures and norms governing behaviour in society.

We conclude this chapter with an example of empowering research.

---

example

A group of fishermen whose territory covered a vast tract of coastline in Tanzania were informed that the authorities blamed environmental destruction on their ignorance. Over a six-day period, both fishermen and fisherwomen were able to control the entire production process of a video to express their experiences and views, undistorted and not taken over by any intervening person or interest group. Participants revealed the involvement of police and dynamite dealers in the wholesale destruction of fish and the coral fishing environment. By the time the video-maker returned to Tanzania for a second video workshop, the first video had mobilized the local community on a huge scale, crossing ethnic divisions, building confidence and inspiring action. A locally formed action group used the video to influence environmental agencies and parliament, empowering local people to campaign for legislative and policy change (Holland and Blackburn, 1998, pp. 156–7).

Conclusion

It is necessary for the empowering evaluation of practice to include, in the planning and implementation of the evaluation, those whose services are being evaluated. The above example illustrates how powerful critical appraisal can be in the hands of people using services, who can use it to achieve their own aims. The term 'critical appraisal' is more appropriate for many participative evaluations, but, whatever the label, the evaluative process is identical.

We have summarized the main stages of participative research, noting some key questions and issues that need to be considered within each. Far from each stage being completed before the next is begun, in practice, constant 'looping back' will normally be necessary, to revise the task of appraisal and its implementation.

---

putting it into practice

Activity 1

Describe each of the following: reflection-in-action, participatory action research, new paradigm research.

Activity 2

Distinguish between qualitative and quantitative methodology.

Activity 3

Specify the main stages of empowering research and describe what is involved in each stage.

---

further reading

Connor, A. (1993) *Monitoring and Evaluation Made Easy: A Handbook for Voluntary Organisations*, Edinburgh, HMSO for the Scottish Office. A practical guide for people wanting to monitor and evaluate the work of the organization.

Fetterman, D.M. (2000) *Foundations of Empowerment Evaluation*, London, Sage. A useful examination of aspects of empowerment evaluation.

Fetterman, D.M. and Wandersman, A. (2004) *Empowerment Evaluation Principles in Practice*, New York, Guildford. Critical discussion of applications of the principles of empowerment evaluation.

Fetterman, D.M., Kaftarian, S.J. and Wandersman, A. (eds) (1996) *Empowerment Evaluation: Knowledge and Tools for Self-Assessment and Accountability*, London, Sage. Fetterman's first essay in this collection (Chapter 1) introduces the theory and practice of empowerment evaluation.

Holland, J. and Blackburn, J. (eds) (1998) *Whose Voice? Participatory Research and Policy Change*, London, Intermediate Technology Publications. A collection of papers on aspects of participatory research.

Marsden, D. and Oakley, P. (eds) (1990) *Evaluating Social Development Projects*, Oxford, Oxfam. A series of chapters critically examining research into social development linked with participatory approaches.

McTaggart, R. (1996) 'Action Research for Aboriginal Pedagogy: Improving Teaching via Investigative Learning', in O. Zuber-Skerritt (ed.) *Action Research for Change and Development*, Aldershot, Avebury, pp.157–78.

McTaggart, R (ed.) (1997) *Participatory Action Research: International Contexts and Consequences*, Albany, State University of New York Press.

Two examples of participatory action research in practice.

Reason, P. (ed.) (1994) *Human Inquiry in Action: Developments in New Paradigm Research*, London, Sage. Illustrations of new paradigm research in a stimulating collection of chapters.

Zuber-Skerritt, O. (ed.) (1996) *Action Research for Change and Development*, Aldershot, Avebury. An examination of what is involved in action research.

10 | Achieving empowerment in social work

Introduction

We have seen in previous chapters how an adequate framework for empowering practice ideally engages simultaneously with different domains of practice: individual practitioners, groups and organizations in society, and service users and carers. We have acknowledged in the process how big a gap there often is between the rhetoric and the reality of empowerment. As a way forward, in this book we have tried to focus on practical ways of empowering people, often prioritizing on increasing their participation. This concluding chapter brings together much of the thinking and evidence-based practice from previous chapters and uses participation by people who use services and carers as the main vehicle for empowering them. It:

- provides a framework for developing an empowering practice
- draws on current research so as to build on evidence-based practice
- summarizes the main areas we need to tackle in order to achieve significant empowerment in and through social work
- deals with the integration of empowering work and covers several domains of empowerment – individuals, groups and organizations, and people who use services and carers.

Empowerment through participation

What can we learn from efforts made since the 1970s to achieve the general goal of empowering people through greater participation? We can make eight points:

1. *Developing mutual empowerment:* An important feature of successful empowerment has been the capacity of individuals to develop collective strength. The Nyaya Sangamam or People's Movement forum in India (Chapter 8) enables people to advocate for themselves and equip themselves with resources to help them-

selves. Similarly, in the UK, forums and networks of carers and people who use services can be locally, regionally or (particularly in the case of carers organizations such as Carers UK, the Princess Royal Trust or Crossroads) nationally based and are an important source of mutual support and strength between individuals and small groups.

2. *Enabling self-advocacy:* Much empowerment has been spurred on by the efforts of people to help themselves, through self-advocacy. There is a tension between advocacy by professionals on behalf of people and self-advocacy by people themselves. Particular progress has been made in the social development field. The NESA initiative in India (Chapter 8) sets out deliberately to blur any distinction between human rights work with individuals and broader socioeconomic development. At the same time, its work is not charity based but development based. This involves NESA not speaking up for communities, but equipping them with the skills and resources to advocate and work for themselves. The desired relationship between professionals and service users is defined fundamentally by whether the service users view their activity as integral, facilitated or autonomous in relation to professionals. If the latter, then there is little more to be said, since they will not want professionals involved in their activities, and this stance must be respected by practitioners themselves. However, in the case of integral or facilitated activities, service users and practitioners may each gain from contact, and Wilson (1986, pp. 84–95) points out many of these benefits. For service users, they include resources such as meeting places, administrative help, transport, publicity, extra help through volunteers and students and credibility through the use of an agency address. For practitioners, the gains may be increased knowledge about the needs of service users and the chance to improve services thereby.

3. *Providing non-compromising professional support:* While users may benefit from learning how to build effective links with existing agency services, it is not in their interest to be taken over and incorporated into such services. As a consequence, they could lose their independent identity and much of their creative enthusiasm (Tyler, 1976, p. 447). Relations between people using services and practitioners should be seen as tender and nurtured accordingly. In Evans et al.'s study (1986) of self-help groups of parents of children with disabilities, they found that professionals could react defensively when parents started becoming enthusi-

astic and assertive about care. In fact, suspicion tended to be mutual. While newsletters from carers to practitioners helped to inform them about what was happening, in two of the groups where problems did not arise, three factors may have contributed: first, the fact that groups already existed in their areas and had prepared practitioners to be more accepting; second, the existence of coordinated leadership by groups with experience; and third, the greater care taken in preparation for joint meetings between parents and practitioners (Evans et al., 1986, p. 43).

4. *Using a professional anti-professional approach:* Parsloe (1986, p. 13) identifies three social work skills: ensuring that service users understand the political as well as the personal nature of their problems; that this is communicated adequately to managers, councillors and the public at large; and that the level of social services are defended. This leads to what Parsloe calls a 'professional anti-professional' approach (p. 14), which includes seeing service users as departmental resources in the context of creating open and sharing relationships with them and advocating both for them and on behalf of the personal social services. In pursuit of this, there is a reciprocal need for social policy to support self-help efforts through legislation. Consultative personnel and skills should also be made available, as well as the willingness to liaise with and facilitate activity, without threatening to take it over.

Tax (1976, p. 450) argues that if traditional primary groups such as the family, church and neighbourhood were given more support, there would not be such a vacuum left by the withering of these for the new self-help groups to fill. Tax is less sure about the value of organizing self-help in, say, a Bureau of Self-help Group Affairs, since self-help should begin with a level of awareness in the community itself that simply encourages groups to develop as they wish.

5. *Building on people's skills to achieve local empowerment:* To be effective, service users need a collaborative relationship with practitioners that recognizes the distinctive contribution which service users can make. Gibson (1979, p. 15) argues that small-scale, local, grassroots action groups are an antidote to the bureaucratic strangulation afflicting our centralized society. Contrary to popular belief, ordinary people without skills, special training or even the confidence to do it can take a lead and run such groups (Gibson, 1979, p. 17). In the process, the relationship between practitioners and laypeople may need to be redefined in favour of the latter (Gibson, 1979, p. 128). Perhaps a degree of

training, support and resources to underpin such activity should be negotiated, where possible, from social work agencies.

6. *Building onto the statutory, informal and voluntary sectors:* The voluntary and informal sectors generally offer less bureaucratic and more flexible means of support and encouragement than do many agencies in the statutory sector. Some service user-led activities, which lack any other formal organizational connections or reference points of their own, will welcome the support offered by a voluntary body and may even prefer it to a link with a statutory agency.

7. *Developing profane practice:* If services exemplify the sacred principles of practice, then initiatives by service users and carers perhaps need to express something profane, that is, free to be critical and highlight poor quality services. Balloch et al. (1985, pp. 105–6) state that people need jobs and relief from poverty and isolation rather than exhortations to help themselves. Parsloe (1986) argues that social work should not evade the social and political issues that surround practice in the community by retreating into individualization, privatization or bureaucratization. Perhaps the same point can be made of the area of user empowerment, which needs to avoid the twin dangers of becoming either the preserve of a few relatively well-off, middle-class, articulate people, or a substitute for professional services.

8. *Benefiting from blurring of practitioner and service user roles:* Undoubtedly, there is an ambiguity about the balance of power between practitioners and service users in many facilitated situations. But this is no more problematic than the ambiguous situations of many participants themselves. For example, there is no denying that it was hard for Dr Mowrer, starting his first self-help therapy integrity group in a mental hospital, to open with the comment that he too had been a patient in a mental hospital. But this cannot deny the reality of his position as a practitioner at the point the group started (Mowrer, 1984, p. 108). Mowrer (1984, p. 145) also expresses more general ambivalence, symptomatic of activity in this field. On one hand, he suggests that, in the mental health field, the stimulus for self-help comes as strongly as it ever did from the grassroots rather than from practitioners. Yet he acknowledges Lieberman and Borman's (1976) comment that many groups have had significant professional involvement in their inception and development (Mowrer, 1984, p. 143).

Although social workers may play a part as initiators, once it gets going, the activity remains largely managed and carried out by people using services. Social work support is thus likely to be more intermittent and the level of resourcing much less than in situations where user activity is an integral part of service provision, rather than standing outside it. But the central feature of empowerment is the type of professional advocacy provided by the social worker. It should be emphasized that empowering activities, which are facilitated in their early stages, may later become autonomous as participants acquire the necessary resources, skills and confidence. Practitioners need to develop the skills to manage the tensions involved in providing services for people where appropriate, without slackening commitment to the overarching goal of empowering them.

A systemic approach to empowering people through participation

We focus now on the task of developing empowerment through enhancing people's participation. The above offers some pointers for practice but creates a somewhat haphazard impression of policy and practice to date. Danso et al. (2003, p. 13) conclude that the growth in children's participation since the 1990s has been accompanied by growing awareness of the complexity of the field. It is possible to conclude that participation and empowerment by people who use services and carers is somewhat marginal (Stickley, 2006) and policy and practice at best challenging and at worst unrealistic or even unattainable (M. Barnes, 2005; Diamond et al., 2003). This would be a mistake. Given the creation of a policy and organizational culture that supports participation, they can be nurtured. However, participation and empowerment are not technical tasks to be accomplished in isolation from personal, social and political circumstances and possibilities of change. They will only be meaningful when regarded as continuing processes, even if the ultimate goal of empowerment is not reached. Policy and practice are socially constructed and there are parallels between empowerment processes in social work (Carr, 2003) and healthcare (Falk-Rafael, 2001).

The empowerment process is likely to offer direct gains to people, in terms of confidence-building, feeling useful, developing skills, and acquiring further resources. There are also indirect gains, such as extending networks to people who are seldom heard, strengthening existing networks and increasing mutual support and the likelihood of collective activities, including making views known and taking action to improve services. The more empowered people are and the more they participate, the more likely it is that the services will be relevant, quality based and effective (Jackson, 2004, p. 10).

While a critical awareness of the barriers to participation and empowerment is necessary, the most appropriate way to help organizations to change is by making it possible to assess the level of participation reached and trying to guide them to enhance this (Wright and Haydon, 2002). It is not sufficient to work with individuals, out of their group, family, organizational, social, political and economic context. Empowerment needs to be practised and theorized in all these aspects in order for its potential to be realized. In other words, empowering practice needs to engage with the social and political as well as with the personal dimensions of people's lives. If these aims can be achieved, empowerment practice will engage with inclusion, participation and justice.

Many different strategies are possible for enhancing participation in an empowering way. Pasteur (2001) has developed a handbook for developing countries, but its style makes its messages applicable to many organizations involved in changing their culture and developing participation. Wright and Haydon (2002) and Wright et al. (2006) have developed an approach to participation by children and young people in developing social care. This is important in order to ensure that people feel empowered through their participation to the point where they make an impact on change in the organization (Wright et al., 2006, p. 12). The framework has wider application across the entire field of social care and social work and a parallel publication on participation by adult service users, including older people, makes this point (Moriarty et al., 2006). They propose a systemic approach to change through tackling the four linked areas of structure, culture, practice and review (Table 10.1). Wright and Haydon emphasize that they will need to be dealt with simultaneously, as the interlocking pieces of a jigsaw. The four areas provide a useful checklist of essential areas needing attention, which we use as headings in this final chapter, as this enables us to draw on other research to expand various points. For the sake of brevity, we shall refer to an organization, although the domains of practice covered in this book include individuals, groups and communities as well, as settings for empowerment.

We need to work out for each particular situation what is entailed in implementing this systemic approach to empowering people through participation. In Table 10.2, we begin this process, making the assumption that a good deal of work is required in the organization to embed practice that genuinely empowers people who use services and carers.

Table 10.1 Systemic approach to empowering people

Building structures How the empowering policies and practices are embedded in infrastructure and working of the organization, resourcing and support of all who participate in empowerment	**Developing cultures** How the staff, people who use services, carers and others share beliefs about the value of empowerment and are committed to empowering practices
Practice/implementation How staff, people who use services, carers and others involved in empowering activities use methods and skills to work together	**Review/evaluation** How all those with a stake in empowerment take part in monitoring and evaluating the extent to which empowerment is achieved

Source: adapted from Wright and Haydon, 2002

Table 10.2 Implementing a systemic strategy for participation by services users and carers

Components of systemic strategy	**What implementing the strategy entails**
Developing a culture of participation	A constantly updated process of engaging the commitment of all staff to the policy
Developing infrastructures to support participation	Putting in place practical ways of moving the policy forward
Developing participation in practice	Working with managers and practitioners to ensure organizational changes take place
Developing effective mechanisms for review	Putting systems in place for the implementation to be reviewed

Building empowering structures

We need to generate enough motivation among key staff in the organization to enable empowerment and participation to proceed. In Table 10.3, we identify six of the main aspects that need to be considered in this process: developing integral structures, resourcing these structures, developing a systemic strategy to support the process, developing links with partners, identifying people capable of, and motivated towards, change (often called 'champions') and, finally, resourcing the entire development (Adams et al., 2005).

Table 10.3 Making empowering policy mainstream

Policy shift	What it entails
Integral structures	Structures relating to participation and empowerment should be integral to the working of the organization, so that staff cannot dismiss them or regard them as non-essential. It is crucial that they are not perceived as extras or 'bolt-ons' (Wright et al., 2006, p. 21)
Structures resourced	Structures should be adequately resourced, so they are not regarded as 'window-dressing' (Wright et al., 2006, p. 21)
Systemic strategy	The written strategy for participation and empowerment should be published and publicized, and emphasize that participation is multilayered and affects the entire organization (Kirby et al., 2003a, pp. 144–5). It should include reference to: • levels of participation, the focus of how, when and where relevant decisions are made • the kinds of decisions that are made • the sorts of participation and empowerment envisaged • the frequency, timing and duration of participation and empowerment activities • naming the categories and groups intended to be involved (Wright et al., 2006, p. 22)
Links with partners	Partnerships with partner groups and organizations should be set up as part of the emphasis on creating structures (Kirby et al., 2003b, p. 31; Wright et al., 2006, p. 23). This helps to give credibility and reality to the changes taking place in the organization
Champions identified	Champions may be found useful in the organization, to promote the agenda of participation and empowerment. They may act as the conscience of the organization. Existing champions should be identified as well as trying to appoint new ones (Kirby et al., 2003b, p. 27). However, there may be merit in approaching this flexibly, rather than prescriptively, because in some parts of the organization, champions – rather than being appointed or chosen – may emerge naturally as the implementation proceeds and this, in the end, may ensure more productive outcomes
Resources committed to support development	Resourcing changes in the organization can be off-putting and if presented in too challenging a way can provide managers with the excuse to do nothing. However, no innovation of this kind can proceed without the organization committing some resources to it. Wright et al. list the kinds of resources involved: training (perhaps preferable to use the expression 'development') for staff, carers and people who use services; support of various kinds for carers and people who use services (aspects such as respite support for carers while they attend activities may be forgotten), reimbursement for those who participate, full access to all activities; facilities for interpreters, signers and language translation of all materials (including braille)

This ambitious agenda requires us to consider what structures are necessary in order for people to participate. Without the necessary structures, little change in the direction of greater participation and empowerment can take place. The support of senior management is essential to ensure the success of a new policy of participation and empowerment (Kirby et al., 2003b, p. 30). The issue of structure potentially covers the entire organization, wherever significant decisions and aspects of management, administration and practice take place. There will be a need for the organization to develop a strategy. This should establish a direction of travel for the organization and will need translating into policies, processes and procedures. It will be necessary for these to be publicized in writing throughout the organization. This will send an important message to all staff about how senior managers view participation. It will be important to try to institutionalize participation and empowerment through internal policy, guidance and procedures as much as possible (Kirby et al., 2003b, p. 40). Procedures will need to include guidance on how consultations, meetings, study days, training courses and other events are handled, bearing in mind the policy of participation. There will be no point in implementing a policy of participation until the organization has put in place policies securing adequate access to events and recompensing people for their participation, for example. However, participation and empowerment should not be seen as the preserve of a group of staff to the exclusion of others, but as everybody's responsibility. In this way, the policy will become mainstream.

Developing an empowering culture

The culture of the organization may be a barrier to participation by people (Wright et al., 2006, p. 13) or may present opportunities (Hutton, 2004). One way to encourage organizational change, as we saw in Chapter 7, is to promote the idea of change at different levels in the organization, which becomes a 'learning organization', with senior managers encouraging staff to develop a participatory culture (Kirby et al., 2003b, pp. 23–4). It is important to recognize that the culture of an organization is an amalgam of the beliefs and attitudes of individuals and groups within the organization, so it is unrealistic to expect that this will change overnight. The goal of empowerment through participation will never be achieved for everybody. It will remain a goal and the most we can expect is to set in motion a process of change that hopefully will affect the organization over a period of time. According to Wright et al. (2006, p. 6), there are six important components of organizational culture, with which to engage over time (Table 10.4). These separate points do not lessen the need for a holistic approach to culture in the organization. One of the important early objectives will be to use a social work tool – reframing – to try to encourage key staff to perceive the culture of the organization not as a barrier but as an area for service development (Wright et al., 2006, p. 14).

Table 10.4 Tackling six aspects of organizational culture

Aspects	Characteristics
Shared understanding	The development of an understanding of the 'culture of participation' (Wright et al., 2006, p. 15), shared between all involved in the setting – managers, practitioners, carers and people who use services – bringing together all those involved and encouraging them to discuss, clarify and hopefully agree on what they mean by participation and empowerment. It is important to overcome barriers of staff perceptions of vulnerable and excluded people, e.g. as unable to make a valid contribution to the organization
Motivating managers	Cultivating the active support of staff in key management roles. It will be important to identify whether sufficient understanding and resources exist to support the goal of participation and empowerment. An audit may be necessary of the existing situation before proceeding. This would have the advantage of highlighting not only areas where further development would help (avoiding the term 'weakness') but also areas of strength that could be drawn on to help development in other parts of the organization
Motivating staff	Bringing staff to the point where they are committed. This is a process of engaging all staff at all levels with the policy. Work will need to be done with staff to establish their level of knowledge and skills in this aspect of their work. Some staff may not be confident and others may have specific anxieties that will need tackling at an early stage in the implementation
Creating a charter	Creating a 'charter' or statement of principles and policies. The need for a written strategy is not always self-evident to staff in advance. It is an opportunity for the objectives of staff to be contributed, as well as those for carers and people who use services. It should not be considered in isolation from structure, practice and review (Wright et al., 2006, p. 19)
Sharing good practice	Identifying evidence that people are participating in different aspects of the work of the organization, as demonstrated in particular policies and documents. It is likely to help the organization to make visible statements external to the organization about existing work going on, with partner agencies. This contributes to changing the culture in the direction of participation and empowerment
Publicizing successes	Making an effort in the organization to publicize the work being done. It is equally important for the organization to publish within the organization details of how the policy and practice of participation and empowerment are already evident

Implementing empowerment through participation

Measures need to be taken to ensure representation from the entire field of potential participants and not just a favoured few, who represent nobody but themselves. This relates to the above points about policies and procedures, which may state a goal of inclusion but in practice may exclude some groups of people, particularly those who are 'seldom heard'. It will be important for capacity building work to be done with staff. If this is not done first, there will be problems when they are faced with practical issues. Measures include giving time to staff to meet with and listen to carers and people who use services, providing induction material and experiences, discussing participation and empowerment work at staff meetings and in supervision sessions, supporting staff in experimenting and reassuring them that this is a 'no blame' culture, in that they can safely make mistakes, giving staff the chance to talk about practice in and out of the organization or setting and, finally, writing up this practice and what is learned from it (Kirby et al., 2003b, p. 36).

There is a need also for practitioners to build the capacity of carers and people who use services to make the best use of opportunities to participate and empower themselves. In order to achieve this, it will be necessary to ensure that the environment is safe and that ways of working do not exclude or put people off. It is important to recognize that people judge practitioners and managers by their actions as well as by their words. Organizational policies may say one thing, but, for example, carers and people who use services may arrive at a building for a meeting and find it inaccessible for one reason or another. This is about creating a 'people-friendly' environment (Wright et al., 2006, p. 34). Similarly, they may not receive papers for the meeting until the last minute, or even on the day, when it is too late for blind people or people with learning difficulties to study it. Or, the meeting may not be preceded by a period of socializing to enable newcomers to acclimatize to the proceedings and may be conducted too fast for all participants to keep up. These are just examples of the many practice considerations that can undo a participation and empowerment strategy at the point of implementation. Wright et al. (2006, p. 27) observe that 'poor participatory practice is one of the most commonly cited obstacles to participation'. The National Youth Agency (2004) identifies key safety components, providing minimum quality standards for people taking part in the work of organizations, which are summarized in Table 10.5.

Table 10.5 Minimum quality standards

Standard	Criteria for judging
Informed consent	Those participating are able to give informed consent on the basis that the rationale for, and extent of, their commitment is made clear before they commit themselves
Safeguarding from risk	The physical and social boundaries and territory where the activity takes place are sufficiently protected to ensure people's safety
Adequate access	Physical access to the area is adequate; also, the timing is suitable (not early morning), the length of the meeting is broken up with adequate breaks and is not too long overall
Payments policy	The organization abides by a written policy in respect of fees and expenses paid to people who take part; the payments are adequate and include accommodation paid in advance where necessary and prompt (as near to immediate as possible) and payment afterwards where appropriate; arrangements are made with benefits agencies so that other benefits are not stopped unnecessarily when people are recompensed for taking part
Feedback on taking part	There is prompt, adequate feedback – written, verbal or both, or in other formats where necessary (e.g. in braille if the person is blind) – following any activities in which a person takes part

Six further points need making:

1. Flexibility needs to be observed in the running of participatory activities to ensure that all people can continue to take part in them (Wright et al., 2006, p. 36).
2. Opportunities need to be created for all those involved in the organization – staff, carers and people who use services – to take part together in staff development, recruitment of new staff and possible promotional activities (Wright et al., 2006, pp. 39–40). All staff should be encouraged to meet with carers and people who use services (Kirby et al., 2003b, p. 35). It is important to make the same policy and practice statements repeatedly in different situations in the organization and setting. Meetings are places where the message about participation and empowerment as benefits can be repeated. Events should be held to promote the policy and raise awareness of the need for change (Kirby et al., 2003b, p. 27).
3. It may be possible for people who use services and carers to contribute to research, either as advisers or taking part in the full process of research (see Chapter 9).

4. Make space in the organization or setting for people to acknowledge problems, barriers, resistances and conflicts associated with
the implementation of participation and empowerment policies
(Kirby et al., 2003b, p. 37). These examples can be used as
learning points in discussions in different parts of the organization
and worked at, without making judgements about individuals and
groups of staff. Difficulties of resistance and conflict can be
discussed and staff asked for suggestions about methods of
managing conflict and ways forward. Ways of tackling barriers
and reconciling areas of lack of progress with the vision should
be discussed and senior staff resources used where necessary to
support work to reduce resistance and conflict. Staff whose attitudes are positively harmful should be challenged (Kirby et al.,
2003b, p. 38). Carers and people who use services should invariably be supported through the process, since theirs is the precar-
ious position and the situation of structural weakness. Inevitably,
their stake in the organization or setting will be more vulnerable
to erosion than that of staff.

5. Individuals and groups, inside and outside the physical base of the
organization or setting, may take part in decision-making activities. Meetings are clearly central in these, but will not be the
sole mechanism for decisions to be made. It is a mistake to
narrow the field of potential participation and empowerment to
include only meetings. Many other opportunities for involvement
exist, such as one-off consultations, teleconferences, telephone
conversations, responding to written communications, emails,
website conference spaces and blogs. Geographical barriers to
access have been reduced considerably by the use of information
technologies to create virtual organizational environments. Participating carers and people who use services may be provided with
mobile phones, personal computers and laptops, with the appropriate software for deaf people and blind people.

6. Events that go well and examples of positive experiences of
participation and empowerment on the part both of staff and
carers and people who use services should be celebrated together.
Incentives should be given to staff, in terms of rewards at work,
for those who have made significant progress in practice.

Review: monitoring and evaluating

Robson et al. (2003) conclude that empowering changes are more
likely to take place in services that continually monitor and review

their policy and practice regarding participation – an activity with the added advantage of highlighting the benefits of empowerment. Wright et al. (2006, p. 8) refer to the need to put in place adequate means to monitor and evaluate all the above areas. For these measures to have much significance, all people who participate need to take part also in processes of reflecting – monitoring and evaluating – the extent to which they feel empowered through participation. Kirby et al. (2003b, p. 39), in a practice-based report in activity format, identify ways of reflecting and self-evaluating.

Guidance states the necessity to identify clear outcomes for participation and empowerment policies and practices. Without these, effective monitoring and evaluation are not possible (Wright et al., 2006, p. 46). Research points to the necessity to ensure benchmarking statements and standards are stated and published throughout the organization and incorporated into procedures for monitoring and evaluating (Kirby et al., 2003b, p. 39). Systems for reviewing need to be adequately resourced and this means providing sufficient time and space for all those involved to become familiar with what is involved, as well as preparing and distributing the necessary support papers (Wright et al., 2006, p. 47). Howard et al. (2002, pp. 3–6) review different approaches to evaluating participation and identify Shier's (2001) model as superior to Hart's ladder of participation (see Chapter 3), in that it sets the five rungs of the ladder against three stages of commitment to the process of empowerment – what Shier calls 'openings, opportunities and obligations'. *Openings* are the least active degree of commitment, posed by the question, 'Are you ready to listen to [that] person?'; *opportunities* are represented in the question, 'do you work in a way that enables you to listen to [that] person?'; *obligations* are met in the question, 'Is it a policy requirement that [this] person must be listened to?' (Howard et al., 2002, p. 5). Lee Jackson (2004) reviews models of evaluating participation and refers to Rocha's (1997) model, which more straightforwardly brings together degrees of participation and degrees of empowerment. Her model is based on a five-rung ladder, which corresponds with the domains set out in Chapter 3 of this book. Combining these two provides a template to evaluate the extent to which empowerment is achieved (Table 10.6).

The key to using monitoring and evaluation tools successfully is to ensure that they ask the right, the critical, questions. It is a good idea to pose demanding questions of the organization and the practitioners about the degree of participation and empowerment achieved, as we illustrated in Table 9.9, for example. Wright et al.

(2006, p. 48) use three levels to chart the process of implementation: emerging, established or advanced. These loosely correspond to the three stages of commitment of Howard et al. (2002) referred to above. They can be plotted against four core areas of service development and delivery identified by Wright and Haydon (2002), producing a grid for evaluating implementation (Table 10.7).

Table 10.6 Achieving empowerment

Level or domain	Criteria for judging achievement
Community and political empowerment	People taking part in community and political activity can give evidence of processes and/or outcomes that are empowering people
Organizational empowerment	Individual service users, carers, practitioners and managers can give evidence of specific ways in which the organization empowers people
Group empowerment	Service users and carers engage in group activities and feel empowered by them
Individual empowerment	Service users and carers take part in activities with professionals; contribute to decisions
Self-empowerment	Individuals feel confident; can engage in self-development; can plan and carry out participatory activities

Table 10.7 Evaluating empowerment through participation

| Areas of service development and delivery | Criteria for judging whether organization is: | | |
	Emerging	Established	Advanced
Established commitment to empowerment through participation	Evidence of meetings taking place	Evidence of detailed plans being discussed	Evidence of agreement to proceed
Planning and developing participation	Evidence of outline plans	Evidence of detailed plans	Evidence of using plans
Ways of working	Evidence of planning	Evidence of piloting in practice	Evidence of regular use
Skills, knowledge and experience required by people and practitioners	Evidence of relevant skills identified	Evidence of skills gained by people and practitioners	Evidence of skills used by people and practitioners

So far we have tackled the evaluation from the viewpoint of the progress of the organization. We need a different tool altogether to monitor and evaluate from the perspective of the carer and the person who uses services. The crucial question is what the outcomes are, for the carer or person who uses services. The experience of the user is required, to comment on the following trigger questions, with follow-up questions being asked where appropriate:

1. Were you informed about what was going to happen?
2. Were you given time to think about it?
3. Were you asked if you wanted to take part?
4. Were you able to choose from alternative ways of taking part?
5. Were you able to suggest your own ways of taking part?
6. Did you have opportunities to change your view in the light of experience?
7. Were you listened to when you took part?
8. Did you receive feedback after you took part?
9. Did anything change as a result of you taking part?
10. If so, what changed as a result of you taking part?

Conclusion

We have seen in this chapter how valuable it is to develop a holistic approach to empowering practice. Social work, in our view, benefits from a structural approach that appreciates the institutionalized and embedded nature of divisions and conflicts between different interests. This is not a universally held view, but it is borne out in work I have done over the past four years with people – adults, children and young people – who are carers and people who are using health and social care and social work services. In essence, this does not seem to me to make it impossible to do joint work, but it does help to have an honest appreciation of the fact that our interests differ. In my case, the position of able-bodied, white, male university lecturer or professor is one of relative structural power, which makes any assertion such as 'we are equal partners' to a carer or person using services at best rhetorical and at worst meaningless. What we can do is openly admit our circumstances and call a temporary truce in our differences, in agreeing to cooperate and collaborate.

Having done this, I have tried to lay out as openly as possible in this chapter a typical set of issues and measures that are likely to be encountered in implementing a participation and empowerment strategy in a social work organization or setting. It is not a matter of applying a set of rules or techniques, but engaging in a difficult process, sometimes a struggle, demanding personal, physical and financial resources. It will not end on a particular date, but once started it should continue, gathering momentum on its way. Empowering practice is an unending process with the aim of eliminating the persistent divisions and inequalities of power and resources that prevent so many people from reaching their full potential.

---

putting it into practice

Activity 1

Specify the four main components of a systemic approach to empowerment of people through participation.

Activity 2

Give details of the main items you would particularly watch when implementing a participatory approach to empowerment.

Activity 3

Specify the main questions you would expect to be asked in reviewing and evaluating a participatory approach to participation.

Further reading

Barker, G., Knaul, F., Cassaniga, N. and Schrader, A. (2000) *Urban Girls: Empowerment in Especially Difficult Circumstances*, London, Intermediate Technology Publications. A critical discussion of empowerment initiatives in a variety of settings.

Danso, C., Greaves, H., Howell, S. et al. (2003) *The Involvement of Children and Young People in Promoting Change and Enhancing the Quality of Social Care*, London, National Children's Bureau. An examination of the practice of participation by young people.

Franklin, A. and Sloper, P. (2006) *Participation of Disabled Children and Young People in Decision-making Relating to Social Care*, DfES 2119, York, University of York. A discussion of the components of participation by disabled children and young people.

Kay, E., Tisdall, M., Davis, J.M. et al. (eds) (2006) *Children, Young People and Social Inclusion: Participation for What?*, Bristol, Policy Press. A stimulating collection of essays on aspects of empowerment, participation and social inclusion of children and young people.

Kirby, P., Lanyon, C., Cronin, K. and Sinclair, R. (2003a) *Building a Culture of Participation: Involving Children and Young People in Policy, Service Planning, Delivery and Evaluation: The Research*, London, Department for Education and Skills. Wide-ranging research into theories and practice of bringing about participation by children and young people.

Kirby, P., Lanyon, C., Cronin, K. and Sinclair, R. (2003b) *Building a Culture of Participation: Involving Children and Young People in Policy, Service Planning, Delivery and Evaluation: The Handbook*, London, Department for Education and Skills. Practical guide, copiously illustrated with examples, showing how participation by children and young people may be enhanced.

Moriarty, J., Rapaport, P., Beresford, P. et al. (2006) *Practice Guide: The Participation of Adult Service Users, Including Older People, in Developing Social Care*, London, SCIE. Guidance on work with adults which uses a similar framework to that developed by Kirby et al. in empowering participation with children.

Wilcox, D. (1994) *A Guide to Effective Participation*, York, Joseph Rowntree Foundation. A highly relevant guide, containing many hints on practice.

Bibliography

ACORD (Agency for Co-operation and Research in Development) (2002) *Capacity Building for Community Based Organisations*, Gumare, Botswana, Acord, PO Box 431, Gumare, Botswana, acord@mail.com.

Adams, R. (1981) 'Pontefract Activity Centre', in R. Adams, S. Allard, J. Baldwin and J. Thomas (eds) *A Measure of Diversion: Case Studies in Intermediate Treatment*, Leicester, National Youth Bureau, pp. 211–47.

Adams, R. (1990) *Self-help, Social Work and Empowerment*, London, BASW/Macmillan – now Palgrave Macmillan.

Adams, R. (1991) *Protests by Pupils: Empowerment, Schooling and the State*, Basingstoke, Falmer.

Adams, R. (1992) *Empowering Clients* (video in Social Work Theories series) Brighton, Pavilion.

Adams, R. (1994) *Prison Riots in Britain and the USA* (2nd edn) Basingstoke, Macmillan – now Palgrave Macmillan.

Adams, R. (1996) *The Personal Social Services: Clients, Consumers or Citizens?*, Harlow, Addison Wesley Longman.

Adams, R. (1997) 'Empowerment, Marketisation and Social Work', in B. Lesnik (ed.) *Change in Social Work*, Aldershot, Arena.

Adams, R. (1998a) *Quality Social Work*, Basingstoke, Macmillan – now Palgrave Macmillan.

Adams, R. (1998b) 'Empowerment and Protest', in B. Lesnik (ed.) *Challenging Discrimination in Social Work*, Aldershot, Ashgate.

Adams, R., Dixon, G., Henderson, T. et al. (2005) *A Strategy for Bringing about Participation by Service Users in the Work of Skills for Care*, Middlesbrough, University of Teesside.

Afshar, H. (ed.) (1998) *Women and Empowerment: Illustrations from the Third World*, Basingstoke, Macmillan – now Palgrave Macmillan.

Agel, J. (ed.) (1971) *Radical Therapist: The Radical Therapist Collective*, New York, Ballantine Books.

Aldridge, J. (2007) 'Picture This: The Use of Participatory Photographic Research Methods with People with Learning Disabilities', *Disability and Society*, **22**(1): 1–17.

Alsop, R. and Heinsohn, N. (2005) Measuring Empowerment: Structuring

Analysis and Framing Indicators, policy research working paper 3510, Washington DC, World Bank.

Altman, D. (1986) *AIDS and the New Puritanism*, London, Pluto Press.

Andrews, J., Manthorpe, J. and Watson, R. (2004) 'Involving Older People in Intermediate Care', *Journal of Advanced Nursing*, **46**(3): 303–10.

Arnstein, S. (1969) 'A Ladder of Citizen Participation', *Journal of the American Institute of Planners*, **35**(4): 216–22.

Asian Resource Centre (1987) *Annual Report 1986–87*, Birmingham, Asian Resource Centre.

Askheim, O.P. (2003) 'Empowerment as Guidance for Professional Social Work: An Act of Balancing on a Slack Tightrope', *European Journal of Social Work*, **6**(3): 229–40.

Askonas, P. and Stewart, A. (eds) 2000) *Social Inclusion: Possibilities and Tensions*, Basingstoke, Macmillan – now Palgrave Macmillan.

Atkinson, D. (2004) 'Research and Empowerment: Involving People with Learning Difficulties in Oral and Life History Research', *Disability and Society*, **19**(7): 691–702.

Atkinson, R. and Willis, P. (2006) Capacity Building: A Practical Guide, paper no. 6, Housing and Community Research Unit, Hobart, University of Tasmania, www.utas.edu.au/sociology/HACRU/.

Aves, G. (1969) *The Voluntary Worker in the Social Services*, London, Allen & Unwin.

Bagguley, P. (1991) *From Protest to Acquiescence: Political Movements of the Unemployed*, Basingstoke, Macmillan – now Palgrave Macmillan.

Baistow, K. (1994) 'Liberation and Regulation? Some Paradoxes of Empowerment', *Critical Social Policy*, **42**(14 3): 34–46.

Balloch, S., Hume, C., Jones, B. and Westland, P. (eds) (1985) *Caring for Unemployed People*, London, Bedford Square Press.

Bamford, T. (1982) *Managing Social Work*, London, Tavistock.

Bamford, C. and Bruce, E. (2000) 'Defining the Outcomes of Community Care: The Perspectives of Older People with Dementia and Their Carers', *Ageing and Society*, **20**(5): 543–70.

Bannister, A. and Huntington, A. (eds) (2002) *Communicating with Children and Adolescents: Action for Change*, London, Jessica Kingsley.

Barber, J.G. (1991) *Beyond Casework*, London, BASW/Macmillan – now Palgrave Macmillan.

Barker, G., Knaul, F., Cassaniga, N. and Schrader, A. (2000) *Urban Girls: Empowerment in Especially Difficult Circumstances*, London, Intermediate Technology Publications.

Barnes, C. (2005) Notes on Capacity Building for Local Service Provider Organisations Controlled and Run by Disabled People Often Referred to as CILs, leeds.ac.uk/disability-studies/archiveuk/ Barnes/IL%20Zone.pdf.

Barnes, C. and Mercer, G. (eds) (1997) *Doing Disability Research*, Disability Press, University of Leeds.

Barnes, C. and Mercer, G. (2006) *Independent Futures: Creating User-led Disability Services in a Disabling Society*, Bristol, Policy Press.

Barnes, C., Mercer G., and Din, I. (2003) Research Review on User Involvement in Promoting Change and Enhancing the Quality of Social Care Services for Disabled People, Centre for Disability Studies, University of Leeds, http://www.leeds.ac.uk/disability-studies/ archiveuk/index.html.

Barnes, M. (2005) 'The Same Old Process? Older People, Participation and Deliberation', *Ageing and Society*, **25**(2): 245–59.

Barnes, M. and Bowl, R. (2001) *Taking Over the Asylum: Empowerment and Mental Health*, Basingstoke, Palgrave Macmillan.

Bar-On, A. and Prinsen, G. (1999) 'Planning, Communities and Empowerment: An Introduction to Participatory Rural Appraisal', *International Social Work*, **42**(3): 277–94.

Beazley, M. and Smith, M. (2004) A Resident-led Evaluation of Community Empowerment on the Castle Vale Estate Including Key Aspects of the Effectiveness of Intervention, Community Capacity, Succession and Sustainability, School of Public Policy, University of Birmingham, http://www.cvhat.org.uh/pir/empowerment%20&%20 resident%20Involvement.pdf.

Begum, N. (2006) Doing it for Themselves: Participation and Black and Minority Ethnic Service Users, participation report 14, London, Social Care Institute for Excellence and Race Equality Unit.

Beresford, P. (1999) 'Making Participation Possible: Movements of Disabled People and Psychiatric System Survivors', in T. Jordan and A. Lent (eds) *Storming the Millennium: The New Politics of Change*, London, Lawrence & Wishart.

Beresford, P. (2001) 'Service Users, Social Policy and the Future of Welfare', *Critical Social Policy*, **21**(4): 494–512.

Beresford, P. and Croft, S. (1986) *Whose Welfare: Private Care or Public Services?*, Brighton, Lewis Cohen Urban Studies.

Beresford, P. and Croft, S. (1993) *Citizen Involvement: A Practical Guide for Change*, London, BASW/Macmillan – now Palgrave Macmillan.

Beresford, P. and Croft, S. (2001) 'Service Users' Knowledges and the Social Construction of Social Work', *Journal of Social Work*, **1**(3): 295–316.

Berger, P. and Luckman, T. (1966) *The Social Construction of Reality: A Treatise in the Sociology of Knowledge*, New York, Doubleday.

Biestek, F. (1961) *The Casework Relationship*, London, Allen & Unwin.

Blackburn, J. and Holland, J. (eds) (1998) *Who Changes? Institutionalizing Participation in Development*, London, Intermediate Technology Publications.

Bonhoeffer, D. (1966) *I Loved this People*, London, SPCK.

Botchway, K. (2001) 'Paradox of Empowerment: Reflections on a Case Study from Northern Ghana', *World Development*, **29**(1): 1135–53.

Boushel, M. and Farmer, E. (1996) 'Work with Families where Children are at Risk: Control and/or Empowerment?', in P. Parsloe (ed.) *Pathways to Empowerment*, Birmingham, Venture, pp. 93–107.

Burton, P. (1993) *Community Profiling: A Guide to Identifying Local Needs*, Bristol, SAUS.

Brandon, D. (1995) *Advocacy: Power to People with Disabilities*, Birmingham, Venture.

Brandon, D. and Brandon, A. (1988) *Putting People First: A Handbook in the Practical Application of Ordinary Living Principles*, London, Good Impressions.

Brandon, D. and Brandon, T. (2001) *Advocacy in Social Work*, Birmingham, Venture.

Brannelly, T. (2006) 'Negotiating Ethics in Dementia Care: An Analysis of an Ethic of Care in Practice', *Dementia: the International Journal of Social Research and Practice*, **5**(2): 197–212.

Braye, S. and Preston-Shoot, M. (1995) *Empowering Practice in Social Care*, Buckingham, Open University.

Bureau, J. and Shears, J. (eds) (2007) *Pathways to Policy: A Toolkit for Grassroots Involvement in Mental Health Policy*, London, Hamlet Trust.

Burke, B. and Dalrymple, J. (2002) 'Intervention and Empowerment', in R. Adams, L. Dominelli and M. Payne (eds) *Critical Practice in Social Work*, Basingstoke, Palgrave Macmillan, pp. 55–62.

Burke, P. and Cigno, K. (eds) (2000) *Learning Disabilities in Children*, Oxford, Blackwell.

Burns, D., Williams, C.C. and Windebank, J. (2004) *Community Self-help*, Basingstoke, Palgrave Macmillan.

Burns, T. and Stalker, G.M. (1961) *The Management of Innovation*, New York, Quadrangle Books.

Cantley, C., Woodhouse, J. and Smith, M. (2005) *Listen to Us: Involving People with Dementia in Planning and Developing Services*, Newcastle, Dementia North.

Carr, E.S. (2003) 'Rethinking Empowerment Theory Using a Feminist Lens: The Importance of Process', *Affilia*, **18**(1): 8–20.

Carr, M., Chen, M. and Jhabvala, R. (eds) (1996) *Speaking Out: Women's Economic Empowerment in South Asia*, London, Intermediate Technology Publications.

Carr, S. (2004a) *Has Service User Participation Made a Difference to Social Care Services?*, position paper 3, London, Social Care Institute for Excellence.

Carr, S. (2004b) 'Just an Illusion', *Care and Health*, **57**: 24–5.

Chamberlain, M. (1981) *Old Wives' Tales*, London, Virago.

Chambers, R. (1997) *Whose Reality Counts? Putting the First Last*, London, ITDG Publishing.

Chan, C.L.W., Chan, Y. and Lou, V.W.Q. (2002) 'Evaluating an Empowerment Group for Divorced Chinese Women in Hong Kong', *Research on Social Work Practice*, **12**(4): 558–69.

Charlton, J.I. (2000) *Nothing About Us Without Us: Disability, Oppression and Empowerment*, Berkeley, CA, University of California Press.

Chesner, A. and Hahn, H. (eds) (2001) *Creative Advances in Groupwork*, London, Jessica Kingsley.

Cheston, R., Bender, M. and Byatt, S. (2000) 'Involving People who Have

Dementia in the Evaluation of Services: A Review', *Journal of Mental Health*, **9**(5): 471–9.

Chiu, L.F. (2004) 'Critical Engagement: The Community Health Educator Model as a Participatory Strategy for Improving Minority Ethnic Health', paper presented at 'Hospitals in a Culturally Diverse Europe' conference, 9–11 December, Amsterdam.

Cissé, M.K., Sokona, Y. and Thomas, J.P. (n.d.) Environnement et Développement du Tiers-Monde, Dakar, Senegal, ENDA-TM Energy Programme, http://www.enda.sn, accessed 25.11.06.

Clarke, J., Cochrane, A. and McLaughlin, E. (eds) (1994) *Managing Social Policy*, London, Sage.

Clarke, M. and Stewart, J. (1992) *Citizens and Local Democracy: Empowerment: A Theme for the 1990s*, Luton, Local Government Management Board.

Cohen, J. and Emanuel, J. (2000) *Positive Participation: Consulting and Involving Young People in Health-related Work: A Planning and Training Resource*, London, Health Development Agency.

Connor, D.M. (1988) 'A New Ladder of Citizen Participation', *National Civic Review*, **77**(3): 249–57.

Cornwall, A. and Jewkes, R. (1995) 'What is Participatory Research?' *Social Science and Medicine*, **41**(12): 1667–76.

Coulshed, V. (1991) *Social Work Practice: An Introduction*, London, BASW/Macmillan – now Palgrave Macmillan.

Craig, G. (1989) 'Community Work and the State', *Community Development Journal*, **24**(1): 3–18.

Craig, G. (1992) *Cash or Care: A Question of Choice?*, Social Policy Research Unit, University of York.

Craig, G. and Mayo, M. (eds) (1995) *Community Empowerment*, London, Zed Books.

Crawford, M., Rutter, D. and Thelwall, S. (2003) User Involvement in Change Management: A Review of the Literature, Report to NHS Service Delivery and Organisation Research and Development Programme.

Croft, S. and Beresford, P. (2000) 'Empowerment', in M. Davies, (ed.) *The Blackwell Encyclopaedia of Social Work*, Oxford, Blackwell, pp. 116–18.

Cunningham, I. (1994) 'Interactive Holistic Research: Researching Self-managed Learning', in P. Reason (ed.) *Human Inquiry in Action: Developments in New Paradigm Research*, London, Sage, pp. 163–81.

Cutler, D. (2002) *Taking the Initiative: Promoting Young People's Involvement in Public Decision Making in the USA*, London, Carnegie Young People's Initiative.

Danso, C., Greaves, H., Howell, S. et al. (2003) The Involvement of Children and Young People in Promoting Change and Enhancing the Quality of Services: A Research Report for SCIE from the National Children's Bureau, London,.

Darvill, G. and Munday, B. (1984) *Volunteers in the Personal Social Services*, London, Tavistock.

Dearden, C. and Becker, S. (2004) *Young Carers in the UK: The 2004 Report*, London, Carers UK.

Deegan, P.E. (1997) 'Recovery and Empowerment for People with Psychiatric Disabilities', *Social Work Health Care*, **25**(3): 11–24.

DFID (Department for International Development) (1997) *Eliminating World Poverty: Making Globalisation Work for the Poor*, White Paper, Cm 5006, London, TSO.

DFID (Department for International Development) (2000) *Poverty Elimination and the Empowerment of Women: Strategies for Achieving the International Development Targets*, London, DFID.

Dew, J.R. (1997) *Empowerment and Education in the Workplace: Applying Adult Education Theory and Practice for Cultivating Empowerment*, Westport, CT, Quorum Books.

Diamond, B., Parkin, G., Morris, K. et al. (2003) 'User Involvement: Substance or Spin?' *Journal of Mental Health*, **12**(6): 613–26.

Doel, M., Carroll, C., Chambers, E. et al. (2007) *Developing Measures for Service User and Carer Participation in Social Care*, London, Social Care Institute for Excellence.

Dominelli, L. (1997) *Sociology for Social Work*, Basingstoke, Macmillan – now Palgrave Macmillan.

Dominelli, L. (2002) *Feminist Social Work Theory and Practice*, Basingstoke, Palgrave Macmillan.

Donnan, L. and Lenton, S. (1985) *Helping Ourselves: A Handbook for Women Starting Groups*, Toronto, Women's Press.

Dorcey, A.H.J. and British Columbia Round Table on the Environment and the Economy (1994) Public Involvement in Government Decision Making: Choosing the Right Model: A Report of the B.C. Round Table on the Environment and the Economy, Victoria, BC, the Round Table.

Dryden, W. and Feltham, C. (1992) *Brief Counselling: A Practical Guide for Beginning Practitioners*, Buckingham, Open University Press.

European Parliament (2000) Charter of Fundamental Rights, EU 2000/C 364/01, Strasbourg, European Parliament.

Evans, L., Forder, A., Ward, L. et al. (1986) *Working with Parents of Handicapped Children: A Guide to Self-help Groups and Casework with Families*, London, Bedford Square Press.

Falk-Rafael, A.R. (2001) 'Empowerment as a Process of Evolving Consciousness: A Model of Empowered Caring', *Advances in Nursing Science*, **24**(1): 1–16.

Faulkener, A. (2004) *The Ethics of Survivor Research: Guidelines for the Ethical Conduct of Research Carried out by Mental Health Service Users and Survivors*, Bristol, Policy Press.

Fetterman, D.M. (2000) *Foundations of Empowerment Evaluation*, London, Sage.

Fetterman, D.M. and Wandersman, A. (2004) *Empowerment Evaluation Principles in Practice*, New York, Guildford.

Fielding, N. (1989) 'No More Help for Self-helpers', *Community Care*, **755**: 7.

Florin, D. and Dixon, J. (2004) 'Public Involvement in Health Care', *British Medical Journal*, **328**: 159–61.

Follett, M.P. (1918) *The New State*, New York, Longmans, Green and Co.

Follett, M.P. (1924) *Creative Experience*, New York, Longmans, Green and Co.

Francis, J. and Netten, A. (2004) 'Raising the Quality of Home Care: A Study of Service Users' Views', *Social Policy and Administration*, **38**(3): 290–305.

Franklin, B. (ed.) (1986) *The Rights of Children*, Oxford, Basil Blackwell.

Franklin, B. (ed.) (2001) *The New Handbook of Children's Rights: Comparative Policy and Practice*, London, Routledge.

Franklin, H.B. (1978) *Prison Literature in America*, Westport, CT, Lawrence Hill.

Freire, P. (1972, reprinted 1986) *Pedagogy of the Oppressed*, Harmondsworth, Penguin.

Freire, P. (1973) *Education for Critical Consciousness*, New York, Continuum.

Freire, P. (1990) 'A Critical Understanding of Social Work', *Journal of Progressive Human Services*, **1**(1): 3–9.

Gartner, A. and Riessman, F. (1977) *Self-help in the Human Services*, London, Jossey-Bass.

General Social Care Council, the Commission for Social Care Inspection, Skills for Care and the Social Care Institute for Excellence (2005) *Eight Principles for Involving Service Users and Carers*, London, SCIE.

Gibson, T. (1979) *People Power: Communities and Work Groups in Action*, Harmondsworth, Penguin.

Gladstone, F.J. (1979) *Voluntary Action in a Changing World*, London, Bedford Square Press.

Goffman, E. (1963) *Asylums: Essays on the Social Situation of Mental Patients and Other Inmates*, Harmondsworth, Penguin.

Gould, N. and Baldwin, M. (eds) (2004) *Social Work, Critical Reflection and the Learning Organisation*, Aldershot, Ashgate.

Green, D. (1991) *Empowering the Parents: How to Break the Schools Monopoly*, London, Inner London Education Authority Health and Welfare Unit.

Gramsci, A. (1971) *Selections from the Prison Notebooks*, New York, International Publishers.

Griffiths, K. (1991) *Consulting with Chinese Communities*, London, King's Fund.

Guijt, I. and Shah, M.K. (eds) (1998) *The Myth of Community: Gender Issues in Participatory Development*, London, Intermediate Technology Publications.

Gutierrez, L., Parsons, R. and Cox, E. (eds) (2003) *Empowerment in Social Work Practice: A Sourcebook*, Belmont, CA, Wadsworth.

Habermas, J. (1977) 'Hannah Arendt's Communications Concept of Power', *Social Research*, **44**(1): 3–24.

Hallowitz, E. and Riessman, F. (1967) 'The Role of the Indigenous Non-professional in a Community Mental Health Neighbourhood', *American Journal of Orthopsychiatry*, (37): 766–78.

Hardy, C. and Leiba-O'Sullivan, S. (1998) 'The Power Behind Empowerment: Implications for Research and Practice', *Human Relations*, **51**(4): 451–83.

Harris, R. (2002) 'Power', in M. Davies (ed.) *The Blackwell Companion to Social Work*, Oxford, Blackwell.

Hart, R. (1992) Children's Participation: From Tokenism to Citizenship, UNICEF Innocenti Essays, no. 4, Florence, International Child Development Centre.

Hawtin, M., Hughes, G. and Percy-Smith, J. (1994) *Community Profiling: Auditing Social Needs*, Buckingham, Open University Press.

Healy, K. (2001) 'Participatory Action Research and Social Work: A Critical Appraisal', *International Social Work*, **44**(1): 93–105.

Heikkilä, M. and Julkunen, I. (2003) *Obstacles to an Increased User Involvement in Social Services*, Strasbourg, Council of Europe.

Heller, T., Reynolds, J., Gomm, R. et al. (eds) (1996) *Mental Health Matters: A Reader*, Basingstoke, Macmillan – now Palgrave Macmillan.

Henderson, P. and Thomas, D. (1980) *Skills in Neighbourhood Work*, London, Allen & Unwin.

Heron, J. (1990) *Helping the Client: A Creative Practical Guide*, London, Sage.

Heslop, M. (2002) *Participatory Research with Older People: A Sourcebook*, London, HelpAge International.

Hilton, M. (2003) *Consumerism in Twentieth Century Britain: The Search for a Historical Movement*, Cambridge University Press.

Hilton, M., Chessel, M.E. and Chatriot, A. (2006) *The Expert Consumer: Associations and Professionals in Consumer Society*, Aldershot, Ashgate.

Holdsworth, L. (1991) *Empowerment: Social Work with Physically Disabled People*, Social Work Monographs, no. 97, University of East Anglia, Norwich.

Holland, J. and Blackburn, J. (eds) (1998) *Whose Voice? Participatory Research and Policy Change*, London, Intermediate Technology Publications.

Holme, A. and Maizels, J. (1978) *Social Workers and Volunteers*, London, Allen & Unwin.

Howard, S., Newman, L., Harris, V. and Harcourt, J. (2002) 'Talking About Youth Participation – Where, When and Why?', Australian Association for Research in Education Conference, 2–5 December, University of Queensland, http://www.aare.edu.au/02pap/how02535.htm, accessed 15.12.06.

Howell, E. (1981) 'Psychotherapy with Women Clients: the Impact of Feminism', in E. Howell and M. Bayes (eds) *Women and Mental Health*, New York, Basic Books, pp. 509–13.

Hugman, R. (1991) *Power in Caring Professions*, Basingstoke, Macmillan – now Palgrave Macmillan.

Humphries, B. (ed.) (1996) *Critical Perspectives on Empowerment*, Birmingham, Venture.

Humphry, D. (1996) *Final Exit: The Practicalities of Self-deliverance and Assisted Suicide for the Dying*, New York, Dell.

Hurvitz, N. (1974) 'Peer Self-help Psychotherapy Groups: Psychotherapy without Psychotherapists', in P.M. Roman and H.M. Trice (eds) *The Sociology of Psychotherapy*, New York, Jason Aronson, pp. 84–137.

Hutchings, A. and Taylor, I. (2007) 'Defining the Profession? Exploring an International Definition of Social Work in the China Context', *International Journal of Social Welfare*, **16**(4): 382–90.

Hutton, A. (2004) What Works in Children and Young People's Participation, unpublished, Ilford, Barnardo's.

Illich, I. (1975) *Medical Nemesis: The Expropriation of Health*, London, Caldar & Boyars.

INVOLVE (2006) *A Guide to Reimbursing and Paying Members of the Public Who are Actively Involved in Research*, London, DH, www.invo.org.uk.

Jack, R. (ed.) (1995) *Empowerment in Community Care*, London, Chapman & Hall.

Jackson, L. (2004) 'Citizenship Education through Community Action', Citizenship and Teacher Education (citizED), winter 2004/5, www.citized.info, accessed 15.12.06.

Jacobs, S. and Popple, K. (eds) (1994) *Community Work in the 1990s*, Nottingham, Spokesman.

Janzon, K., and Law, S. (2003) Older People Influencing Social Care: Aspirations and Realities, research review on User Involvement in Promoting Change and Enhancing the Quality of Social Care Services, final report for SCIE.

Johansson, H. and Hvinden, B. (2005) 'Welfare Governance and the Remaking of Citizenship', in J. Newman (ed.) *Remaking Governance: Peoples, Politics and the Public Sphere*, Bristol, Policy Press, pp. 101–18.

Johnson, A. (2006) 'Community Engagement in Determining Health Policy: Perpetual Allure, Persistent Challenge', lecture to Doctors Reform Society, Australia, Department of Public Health, Flinders University, Adelaide.

Kabeer, N. (1999) 'Resources, Agency, Achievements: Reflections on the Measurement of Women's Empowerment', *Development and Change*, **30**(3): 435–64.

Kam, P.K. (2002) 'From Disempowering to Empowering: Changing the Practice of Social Service Professionals with Older People', *Hallym International Journal of Aging*, **4**(2): 161–83.

Katz, A.H. and Bender, E.I. (1976) *The Strength in Us: Self-help Groups in the Modern World*, New York, New Viewpoints/Franklin Watts.

Kemshall, H. and Littlechild, R. (eds) (2000) *User Involvement and Participation in Social Care: Research Informing Practice*, London, Jessica Kingsley.

Kesoy, M. (2005) 'Retheorising Empowerment-through-Participation as a Performance in Space: Beyond Tyranny to Transformation', *Signs: Journal of Women in Culture and Society*, **30**: 2037–65.

Key, M., Hudson, P. and Armstrong, J. (1976) *Evaluation Theory and Community Work*, London, Young Volunteer Force Foundation.

Kiden, M. (2004) Evaluation/Appraisal of South Sudan Women Concern Capacity Building Programme, www.baringfoundation.org. uk/intevalSSWC.pdf, accessed 25.11.06.

Killilea, M. (1976) 'Mutual Help Organisations: Interpretations in the Literature', in G. Caplan and K. Killilea (eds) *Support Systems and Mutual Help: Multidisciplinary Explorations*, New York, Grune & Stratton, pp. 37–87.

Kirby, P., Lanyon, C., Cronin, K. and Sinclair, R. (2003a) Building a Culture of Participation: Involving Children and Young People in Policy, Service Planning, Delivery and Evaluation, Research Report, London, Department for Education and Skills.

Kirby, P., Lanyon, C., Cronin, K. and Sinclair, R. (2003b) *Building a Culture of Participation: Involving Children and Young People in Policy, Service Planning, Delivery and Evaluation, The Handbook*, London, Department for Education and Skills.

Kleiman, M.A., Mantell, J.E. and Alexander, E. S. (1976) 'Collaboration and its Discontents: The Perils of Partnership', *Journal of Applied Behavioural Science*, (12) Part 3: 403–10.

Knight, B. and Hayes, R. (1981) *Self-help in the Inner City*, London, London Voluntary Service Council.

Kropotkin, P. (1902) *Mutual Aid: A Factor in Evolution*, Boston, Porter Sargeant.

Krzowski, S. and Land, P. (1988) *In our Experience: Workshops at the Women's Therapy Centre*, London, Women's Press.

Kuhn, T.S. (1970) *The Structure of Scientific Revolutions* (2nd edn) University of Chicago Press.

Kumar, G.P. (2004) *From Involvement to Empowerment: People Living with HIV/AIDS in Asia Pacific*, Colombo, Sri Lanka, United Nations Development Programme, www.youandaids.org/unfiles/frominvtoemp.pdf.

Labonte, R. (1993) *Health Promotion and Empowerment: Practice Frameworks*, Toronto, Centre for Health Promotion/Participation/ Action.

Lawson, M. (1991) 'A Recipient's View', in S. Ramon (ed.) *Beyond Community Care: Normalisation and Integration Work*, London, Mind/Macmillan – now Palgrave Macmillan, pp. 62–83.

Leadbetter, M. (2002) 'Empowerment and Advocacy', in R. Adams, L. Dominelli and M. Payne (eds) *Social Work: Themes, Issues and Critical Debates* (2nd edn) Basingstoke, Palgrave Macmillan, pp. 200–8.

Lee, J.A.B. (2001) *The Empowerment Approach to Social Work Practice: Building the Beloved Community* (2nd edn) New York, Columbia University Press.

Leonard, P. (1997) *Postmodern Welfare: Reconstructing and Emancipatory Project*, London, Sage.

Lerner, M.P. (1979) 'Surplus Powerlessness', *Social Policy*, Jan/Feb, pp. 19–27.

Lewin, K. (1948) 'Action Research and Minority Problems', in G.W. Lewin (ed.) *Resolving Social Conflicts: Selected Papers in Group Dynamics*, New York, Harper Row, pp. 201–16.

Lieberman, M. and Borman, L.D. (1976) 'Self-help and Social Research', *Journal of Applied Behavioural Science*, **12**, Part 3: 455–63.

Lindenfield, G. (1986) *Assert Yourself*, London, Thorson.

Lindenfield, G. and Adams, R. (1984) *Problem Solving Through Self-help Groups*, Ilkley, Self-Help Associates.

Linhorst, D.M. (2006) *Empowering People with Severe Mental Illness*, Oxford, Oxford University Press.

Living Options in Practice (1992) Achieving User Participation, project paper no. 3, London, King's Fund.

Lofland, J. and Lofland, L. (1984) *Analysing Social Settings*, Belmont, CA, Wadsworth.

Lord, J. and Hutchison, P. (1993) 'The Process of Empowerment: Implications for Theory and Practice', *Canadian Journal of Community Mental Health*, **12**(1): 5–22.

Lowry, M. (1983) 'A Voice from the Peace Camps: Greenham Common and Upper Heyford', in Thompson, D. (ed.) *Over Our Dead Bodies: Women Against the Bomb*, London, Virago, pp. 73–7.

Lukes, S. (1974) *Power: A Radical View*, Basingstoke, Macmillan – now Palgrave Macmillan.

Lupton, C. and Nixon, P. (1999) *Empowering Practice? A Critical Appraisal of the Family Group Conference Approach*, Bristol, Policy Press.

Masters, J. (1995) 'The History of Action Research', in I. Hughes (ed.) Action Research Electronic Reader, University of Sydney, http://www.behs.cchs.usyd.edu.au/arow/reader/masters.htm, accessed 28.9.2007.

McTaggart, R. (1989) 'Sixteen Tenets of Participatory Action Research', paper presented to 3er Encuentro Mundial Investigacion Participatva, Managua, Nicaragua, 3–9 September.

McTaggart, R. (ed.) (1997) *Participatory Action Research: International Contexts and Consequences*, Albany, State University of New York Press.

McTaggart, R. (1999) 'Reflection on the Purposes of Research, Action and Scholarship: A Case of Cross-cultural Participatory Action Research', *Systemic Practice and Action Research*, **12**(5): 493–511.

McWhirter, E.H. (1997) 'Empowerment, Social Activism and Counselling', *Counselling and Human Development*, **29**(8): 1–14.

Manville, B. and Ober, J. (2003) 'Beyond Empowerment: Building a Company of Citizens', *Harvard Business Review*, **81**(1): 48–53.

Marieskind, H.I. (1984) 'Women's Self-help Groups', in A. Gartner and F. Riessman (eds) *Self-help in the Human Services*, London, Jossey-Bass, pp. 27–32.

Marsden, D. and Oakley, P. (eds) (1990) *Evaluating Social Development Projects*, Oxford, Oxfam.

Mayer, J. and Timms, N. (1970) *The Client Speaks*, London, Routledge & Kegan Paul.

Mayo, M. (2000) *Cultures, Communities, Identities: Cultural Strategies for Participation and Empowerment*, Basingstoke, Macmillan – now Palgrave Macmillan.

Mayoux, L. (2000) Micro-finance and the Empowerment of Women: A Review of the Key Issues, e paper, www.ilo.org/public/english/ employment/finance/download/wpap23.pdf.

Meetham, K. (1995) 'Empowerment and Community Care for Older People', in N. Nelson and S. Wright (eds) *Power and Participatory Development: Theory and Practice*, London, Intermediate Technology Publications, pp. 133–43.

Mezirow, J. (1983) 'A Critical Theory of Adult Learning and Education', in M. Tight (ed.) *Adult Learning and Education*, London, Croom Helm, pp. 124–38.

Moeller, M.L. (1983) *The New Group Therapy*, Princeton, NJ, Van Nostrand.

Mohan, G. and Stokke, K. (2000) 'Participatory Development and Empowerment: The Dangers of Localism', *Third World Quarterly*, **21**(2): 247–68.

Mok, B.H., Cheung, Y.W. and Cheung, T.S. (2006) 'Empowerment Effect of Self-help Group Participation in a Chinese Context', *Journal of Social Service Research*, **32**(3): 87–108.

Moriarty, J., Rapaport, P., Beresford, P. et al. (2006) *Practice Guide: The Participation of Adult Service Users, Including Older People, in Developing Social Care*, London, SCIE.

Morris, J. (1993) *Independent Lives? Community Care and Disabled People*, Basingstoke, Macmillan – now Palgrave Macmillan.

Morris, J. (1997) 'Care or Empowerment? A Disability Rights Perspective', *Social Policy and Administration*, **31**(1): 54–60.

Morse, R.S. (2007) 'Mary Follett, Prophet of Participation' *International Journal of Public Participation*, **1**(1): 1–16.

Mowrer, O.H. (1984) 'The Mental Health Professions and Mutual Help Programs: Co-optation or Collaboration?', in A. Gartner and F. Riessman (eds) *The Self-help Revolution*, New York, Human Sciences Press, pp. 139–54.

Mullender, A. and Ward, D. (1991) *Self-directed Groupwork: Users Take Action for Empowerment*, London, Whiting & Birch.

Nairne, K. and Smith, G. (1984) *Dealing with Depression*, London, Women's Press.

National Youth Agency (2004) *Involving Children and Young People: An Introduction*, Leicester, National Youth Agency.

Nelson, G., Lord, J. and Ochocka, J. (2001) 'Empowerment and Mental Health in the Community: Narratives of Psychiatric Consumers/ Survivors', *Journal of Community and Applied Social Psychology*, **11**(2): 125–42.

Newman, J. (2005) 'Participative Governance and the Remaking of the Public Sphere', in J. Newman (ed.) *Remaking Governance: Peoples, Politics and the Public Sphere*, Bristol, Policy Press, pp. 119–38.

Ng, S.M. and Chan, C.L.W. (2005) 'Intervention', in R. Adams, L. Dominelli and M. Payne (eds) *Social Work Futures: Crossing Boundaries, Transforming Practice*, Basingstoke, Palgrave Macmillan.

OECD (2005) 'Evaluating Public Participation in Policy Making' *Governance*, **2005**(21): 1–130.

Ochieng, R. (2002) 'Information and Communication Technologies as a Tool for Women's Empowerment and Social Transformation', in inaugural issue of Feminist Africa, online journal of African Gender Institute, January, pp. 1–6, www.feministafrica.org.

Ohri, A., Manning, B. and Curno, P. (eds) (1982) *Community Work and Racism*, London, ACW/Routledge.

Oka, T. (1994) 'Self-help Groups in Japan: Trends and Traditions', *Prevention in Human Services*, **2**(1): 69–95.

Oliver, M. (1990) *The Politics of Disablement*, Basingstoke, Macmillan – now Palgrave Macmillan.

Orme, J. (2001) *Gender and Community Care: Social Work and Social Care Perspectives*, Basingstoke, Palgrave Macmillan.

O'Sullivan, T. (1994) 'Why Don't Social Workers Work in Partnership With People?', unpublished paper, University of Humberside, Hull.

Owusu-Bempah, K. (2001) 'Racism: An Important Factor in Practice with Ethnic Minority Children and Families', in P. Foley, J. Roche and S. Tucker (eds) *Children in Society: Contemporary Theory, Policy and Practice*, Basingstoke, Palgrave – now Palgrave Macmillan, pp. 42–51.

Page, R. (1992) 'Empowerment, Oppression and Beyond: A Coherent Strategy? A Reply to Ward and Mullender', *Critical Social Policy*, **12**(35): 89–92.

Page, R. and Clark, G.A. (1977) *Who Cares? Young People in Care Speak Out*, London, National Children's Bureau.

Parsloe, P. (1986) 'What Skills do Social Workers Need?', *in Skills for Social Workers in the 1980s*, Birmingham, BASW, pp. 7–15.

Parsloe, P. (ed.) (1996) *Pathways to Empowerment*, Birmingham, Venture.

Pasteur, K. (2001) *Changing Organisations for Sustainable Livelihoods: A Map to Guide Change*, Brighton, Institute of Development Studies, University of Sussex.

Patmore, C. (2001) 'Can Managers Research their own Services? An Experiment in Consulting Frail, Older Community Care Clients', *Managing Community Care*, **9**(5): 8–17.

Pattie, C., Seyd, P. and Whiteley, P. (2004) *Citizenship in Britain: Values, Participation and Democracy*, Cambridge, Cambridge University Press.

Patton, M.Q. (1982) *Practical Evaluation*, Beverly Hills, Sage.

Payne, M. (1991) *Modern Social Work Theory: A Critical Introduction*, Basingstoke, Macmillan – now Palgrave Macmillan.

Payne, M. (1997) *Modern Social Work Theory* (2nd edn) Basingstoke, Macmillan – now Palgrave Macmillan.

Payne, M., Adams, R. and Dominelli, L. (2002) 'On Being Critical in Social Work', in R. Adams, L. Dominelli and M. Payne (eds) *Critical Practice in Social Work*, Basingstoke, Palgrave Macmillan, pp. 1–12.

Pedler, M., Burgoyne, J. and Boydell, T. (1996) *The Learning Company: A Strategy for Sustainable Development*, Maidenhead, McGraw-Hill.

Peled, E., Eisikovits, Z., Enosh, G. and Winstok, Z. (2000) 'Choice and Empowerment for Battered Women Who Stay: Towards a Constructivist Model', *Social Work*, **45**(1): 9–25.

Perkins, D.P. and Zimmerman, M.A. (1995) 'Empowerment Theory, Research and Application', *American Journal of Community Psychology*, **23**(5): 569–79.

Phillips S. and Orsini, M. (2002) Making the Links: Citizen Involvement in Policy Processes, discussion paper, Ottawa, Canadian Policy Research Networks, info@cprn.org.

Phillipson, J. (1992) *Practising Equality: Women, Men and Social Work*, Improving Social Work Education and Training, no. 10, London, CCETSW.

Plummer, D. (2001) *Helping Children to Build Self-esteem: A Photocopiable Activities Book*, London, Jessica Kingsley.

Preston-Shoot, M. (1987) *Effective Groupwork*, London, BASW/Macmillan.

Price, J. (1996) 'The Marginal Politics of Our Bodies? Women's Health, the Disability Movement, and Power', in B. Humphries (ed.) *Critical Perspectives on Empowerment*, Birmingham, Venture, pp. 35–51.

Pugh, G. and De Ath, W. (1989) *Working Towards Partnership in the Early Years*, London, National Children's Bureau.

Pugh, G., Aplin, G., De Ath, E. and Moxon, M. (1987) *Partnership in Action: Working with Parents in Pre-school Centres*, London, National Children's Bureau.

Rajani, R. (2001) *The Participation Rights of Adolescents: A Strategic Approach*, New York, UNICEF.

Ramcharan, P., Roberts, G., Grant, G. and Borland, J. (eds) (1997) *Empowerment in Everyday Life*, London, Jessica Kingsley.

Rappaport, J. (1984) 'Studies in Empowerment: Introduction to the Issue', *Prevention in Human Services*, **3**(2/3): 1–7.

Reason, P. (ed.) (1994) *Human Inquiry in Action: Developments in New Paradigm Research*, London, Sage.

Reason, P. and Rowan, J. (eds) (1981) *Human Inquiry: A Sourcebook of New Paradigm Research*, Chichester, John Wiley.

Rees, S. (1991) *Achieving Power: Practice and Policy in Social Welfare*, London, Allen & Unwin.

Rissel, C. (1994) 'Empowerment: The Holy Grail of Health Promotion?', *Health Promotion International*, **9**(1): 39–47.

Robinson, D. and Henry, S. (1977) *Self-Help and Health: Mutual Aid for Modern Problems*, New York, Jason Aronson.

Robson, P., Begum, N. and Locke, M. (2003) *Developing User Involvement: Working Towards User-centred Practice in Voluntary Organisations*, Bristol, Policy Press.

Rocha, E.M. (1997) 'A Ladder of Empowerment', *Journal of Education, Planning and Research*, (17): 31–44.

Rogers, A., Pilgrim, D. and Lacey, R. (eds) (1993) *Experiencing Psychiatry: Users' Views of Services*, Basingstoke, Macmillan/Mind.

Rogers, E.S., Chamberlin, J., Ellison, M.L. and Crean, T. (1997) 'A Consumer-constructed Scale to Measure Empowerment among Users of Mental Health Services', *Psychiatric Services*, **48**(8): 1042–7.

Rojek, C. (1986) 'The "Subject" in Social Work', *British Journal of Social Work*, **16**(1): 65–79.

Rose, D., Fleischmann, P., Tonkiss, F. et al. (2003) Review of the Literature: User and Carer Involvement in Change Management in a Mental Health Context, report to NHS Service Delivery and Organisation Research and Development Programme.

Roulstone, A., Hudson, V., Kearney, J. et al. (2006) *Working Together: Carer Participation in England, Wales and Northern Ireland*, SCIE position paper 5, Bristol, Policy Press.

Rowbotham, S., Segal, L. and Wainwright, H. (1980) *Beyond the Fragments: Feminism and the Making of Socialism*, London, Merlin.

Rutherford, J. (ed.) (1990) *Identity: Community, Culture, Difference*, London, Lawrence & Wishart.

Saegert, S. and Winkel, G. (1996) 'Paths to Community Empowerment: Organising at Home', *American Journal of Community Psychology*, **24**(4): 517–50.

Sainsbury, E. (1989) 'Participation and Paternalism', in S. Shardlow (ed.) *The Values of Change in Social Work*, London, Tavistock/Routledge, pp. 98–113.

Salaman, G., Adams, R. and O'Sullivan, T. (1994) *Learning How to Learn: Managing Personal and Team Effectiveness, Book 2, Management Education Scheme by Open Learning*, Milton Keynes, Open University Press.

Saleeby, D. (ed.) (2005) *The Strengths Perspective in Social Work Practice*, London, Allyn & Bacon.

Salmon, P. and Hall, G.M. (2004) 'Patient Empowerment or the Emperor's New Clothes', *Journal of the Royal Society of Medicine*, **97**(2): 53–6.

Sarbin, T.R. and Adler, N. (1971) 'Self-reconstitution Processes: A Preliminary Report', *Psychoanalytic Review*, **57**, Part 4: 599–615.

Scheel, M.J. and Rieckmann, T. (1998) 'An Empirically Derived Description of Self-efficacy and Empowerment for Parents of Children Identified as Psychologically Disordered', *American Journal of Family Therapy*, **26**(1): 15–27.

Schlossberg, M. and Shuford, E. (2005) 'Delineating "Public" and "Participation" in PPGIS', *URISA Journal*, **16**(2): 15–26.

Schön, D. A. (1973) *Beyond the Stable State: Public and Private Learning in a Changing Society*, Harmondsworth, Penguin.

Schön, D.A. (1991) *The Reflective Practitioner: How Professionals Think in Action*, Aldershot, Avebury.

Scraton, P., Sim, J. and Skidmore, P. (1991) *Prisons under Protest*, Milton Keynes, Open University Press.

Sedgwick, P. (1982) *Psychopolitics*, London, Pluto Press.

Seligman, M.E.P. (1975) *Helplessness: On Depression, Development and Death*, San Francisco, Freeman.

Servian, R. (1996) *Theorising Empowerment: Individual Power and Community Care*, Bristol, Policy Press.

Shera, W. and Wells, L.M. (eds) (1999) *Empowerment Practice in Social Work*, Toronto, Canadian Scholars Press.

Shier, H. (2001) 'Pathways to Participation: Openings, Opportunities and Obligations', *Children and Society*, **15**(2): 107–17.

Shor, I. (1992) *Empowering Education: Critical Teaching for Social Change*, London, University of Chicago Press.

Simces, Z. (2003) *Exploring the Link Between Public Involvement/ Citizen Engagement and Quality Health Care: A Review and Analysis of the Current Literature*, Ottawa, Health Canada, Human Resources Strategies Division.

Simon, B.J. (1994) *The Empirical Tradition in American Social Work: A History*, New York, Columbia University Press.

Sinclair, E. (1988) 'The Formal Evidence', in *National Institute for Social Work, Residential Care: A Positive Choice*, London, HMSO.

Sixsmith, J. and Boneham, M. (2003) 'Older Men's Participation in Community Life: Notions of Social Capital, Health, and Empowerment', *Ageing International*, **28**(4): 372–88.

Sleeter, C. (1991) *Empowerment Through Multi-cultural Education*, Albany, State University of New York Press.

Slocum, R., Wichhart, L., Rocheleau, D. and Thomas-Slayter, B. (eds) (1995)

Power, Process and Participation: Tools for Change, London, Intermediate Technology Publications.

Smiles, S. (1875) *Thrift*, London, Harper & Bros.

Smiles, S. (1890) *Self-help: With Illustrations of Conducts and Perseverance*, London, John Murray.

SSI (Social Services Inspectorate) (1991) *Women in Social Services: A Neglected Resource*, London, HMSO.

Solomon, B.B. (1976) *Black Empowerment: Social Work in Oppressed Communities*, New York, Columbia University Press.

Solomon, B.B. (1986) 'Social Work with Afro-Americans', in A. Morales and B. Sheafor (eds) *Social Work: A Profession of Many Faces*, Boston, Allyn & Bacon, pp. 501–21.

Spreitzer, G.M., Kizilos, M.A. and Nason, S.W. (1997) 'A Dimensional Analysis of the Relationship between Psychological Empowerment and Effectiveness, Satisfaction and Strain', *Journal of Management*, **23**(5): 679–704.

Stanton, A. (1990) 'Empowerment of Staff: A Prerequisite for the Empowerment of Users?', in P. Carter, T. Jeffs and M. Smith (eds) *Social Work and Social Welfare Yearbook 2*, Buckingham, Open University Press, pp. 122–33.

Steel, R. (2004) *Involving the Public in NHS, Public Health, and Social Care Research: Briefing Notes for Researchers* (2nd edn) Eastleigh, INVOLVE (first edition Hanley et al. 2003) available: Support Unit, Wessex House, Upper Market Street, Eastleigh, Hants, SO50 9FD, tel. 02380 651088, admin@invo.org.uk.

Steeves, H.L. and Melkote, S.R. (2001) *Communication for Development in the Third World: Theory and Practice for Empowerment* (2nd edn) London, Sage.

Steiner, C. (1974) 'Radical Psychiatry: Principles', in Radical Therapist/ Rough Times Collective (eds) *The Radical Therapist*, Harmondsworth, Pelican, pp. 15–19.

Steiner, C. (ed.) (1975) *Readings in Radical Psychiatry*, New York, Grove Press.

Stevenson, O. (1996) 'Old People and Empowerment: The Position of Old People in Contemporary British Society', in P. Parsloe (ed.) *Pathways to Empowerment*, Birmingham, Venture, pp. 81–91.

Stewart, A. (1994) *Empowering People*, London, Pitman.

Stewart, F. (2003) 'Evaluating Evaluation in a World of Multiple Goals, Interests and Models', conference paper, 5th biennial conference, 'Evaluation and Development', 15–16 July, Washington DC, World Bank Support Unit.

Stewart, F. and Wang, M. (2003) *Do PRSBs Empower Poor Countries and Disempower the World Bank or Is It the Other Way Round?*, Oxford, Queen Elizabeth House.

Stewart, R. and Bhagwanjee, A. (1999) 'Promoting Group Empowerment and Self-reliance through Participatory Research: A Case Study of People with Physical Disability', *Disability and Rehabilitation*, **21**(7): 338–45.

Stickley, T. (2006) 'Should Service User Involvement be Consigned to History? A Critical Realist Perspective', *Journal of Psychiatric and Mental Health Nursing*, **13**(5): 570–7.

Stokes, B. (1981) *Helping Ourselves: Local Solutions to Global Problems*, London, Norton.

Survivors Speak Out (1988) *Self-Advocacy Action Pack – Empowering Mental Health Service Users*, London, Survivors Speak Out.

Swift, C. and Levin, G. (1987) 'Empowerment: An Emerging Mental Health Technology', *Journal of Primary Prevention*, **8**(1/2): 71–94.

Tax, S. (1976) 'Self-help Groups: Thoughts on Public Policy', *Journal of Applied Behavioural Science*, (12) Part 3: 448–54.

Taylor, G. (1999) 'Empowerment, Identity and Participatory Research: Using Social Action Research to Challenge Isolation for Deaf and Hard of Hearing People from Minority Ethnic Communities', *Disability and Society*, **14**(3): 369–84.

Tew, J. (2006) 'Understanding Power and Powerlessness', *Journal of Social Work*, **6**(1): 33–51.

Thomas, M. and Pierson, J. (1995) *Dictionary of Social Work*, London, Collins Educational.

Thomas, K.W. and Velthouse, B.A. (1990) 'Cognitive Elements of Empowerment: An Interpretive Model of Intrinsic Task Motivation', *Academy of Management Review*, **15**: 666–81.

Thompson, N. and Thompson, S. (2004) 'Empowering Older People: Beyond the Care Model', *Journal of Social Work*, **1**(1): 61–76.

Thompson, N. (1993) *Anti-discriminatory Practice*, London, BASW/Macmillan – now Palgrave Macmillan.

Thompson, N. (1997) *Anti-discriminatory Practice* (2nd edn) London, BASW/Macmillan – now Palgrave Macmillan.

Thompson, N. (1998) *Promoting Equality: Challenging Discrimination and Oppression in the Human Services*, Basingstoke, Macmillan – now Palgrave Macmillan.

Thorpe, M. (1993) *Evaluating Open and Distance Learning* (2nd edn) Harlow, Longman.

Thursz, D., Nusberg, C. and Prather, J. (eds) (1995) *Empowering Older People: An International Approach*, Westport, CT, Greenwood Publishing.

Tibbitts, F. (2002) 'Understanding What We Do: Emerging Models for Human Rights Education', *International Review of Education*, **48**(3/4): 159–71.

Towell, D. (ed.) (1988) *An Ordinary Life in Practice*, London, King Edward's Hospital Fund.

Tracy, G.S. and Gussow, Z. (1976) 'Self-help Groups: A Grassroots Response to a Need for Services', *Journal of Applied Behavioural Science*, (12) Part 3: 381–96.

Tully, C.T. (2000) *Lesbians, Gays and the Empowerment Perspective*, New York, Columbia University Press.

Turner, M. and Beresford, P. (2005) *User Controlled Research: Its Meanings and Potential*, Eastleigh, Hants, INVOLVE.

Twelvetrees, A. (1991) *Community Work* (2nd edn) London, BASW/Macmillan – now Palgrave Macmillan.

Tyler, R.W. (1976) 'Social Policy and Self-help Groups', *Journal of Behavioural Science*, (23) Part 3: 444–8.

Ulrich, R.S. (2006) 'Evidence-based Design for Better Healthcare Buildings', Joined Up Management: Development, Diversity, Delivery, annual conference of Institute of Healthcare Management, Manchester.

United Nations (1989) *Convention on the Rights of the Child*, Geneva, United Nations.

User-Centred Services Group (1993) *Building Bridges Between People Who Use and People Who Provide Services*, London, NISW.

Walker, H. and Beaumont, B. (1981) *Probation Work: Critical Theory and Socialist Practice*, Oxford, Blackwell.

Wallerstein, N. (1992) 'Powerlessness, Empowerment and Health: Implications for Health Promotion Programs', *American Journal of Health Promotion*, **6**(3): 197–205.

Ward, D. and Mullender, A. (1991) 'Empowerment and Oppression: An Indissoluble Pairing for Contemporary Social Work', *Critical Social Policy*, **32**(11 2): 21–30.

Waring, M. (2004) 'Civil Society, Community Participation and Empowerment in the Era of Globalization', *Spotlight*, (1), 1–8 May.

Watt, S., Higgins, C. and Kendrick, A. (2000) 'Community Participation in the Development of Services: A Move Towards Community Empowerment', *Community Development Journal*, **35**: 120–32.

Weber, M. (1997) *The Theory of Social and Economic Organisation*, New York, Free Press.

Weeks, L., Shane, C., MacDonald, F., Hart, C. and Smith, R. (2006) 'Learning from the Experts: People with Learning Difficulties Training and Learning from Each Other', *British Journal of Learning Disabilities*, **34**(1): 49–55.

Whitaker, D.S. (1985) *Using Groups to Help People*, London, Tavistock/Routledge.

Wiedemann, P.M. and Femers, S. (1993) 'Public Participation in Waste Management Decision Making: Analysis and Management of Conflicts', *Journal of Hazardous Materials*, **33**(3): 355–68.

Wilcox, D. (1994) *A Guide to Effective Participation*, York, Joseph Rowntree Foundation.

Wilkes, L., White, K. and O'Riordan, (2000) 'Empowerment through Information: Supporting Rural Families of Oncology Patients in Palliative Care', *Australian Journal of Rural Health*, **8**(1): 1–46.

Wilkinson, M.D. (2004) 'Devolving Governance: Area Committees and Neighbourhood Management', report of a seminar held in March, The Mansion House, Doncaster, York, Joseph Rowntree Foundation.

Williams, V. (2003) 'Has Anything Changed? User Involvement in Promoting Change and Enhancing the Quality of Services for People with Learning Difficulties', final report for SCIE.

Wilson, J. (1986) *Self-help Groups: Getting Started – Keeping Going*, Harlow, Longman.

Wilson, J. (1988) *Caring Together: Guidelines for Carers' Self-help and Support Groups*, London, King's Fund.

Wise, S. (1995) 'Feminist Ethics in Practice', in R. Hugman and D. Smith (eds) *Ethical Issues in Social Work*, London, Routledge.

Wolfendale, S. (1992) *Empowering Parents and Teachers: Working for Children*, London, Cassell.

Wolfenden, Lord (1978) *The Future of Voluntary Organisations: Report of the Wolfenden Committee*, London, Croom Helm.

Wolfensberger, W. (1972) *The Principle of Normalisation in Human Services*, Toronto, National Institute on Mental Retardation.

Wolfensberger, W. (1982) 'Social Role Valorisation: A Proposed New Term for the Principle of Normalisation', *Mental Retardation*, **21**(6): 234–9.

Women in MIND (1986) *Finding Our Own Solutions: Women's Experience of Mental Health Care*, London, MIND.

Wood, G.G. and Middleham, R.R. (1992) 'Groups to Empower Battered Women', *Affilia*, **7**(4): 82–95.

Wood, G.G. and Tully, C.T. (2006) *The Structural Approach to Direct Practice in Social Work: A Social Constructionist Perspective* (3rd edn) New York, Columbia University Press.

Wright, P. and Haydon, D. (2002) *Taking Part Toolkit: Promoting the Real Participation of Children and Young People*, Ilford, Barnardo's.

Wright, P., Turner, C., Clay, D. and Mills, H. (2006) *Guide to the Participation of Children and Young People in Developing Social Care*, London, SCIE.

Yip, K.-S. (2004) 'The Empowerment Model: A Critical Reflection of Empowerment in Chinese Culture', *Social Work*, **49**(3): 478–86.

Zimmerman, M. and Rappaport, J. (1988) 'Citizen Participation, Perceived Control and Psychological Empowerment', *American Journal of Community Psychology*, **16**(5): 725–50.

Zweig, M. (1971) 'Is Women's Liberation a Therapy Group?', in J. Agel (ed.) *Radical Therapist: The Radical Therapist Collective*, New York, Ballantine Books.

Index